Orion Books Ltd
Orion House
5 Upper St Martin's Lane
London WC2H 9EA

Alex Graham's Fred Basset 2005

First published by Orion in 2005

Drawings by Michael Martin

Cover illustrations by Alex Graham

ISBN 0 75286 496 3

Printed and bound in Great Britain by
Butler & Tanner Ltd, Frome and London

www.orionbooks.co.uk

Light the touchpaper...
...stand well clear...
...and watch me go like a rocket!
MGM

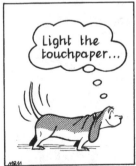

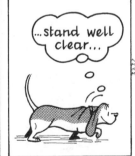

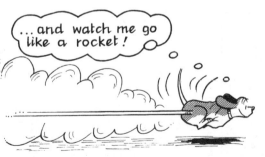

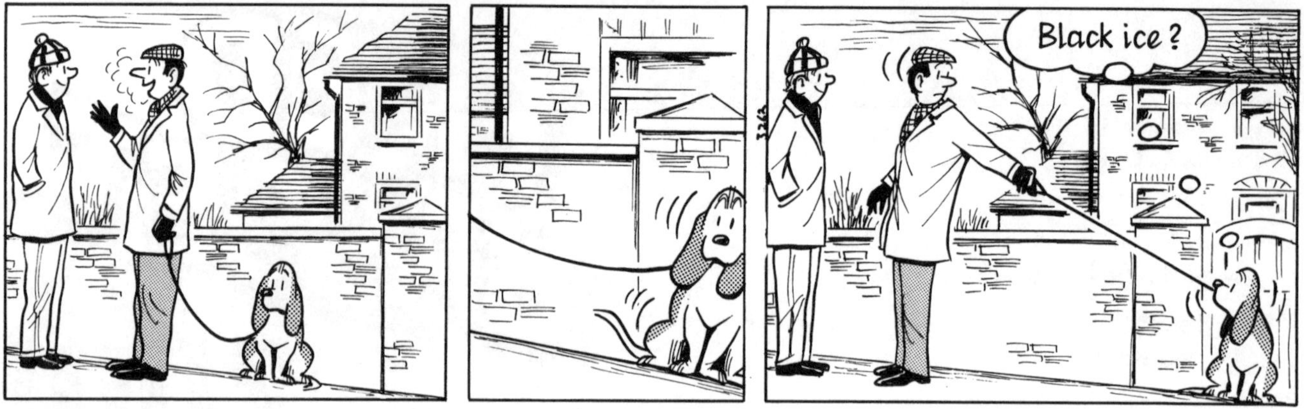
Black ice?

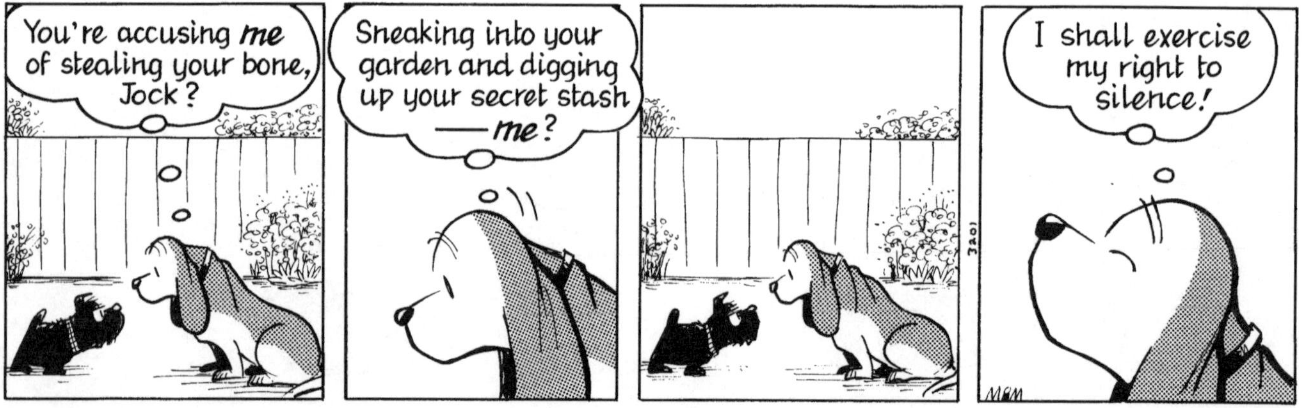
You're accusing *me* of stealing your bone, Jock?
Sneaking into your garden and digging up your secret stash — *me*?
I shall exercise my right to silence!

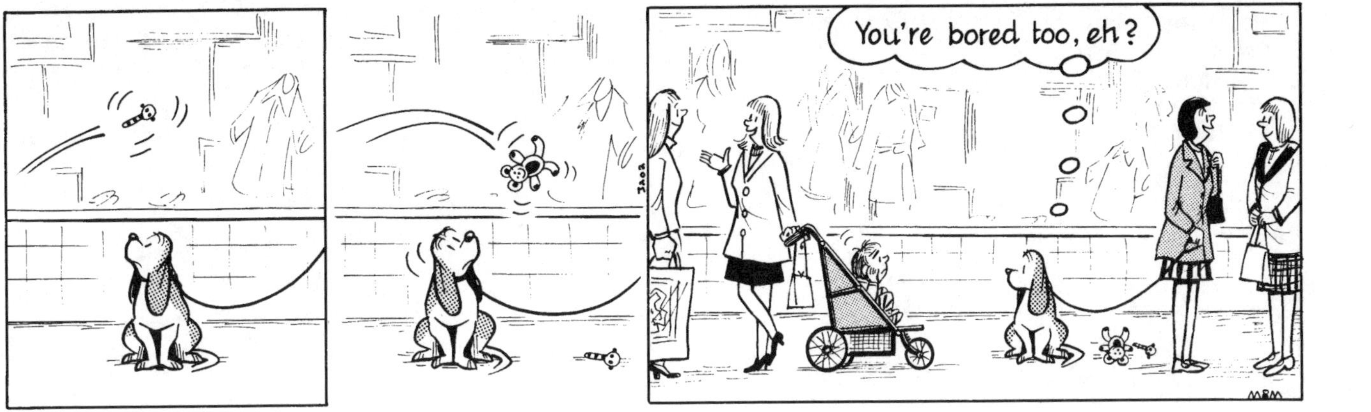
You're bored too, eh?

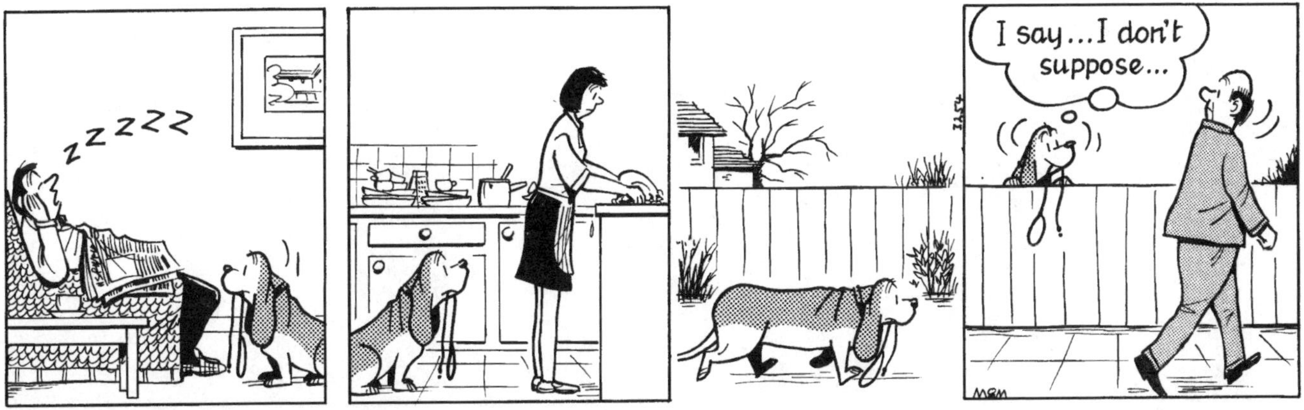
zzZZZZ
I say…I don't
suppose…

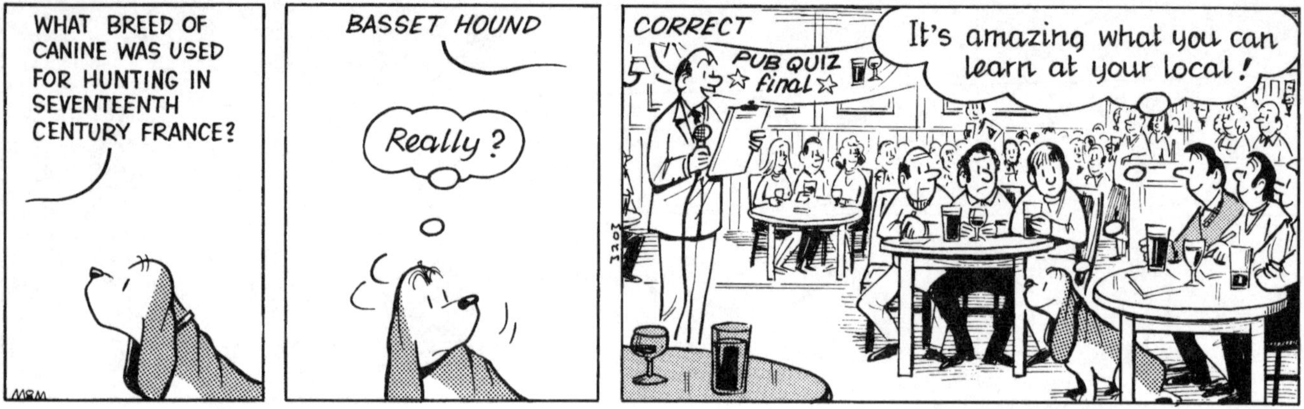
WHAT BREED OF CANINE WAS USED FOR HUNTING IN SEVENTEENTH CENTURY FRANCE?
BASSET HOUND
Really?
CORRECT
PUB QUIZ ☆ final ☆
It's amazing what you can learn at your local!

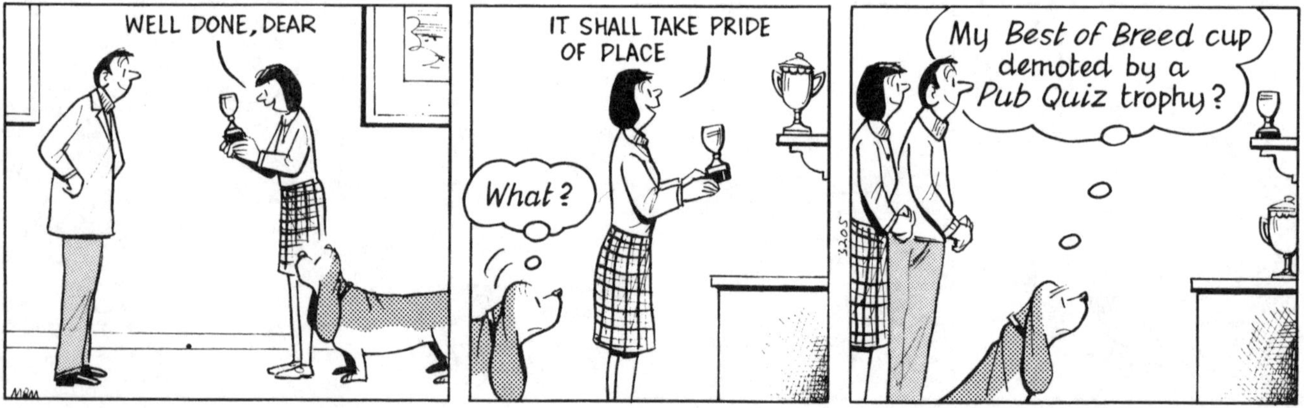
WELL DONE, DEAR
IT SHALL TAKE PRIDE OF PLACE
What?
My *Best of Breed* cup demoted by a *Pub Quiz* trophy?

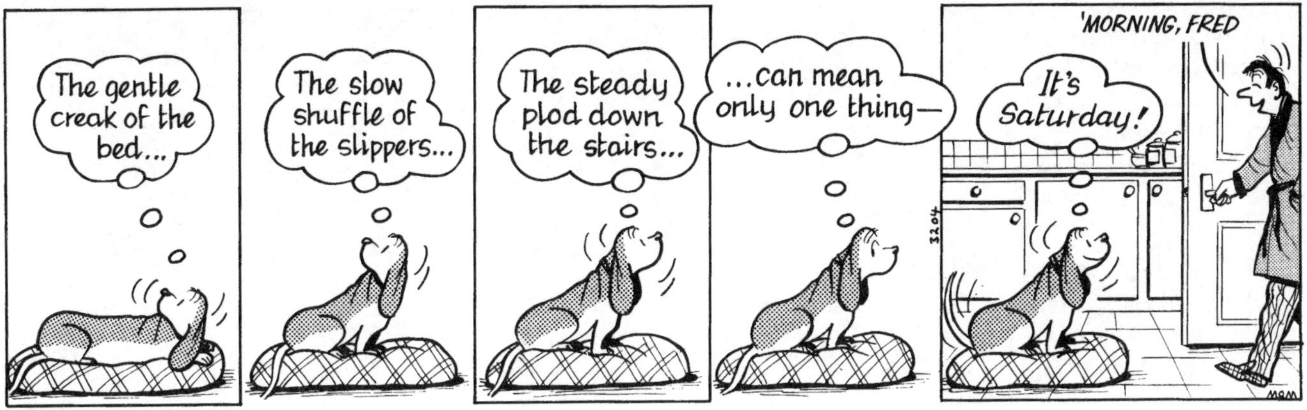
The gentle creak of the bed...
The slow shuffle of the slippers...
The steady plod down the stairs...
...can mean only one thing—
'MORNING, FRED
It's Saturday!

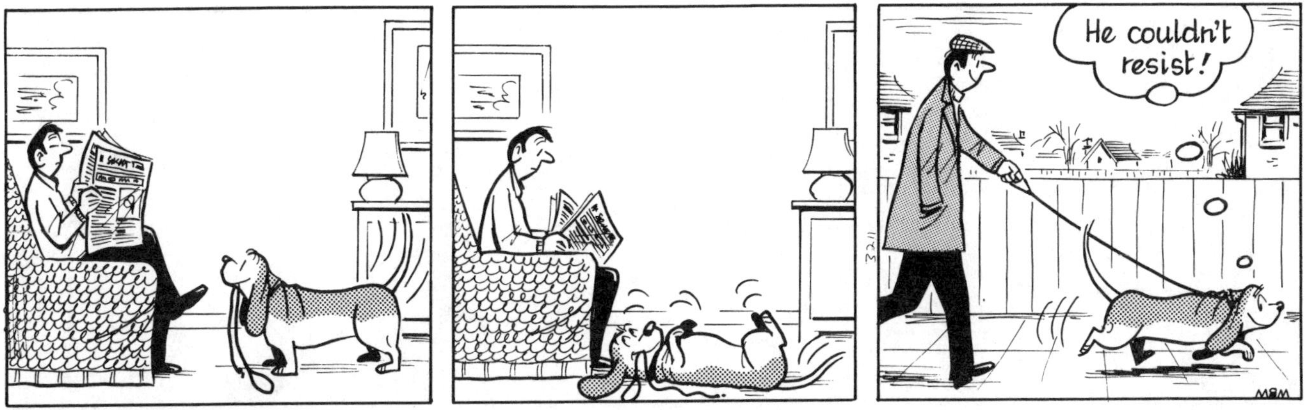
He couldn't resist!

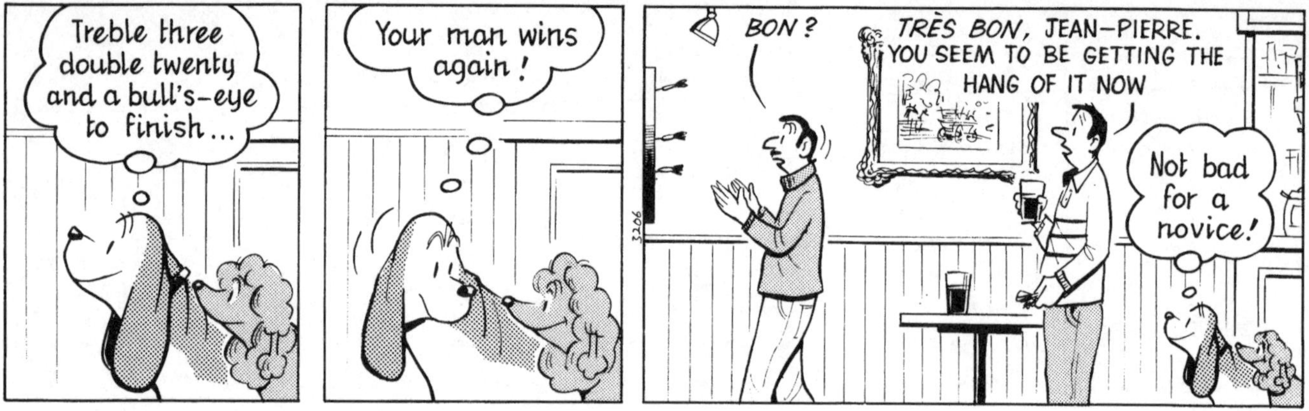
Treble three double twenty and a bull's-eye to finish...
Your man wins again!
BON?
TRÈS BON, JEAN-PIERRE. YOU SEEM TO BE GETTING THE HANG OF IT NOW
Not bad for a novice!

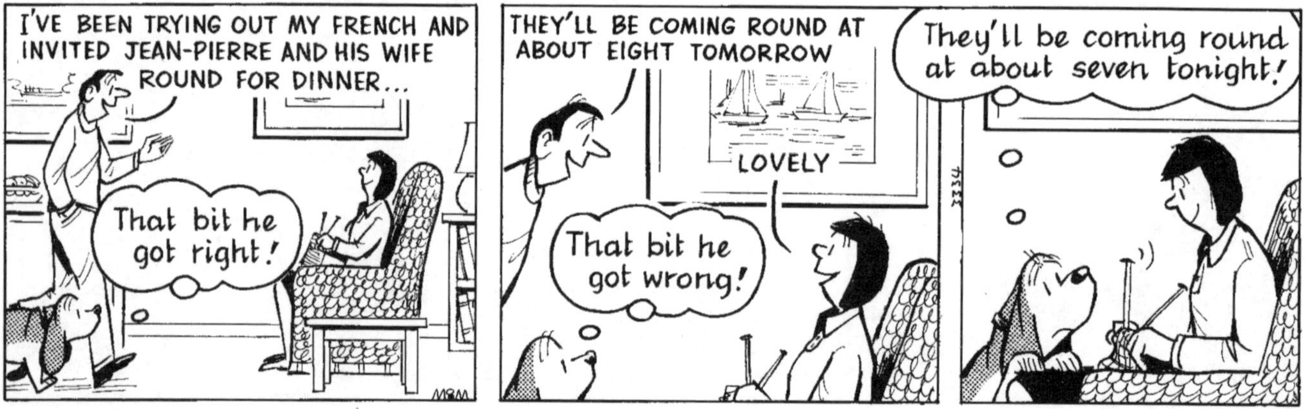
I'VE BEEN TRYING OUT MY FRENCH AND INVITED JEAN-PIERRE AND HIS WIFE ROUND FOR DINNER...
That bit he got right!
THEY'LL BE COMING ROUND AT ABOUT EIGHT TOMORROW
LOVELY
That bit he got wrong!
They'll be coming round at about seven tonight!

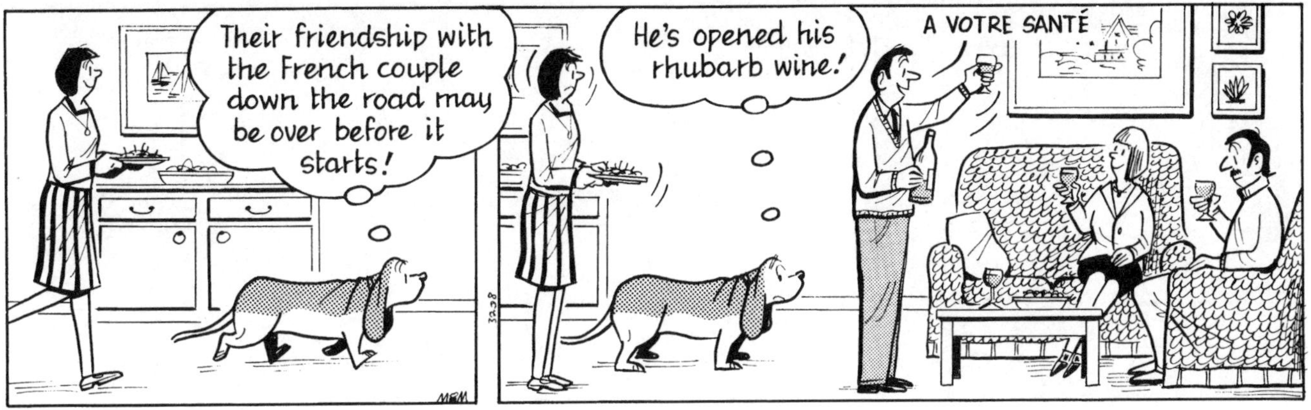
Their friendship with the French couple down the road may be over before it starts!
He's opened his rhubarb wine!
A VOTRE SANTÉ
MBM

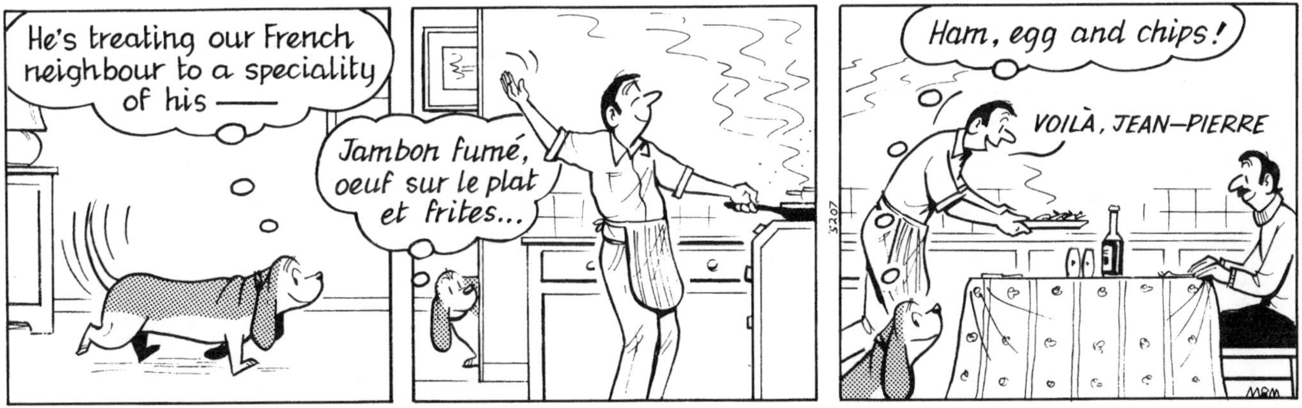
He's treating our French neighbour to a speciality of his ——
Jambon fumé, oeuf sur le plat et frites...
Ham, egg and chips!
VOILÀ, JEAN—PIERRE
MBM

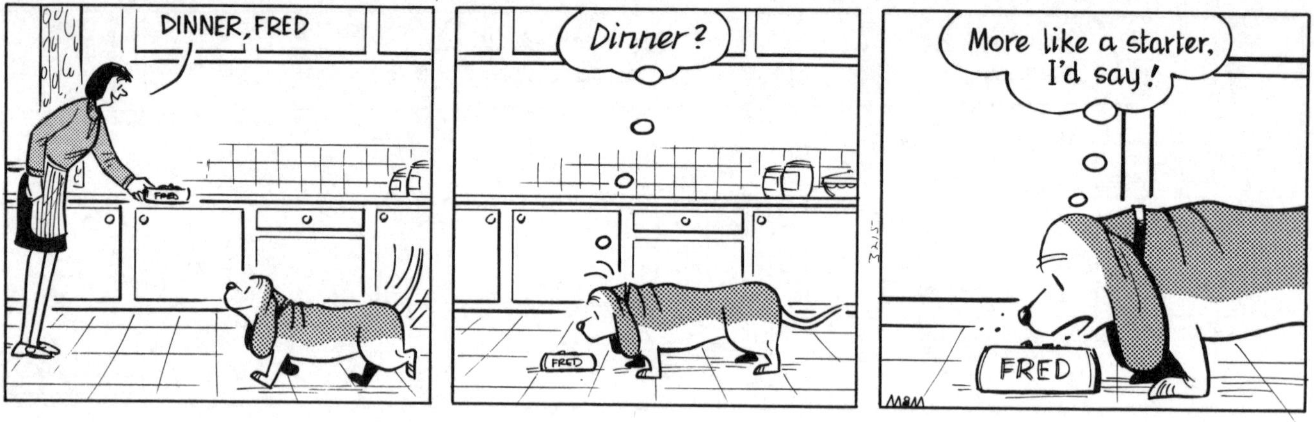
DINNER, FRED
FRED
Dinner?
FRED
More like a starter, I'd say!
FRED

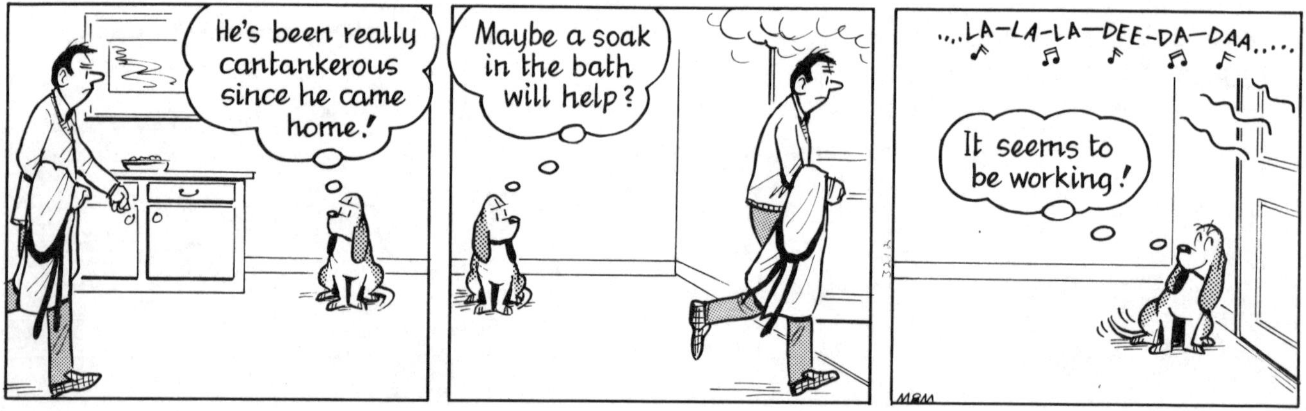
He's been really cantankerous since he came home!
Maybe a soak in the bath will help?
...LA-LA-LA-DEE-DA-DAA....
It seems to be working!

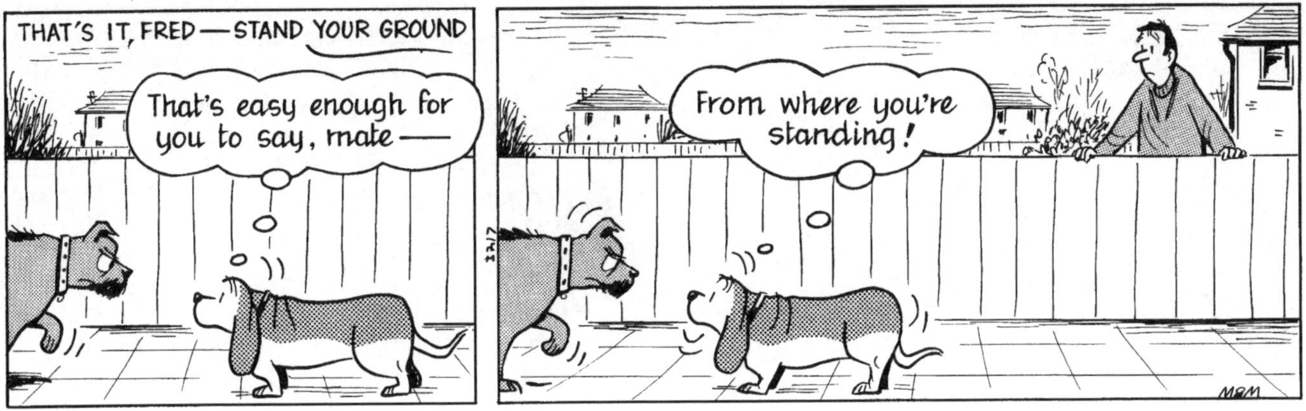
THAT'S IT, FRED — STAND YOUR GROUND
That's easy enough for you to say, mate —
From where you're standing!
MBM

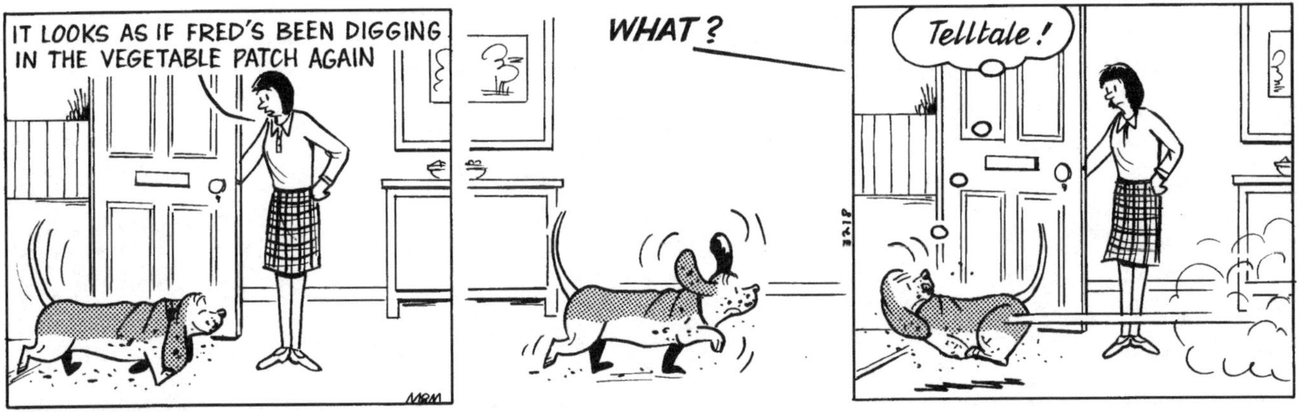
IT LOOKS AS IF FRED'S BEEN DIGGING IN THE VEGETABLE PATCH AGAIN
WHAT?
Telltale!
MBM

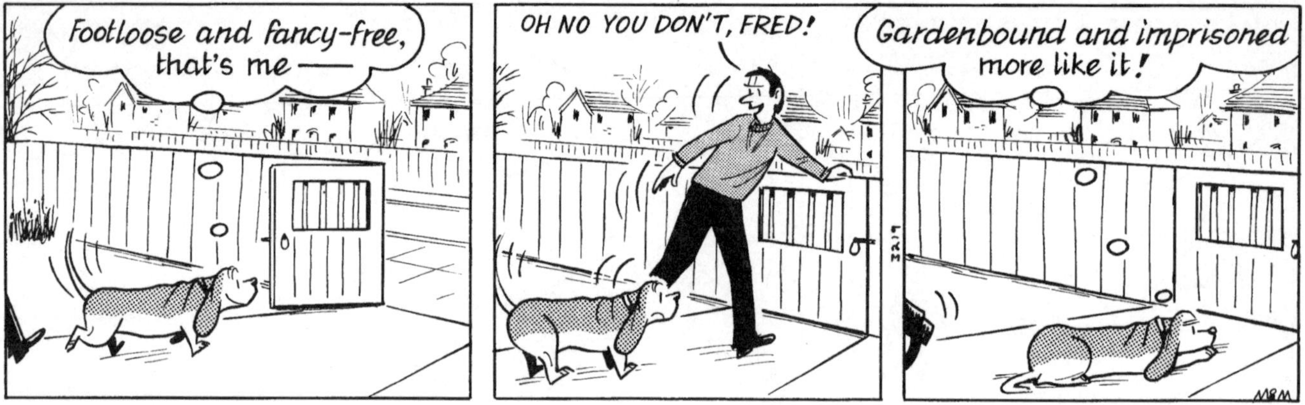
Footloose and fancy-free, that's me ——
OH NO YOU DON'T, FRED!
Gardenbound and imprisoned more like it!
3219
M&M

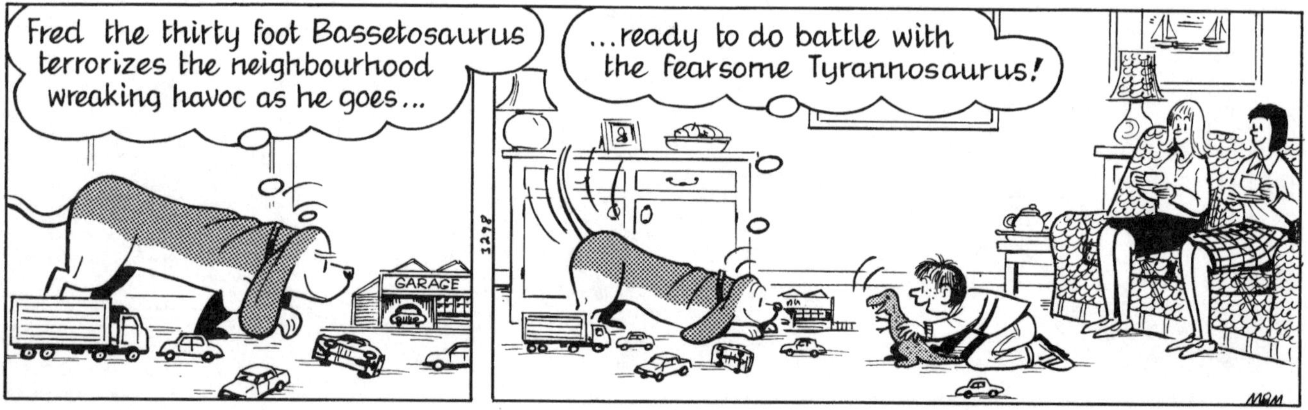
Fred the thirty foot Bassetosaurus terrorizes the neighbourhood wreaking havoc as he goes...
GARAGE
3298
...ready to do battle with the fearsome Tyrannosaurus!
M&M

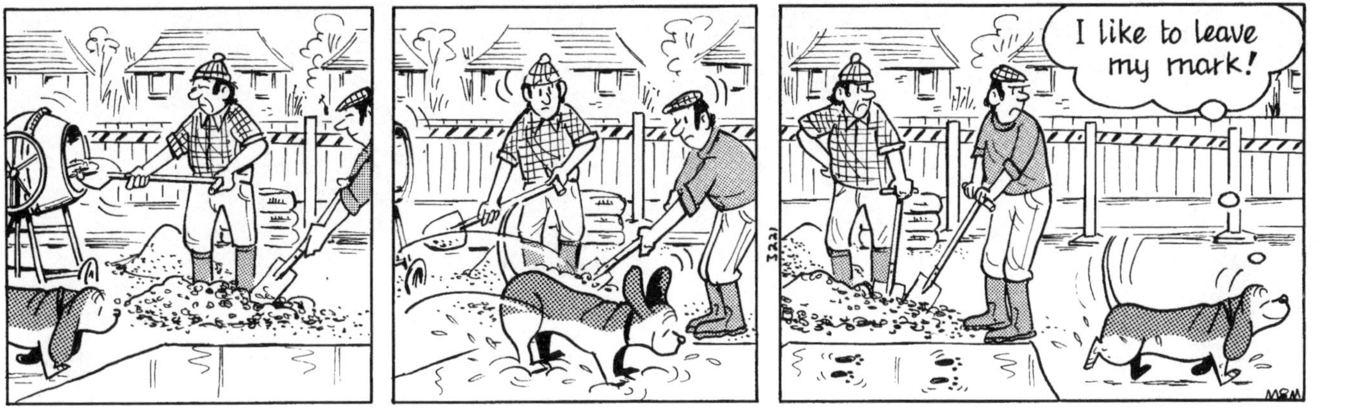
I like to leave my mark!

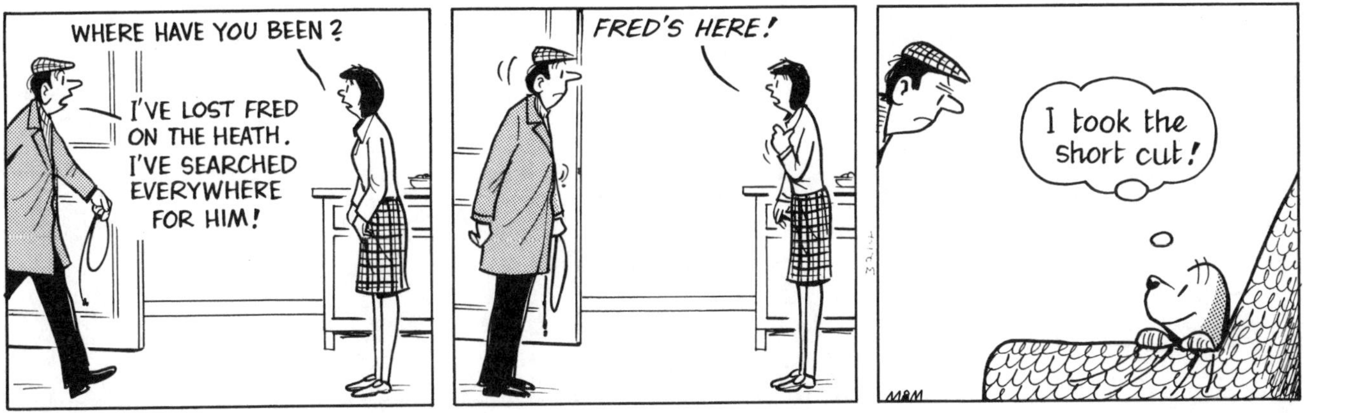
WHERE HAVE YOU BEEN?
I'VE LOST FRED ON THE HEATH. I'VE SEARCHED EVERYWHERE FOR HIM!
FRED'S HERE!
I took the short cut!

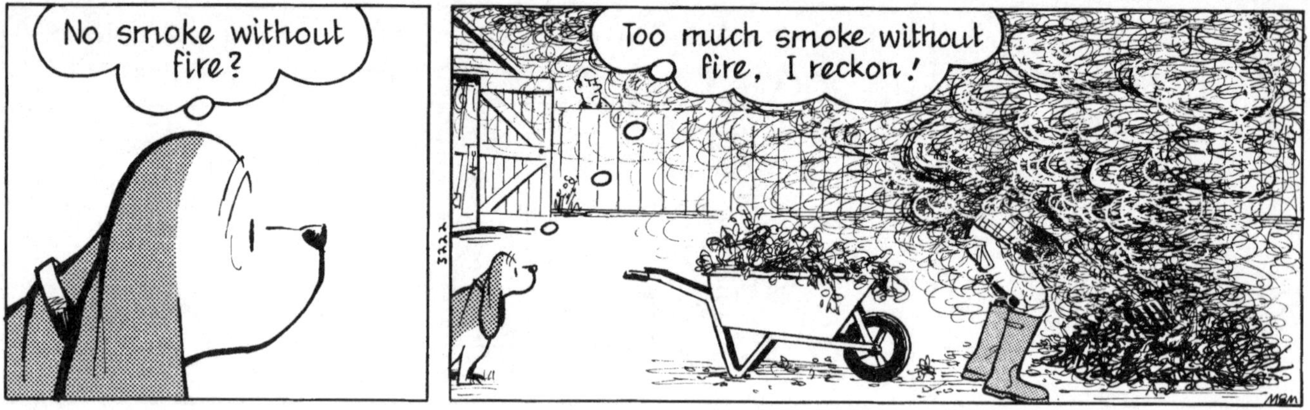
No smoke without fire?
Too much smoke without fire, I reckon!

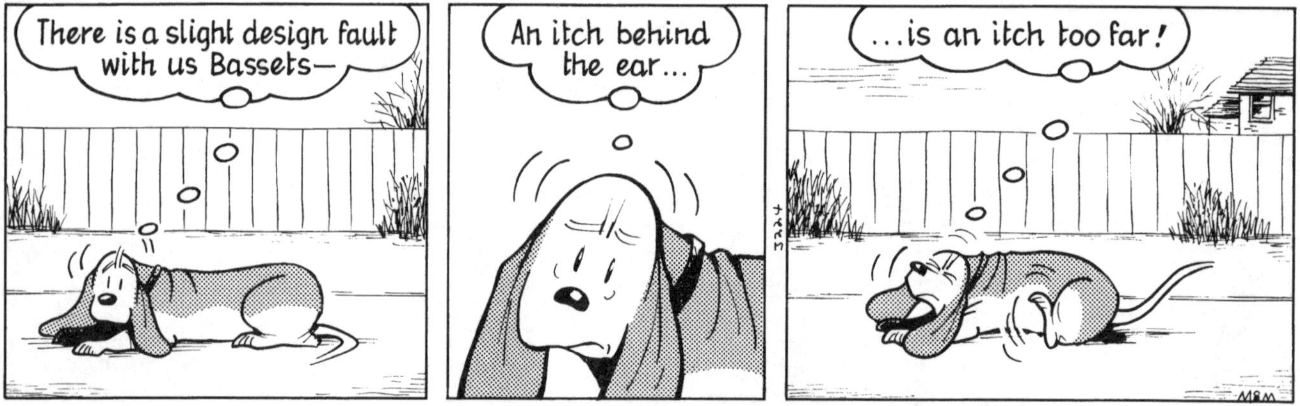
There is a slight design fault with us Bassets—
An itch behind the ear...
...is an itch too far!

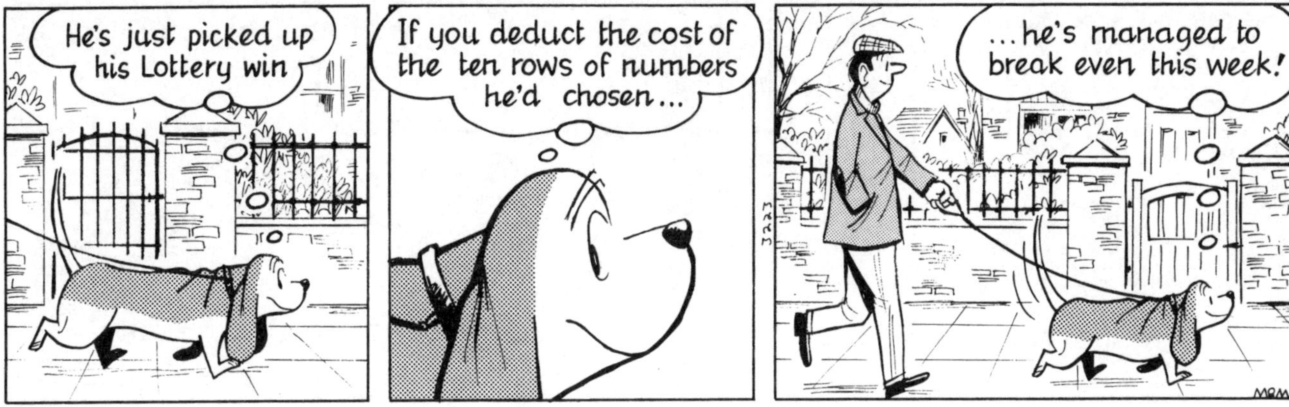
He's just picked up his Lottery win
If you deduct the cost of the ten rows of numbers he'd chosen...
...he's managed to break even this week!

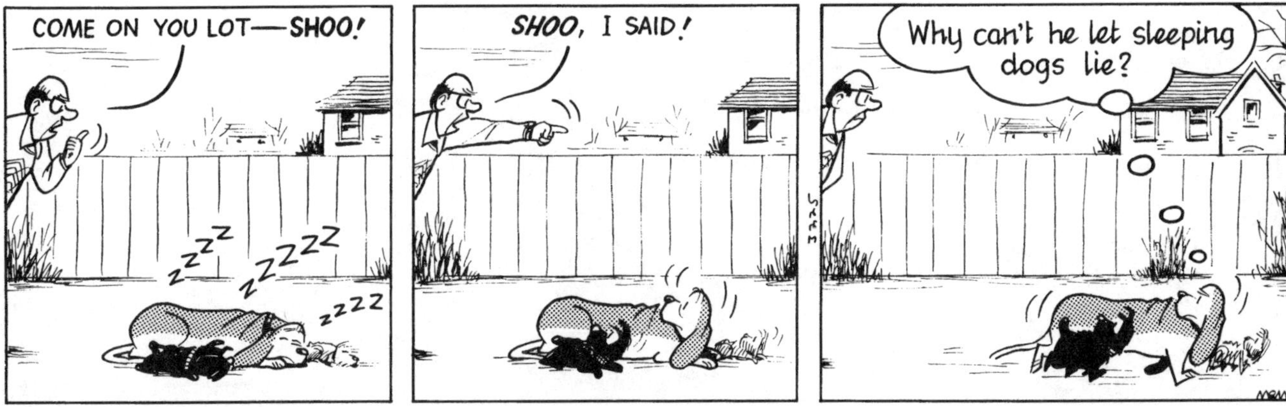
COME ON YOU LOT—SHOO!
ZZZZ ZZZZZZ ZZZZ
SHOO, I SAID!
Why can't he let sleeping dogs lie?

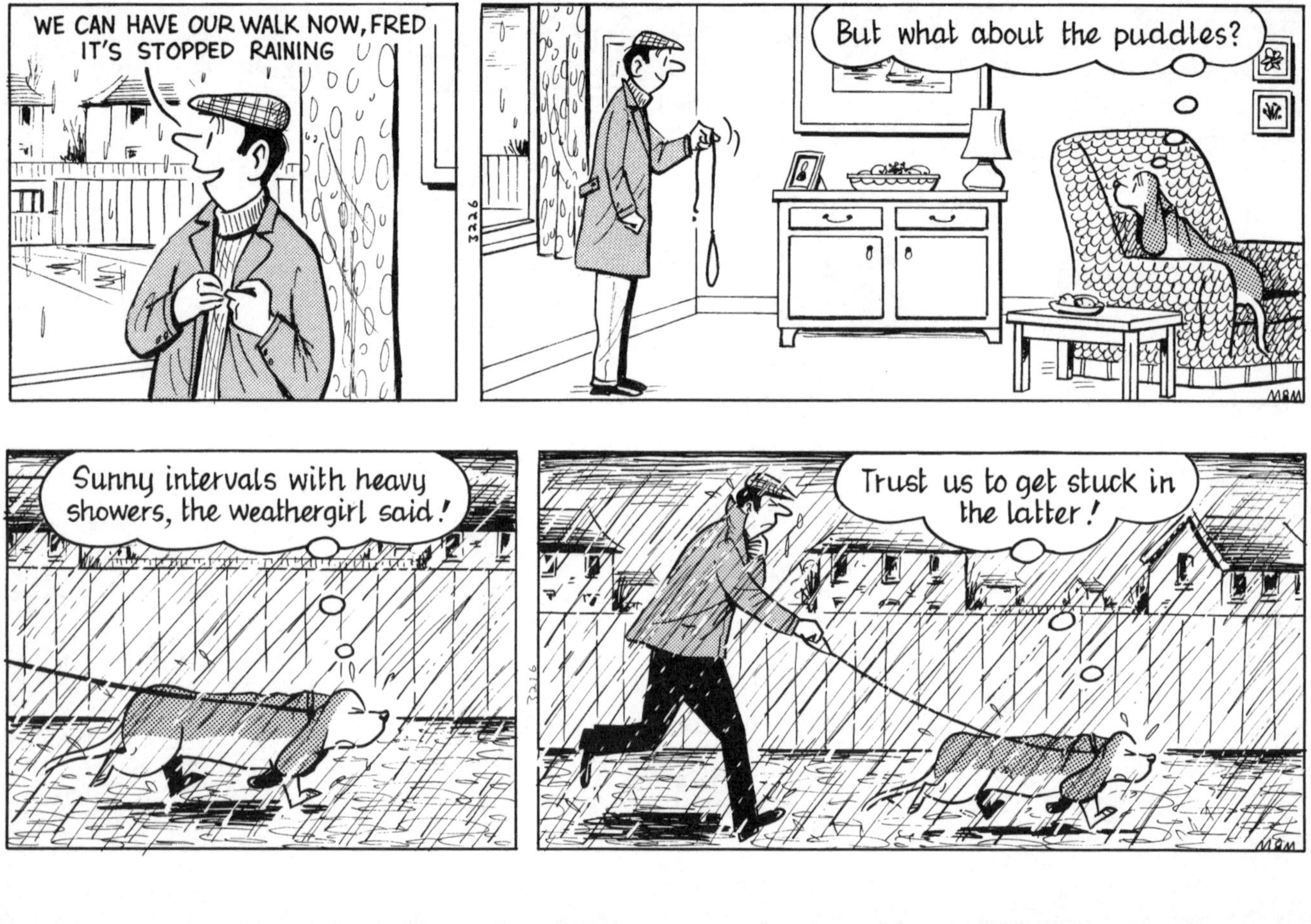
WE CAN HAVE OUR WALK NOW, FRED IT'S STOPPED RAINING
But what about the puddles?
Sunny intervals with heavy showers, the weathergirl said!
Trust us to get stuck in the latter!

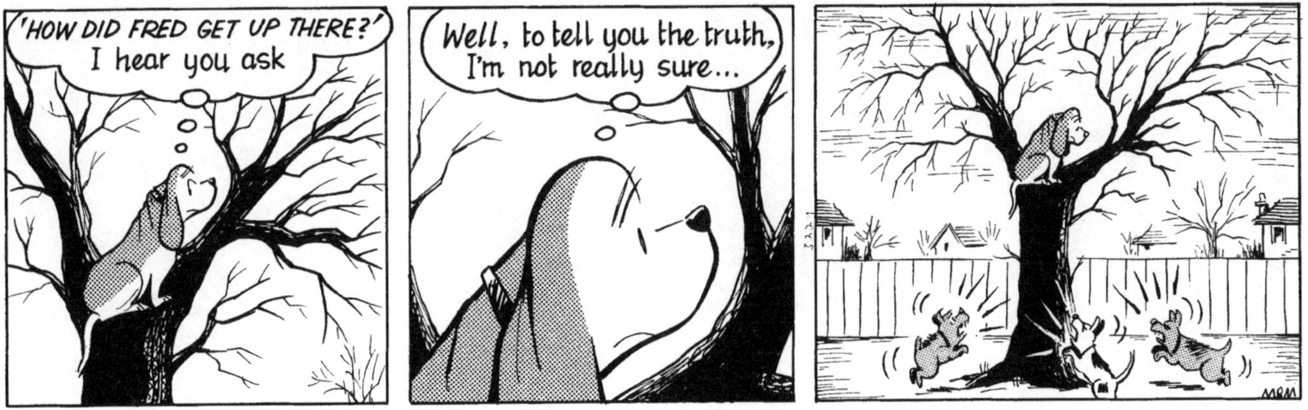
'HOW DID FRED GET UP THERE?' I hear you ask
Well, to tell you the truth, I'm not really sure...

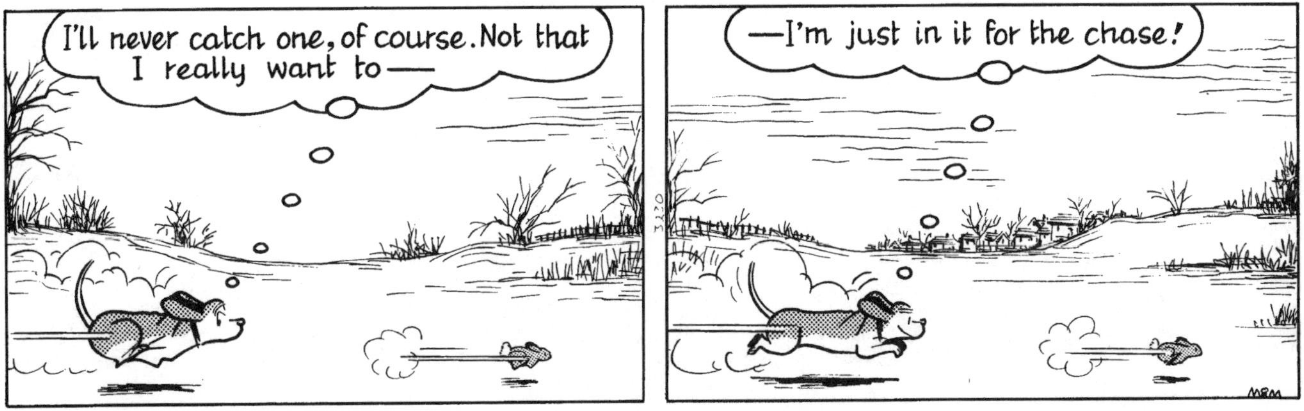
I'll never catch one, of course. Not that I really want to —
—I'm just in it for the chase!

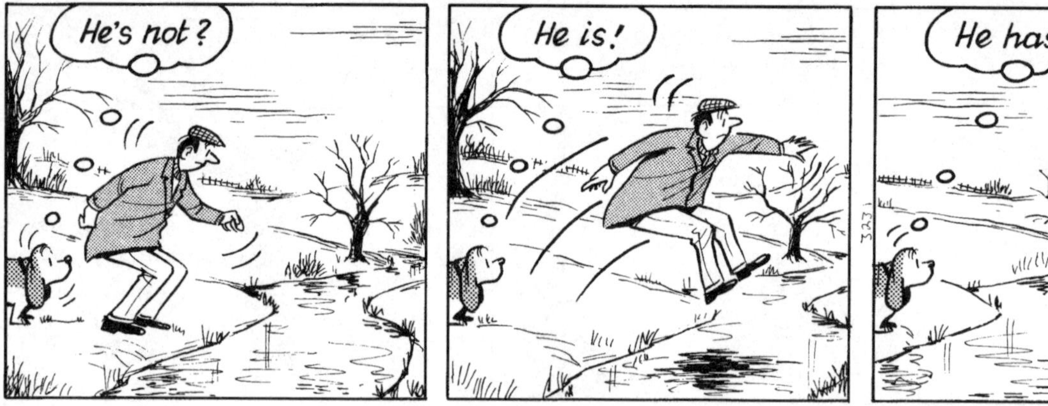
He's not?
He is!
He has!

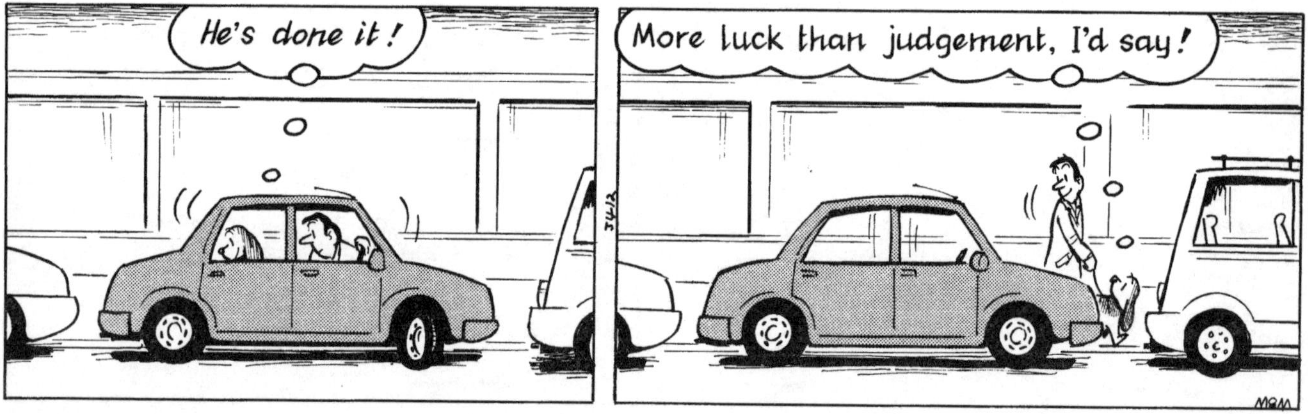
He's done it!
More luck than judgement, I'd say!

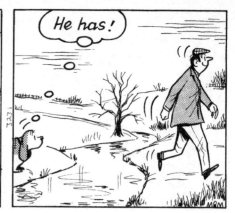

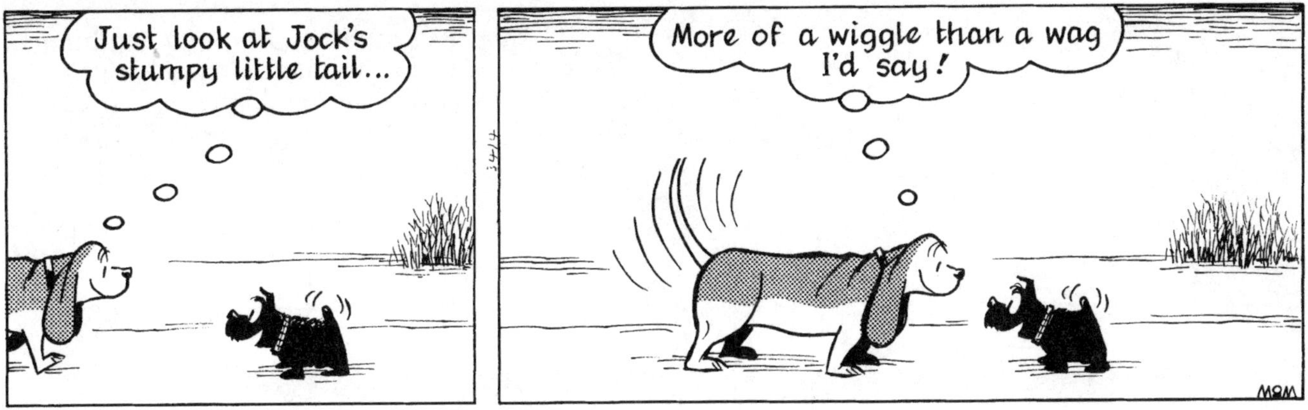
Just look at Jock's stumpy little tail...
More of a wiggle than a wag I'd say!

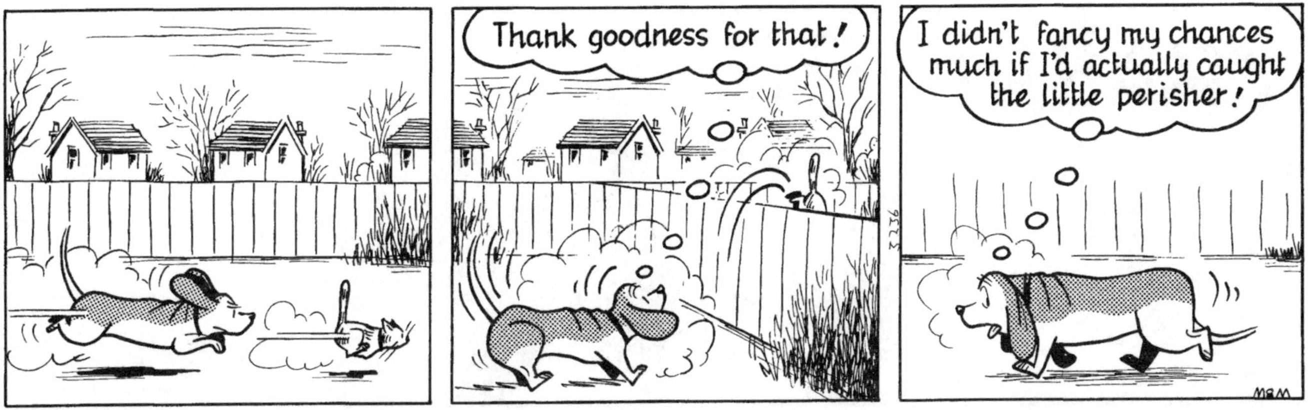
Thank goodness for that!
I didn't fancy my chances much if I'd actually caught the little perisher!

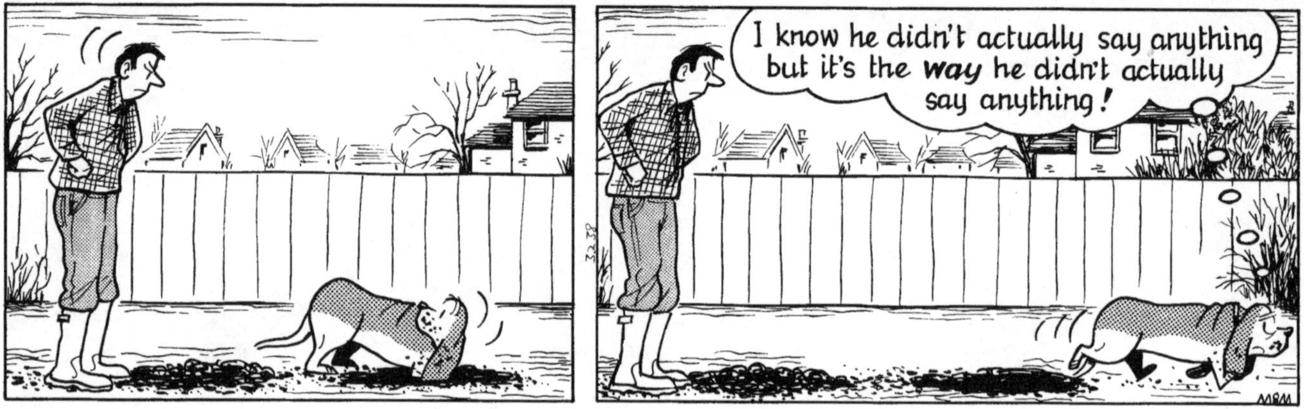
I know he didn't actually say anything but it's the **way** he didn't actually say anything!

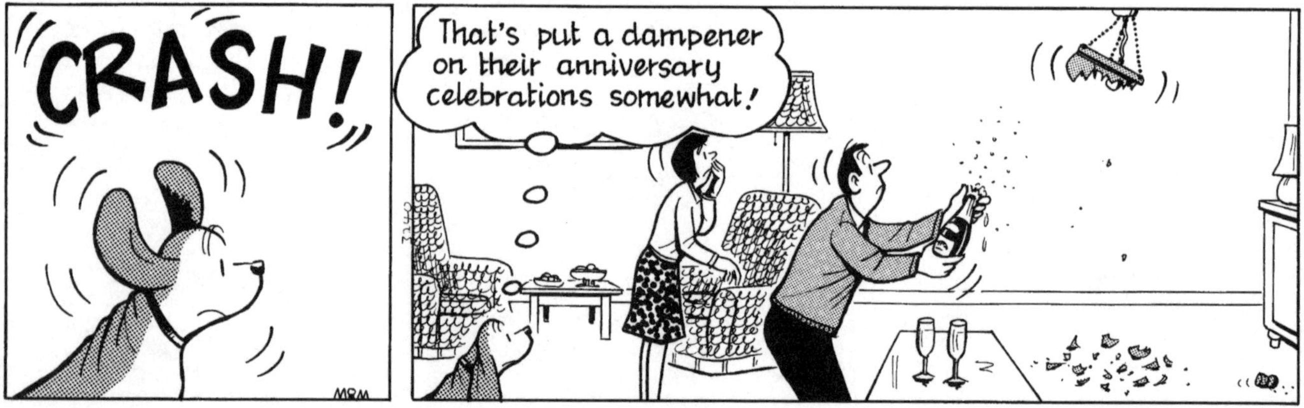
CRASH!
That's put a dampener on their anniversary celebrations somewhat!

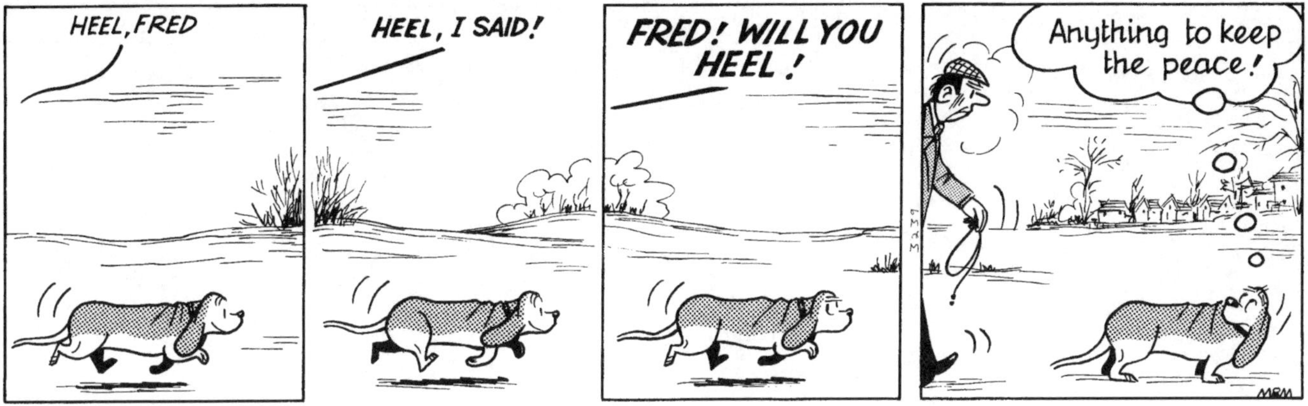
HEEL, FRED
HEEL, I SAID!
FRED! WILL YOU HEEL!
Anything to keep the peace!
MBM

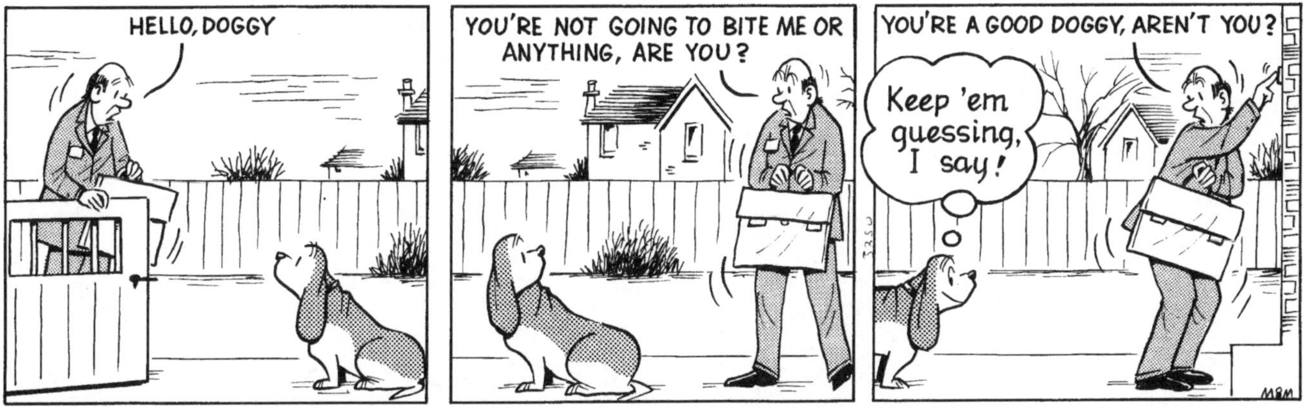
HELLO, DOGGY
YOU'RE NOT GOING TO BITE ME OR ANYTHING, ARE YOU?
YOU'RE A GOOD DOGGY, AREN'T YOU?
Keep 'em guessing, I say!
MBM

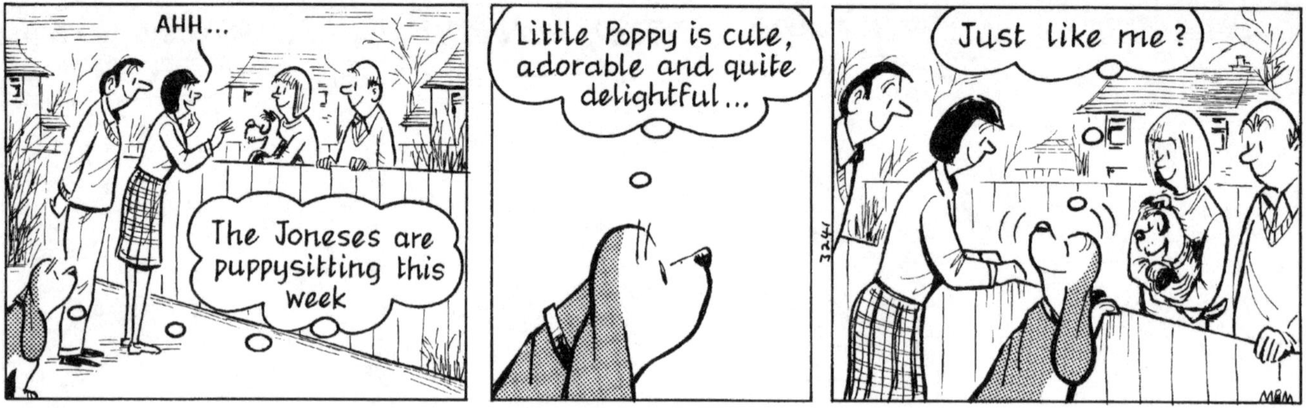
AHH...
The Joneses are puppysitting this week
Little Poppy is cute, adorable and quite delightful...
3241
Just like me?

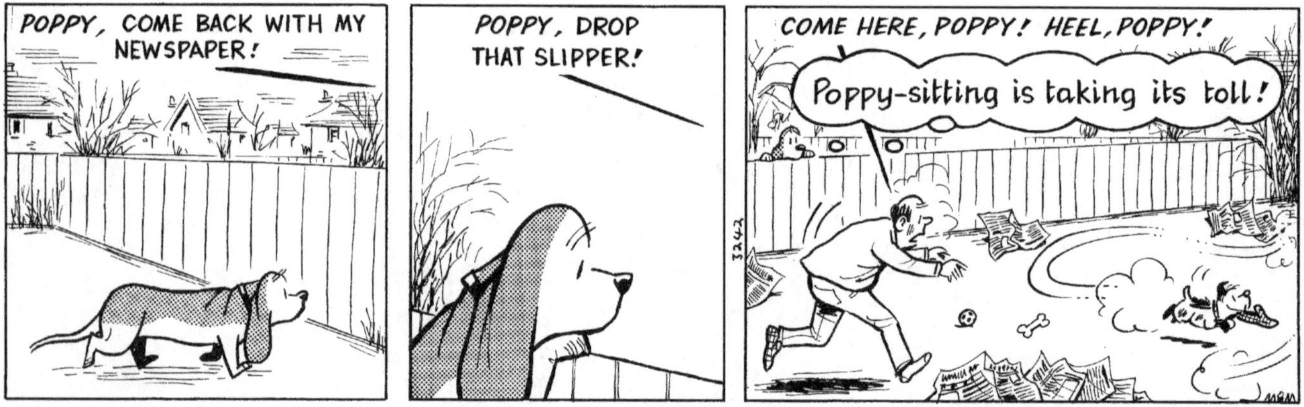
POPPY, COME BACK WITH MY NEWSPAPER!
POPPY, DROP THAT SLIPPER!
3242
COME HERE, POPPY! HEEL, POPPY!
Poppy-sitting is taking its toll!

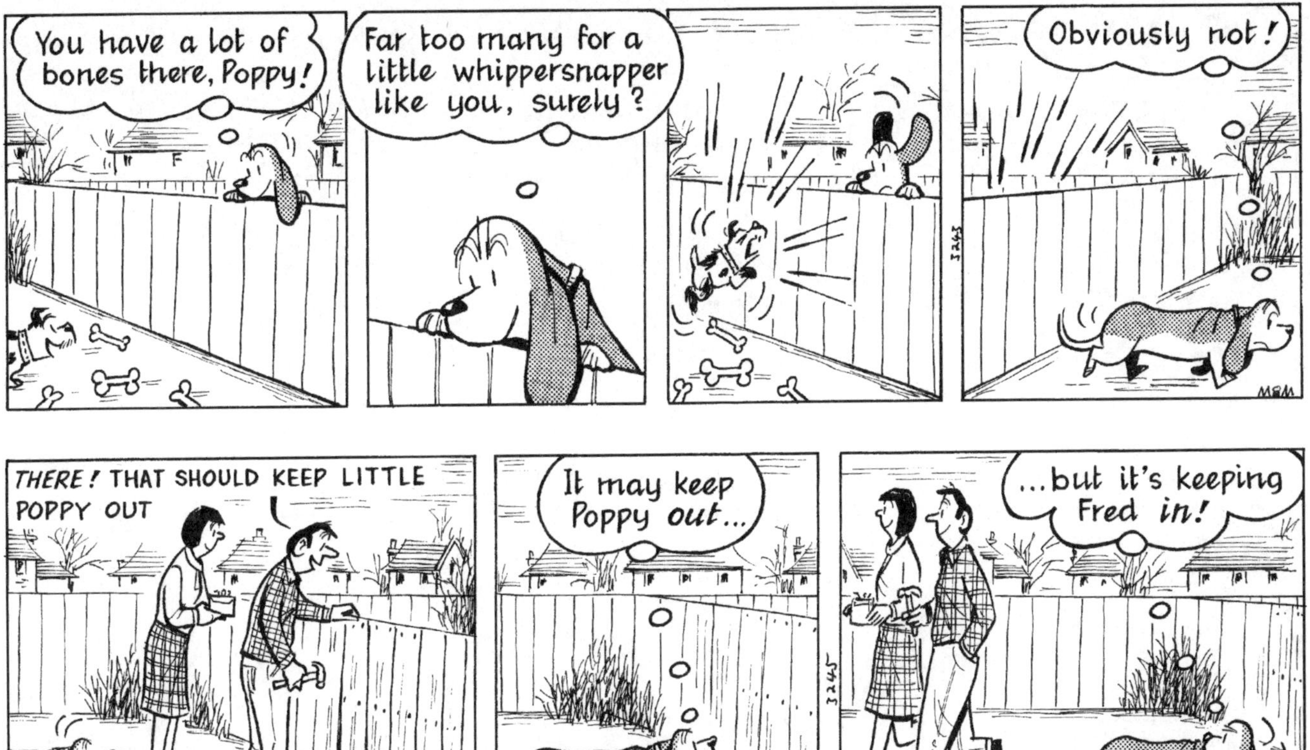
You have a lot of bones there, Poppy!
Far too many for a little whippersnapper like you, surely?
Obviously not!
MGM
3245
THERE! THAT SHOULD KEEP LITTLE POPPY OUT
It may keep Poppy out...
...but it's keeping Fred in!
3245
MGM

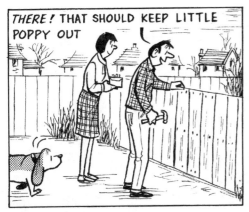

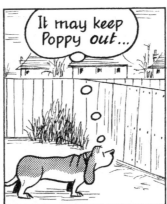

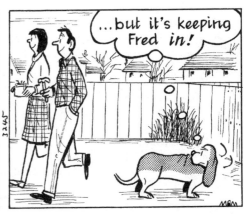

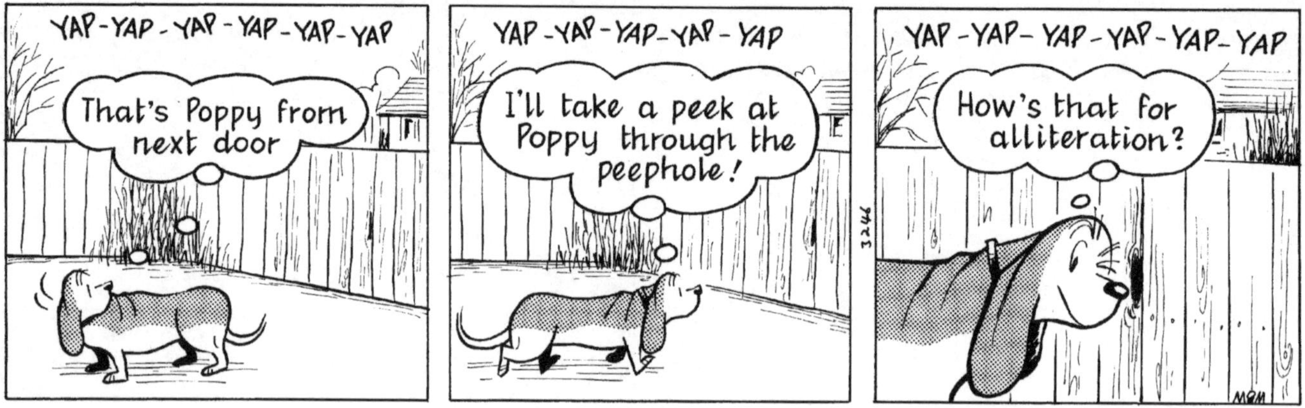
YAP-YAP-YAP-YAP-YAP-YAP
That's Poppy from next door
YAP-YAP-YAP-YAP-YAP
I'll take a peek at Poppy through the peephole!
YAP-YAP-YAP-YAP-YAP-YAP
How's that for alliteration?

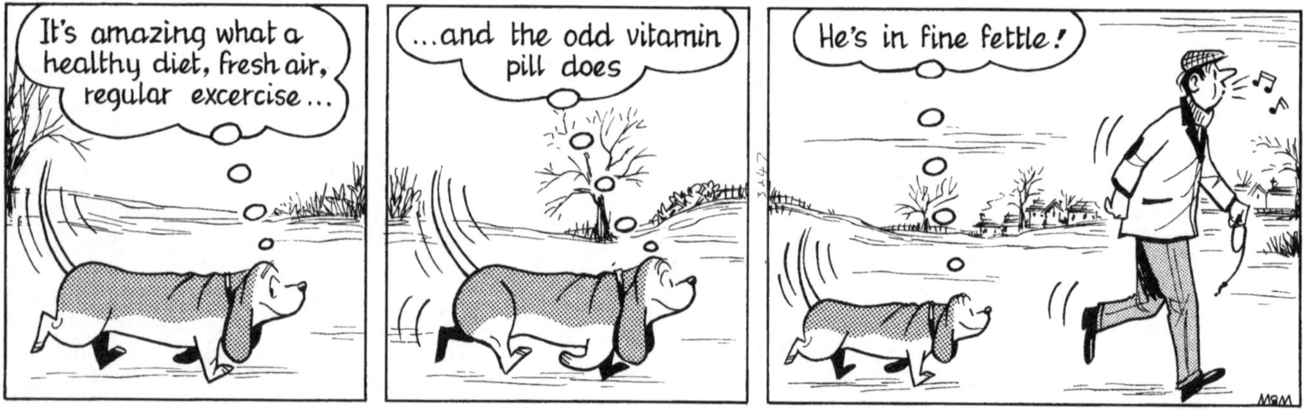
It's amazing what a healthy diet, fresh air, regular excercise...
...and the odd vitamin pill does
He's in fine fettle!

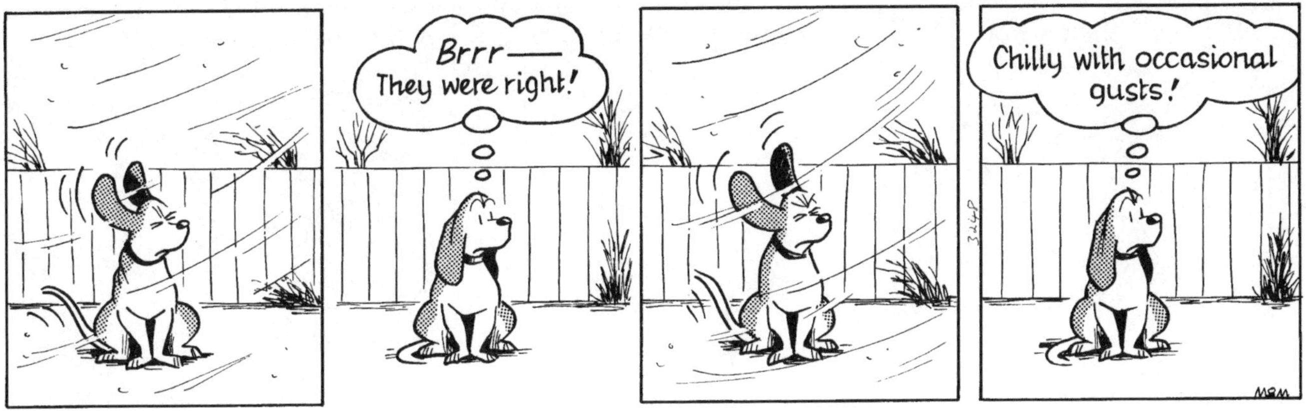
Brrr——
They were right!
Chilly with occasional gusts!

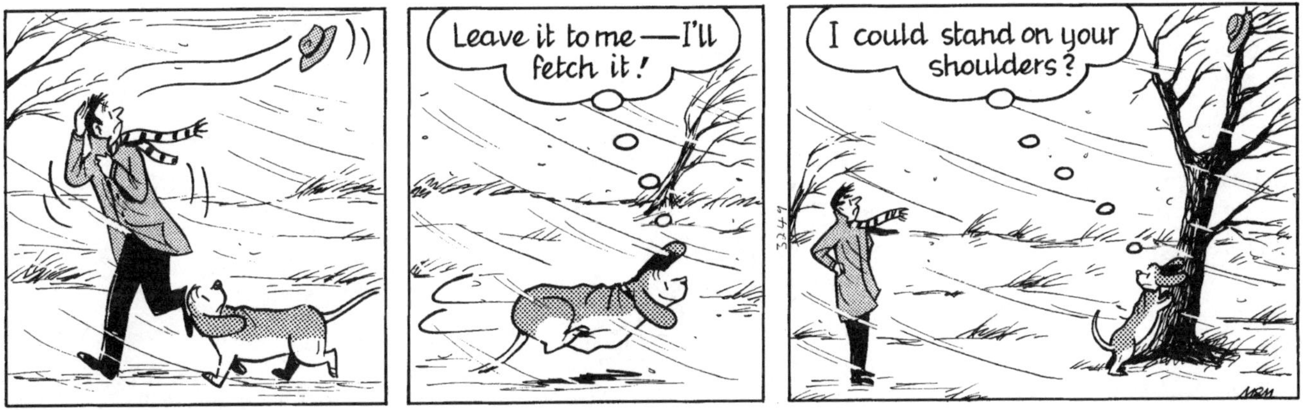
Leave it to me——I'll fetch it!
I could stand on your shoulders?

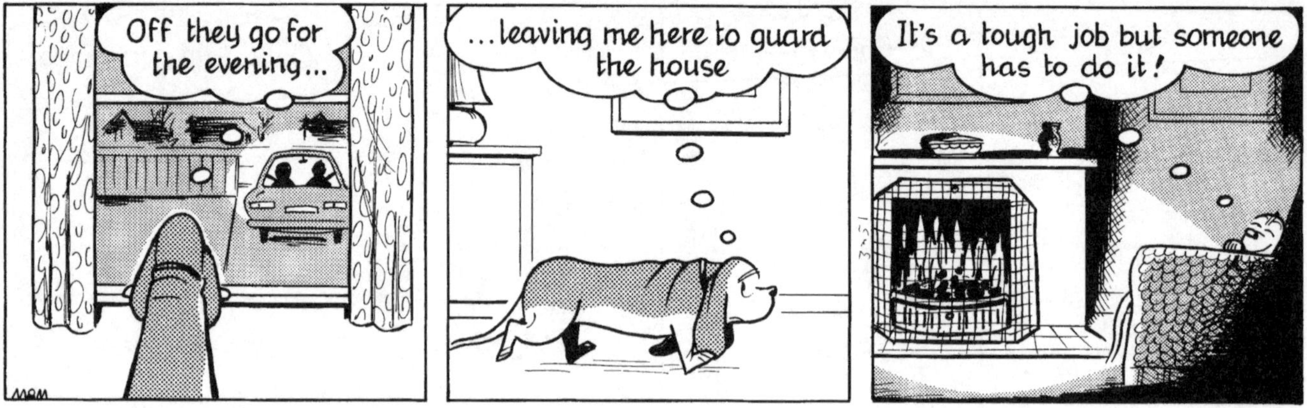
Off they go for the evening...
...leaving me here to guard the house
It's a tough job but someone has to do it!

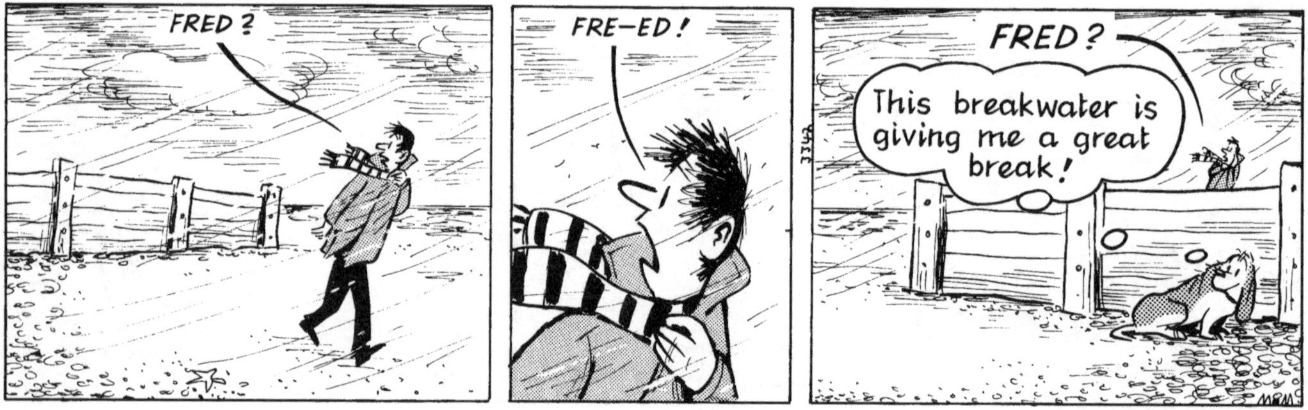
FRED?
FRE-ED!
FRED?
This breakwater is giving me a great break!

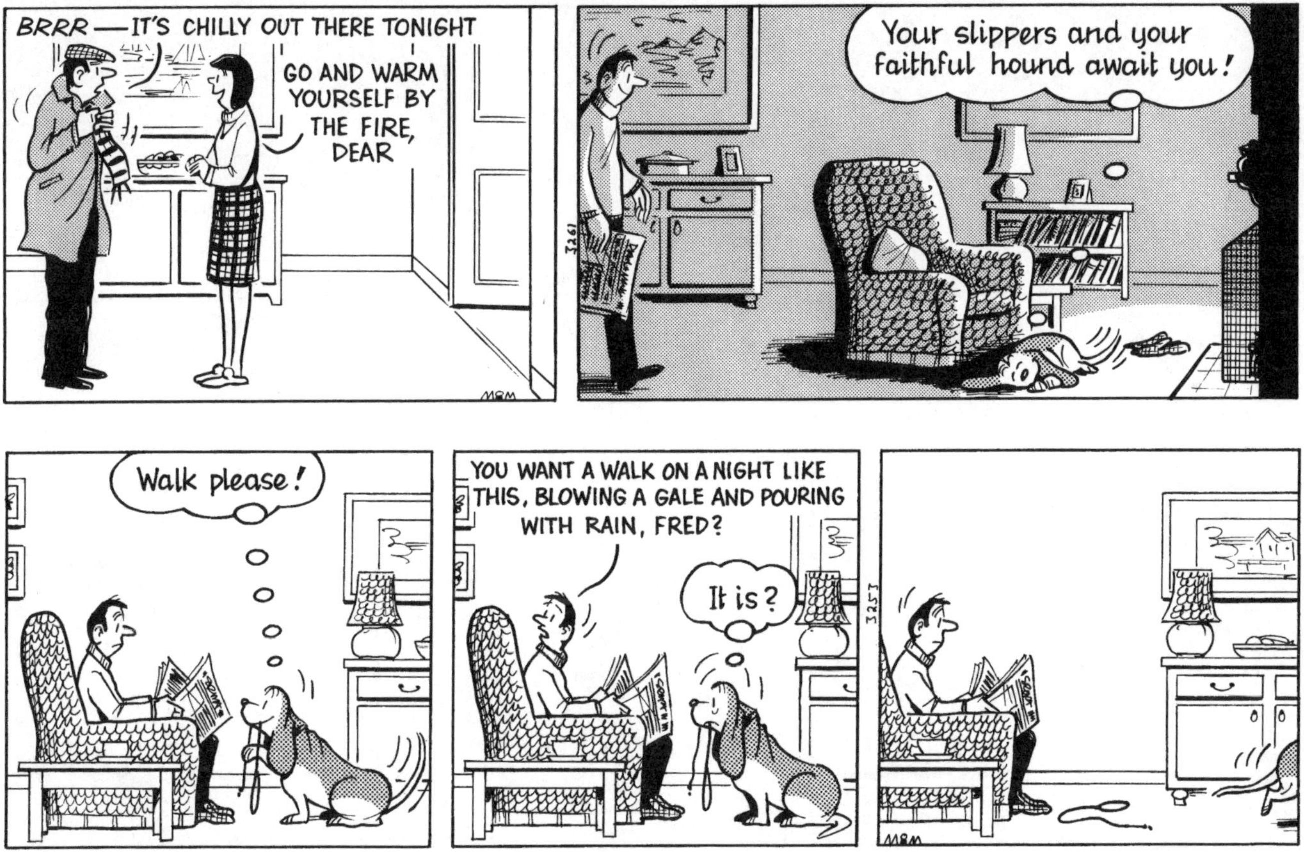
BRRR—IT'S CHILLY OUT THERE TONIGHT
GO AND WARM YOURSELF BY THE FIRE, DEAR
Your slippers and your faithful hound await you!
Walk please!
YOU WANT A WALK ON A NIGHT LIKE THIS, BLOWING A GALE AND POURING WITH RAIN, FRED?
It is?

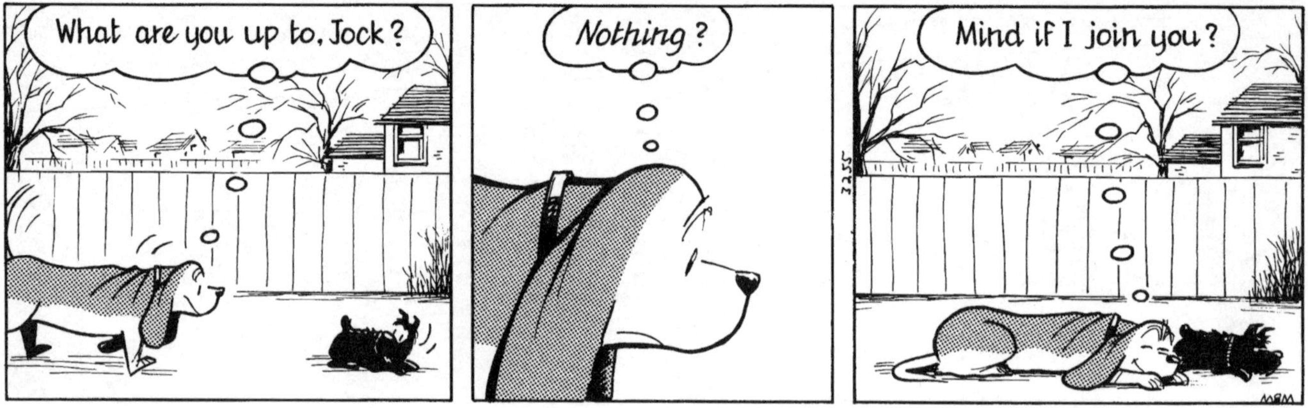
What are you up to, Jock?
Nothing?
Mind if I join you?

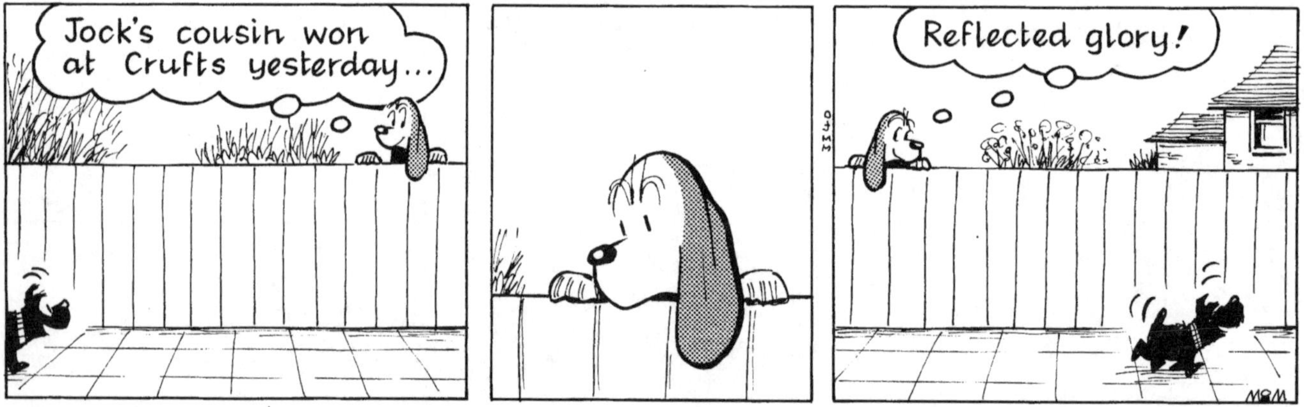
Jock's cousin won at Crufts yesterday...
Reflected glory!

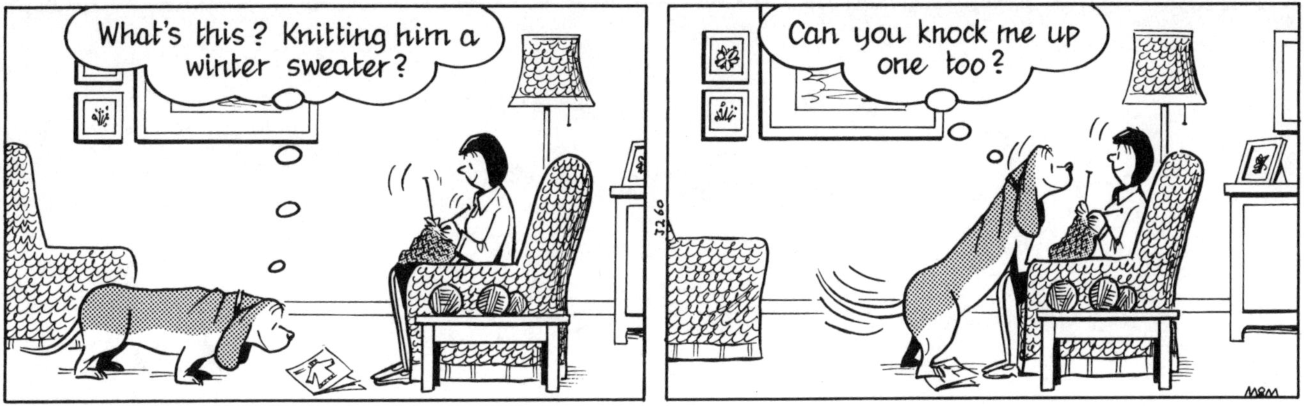
What's this? Knitting him a winter sweater?
Can you knock me up one too?

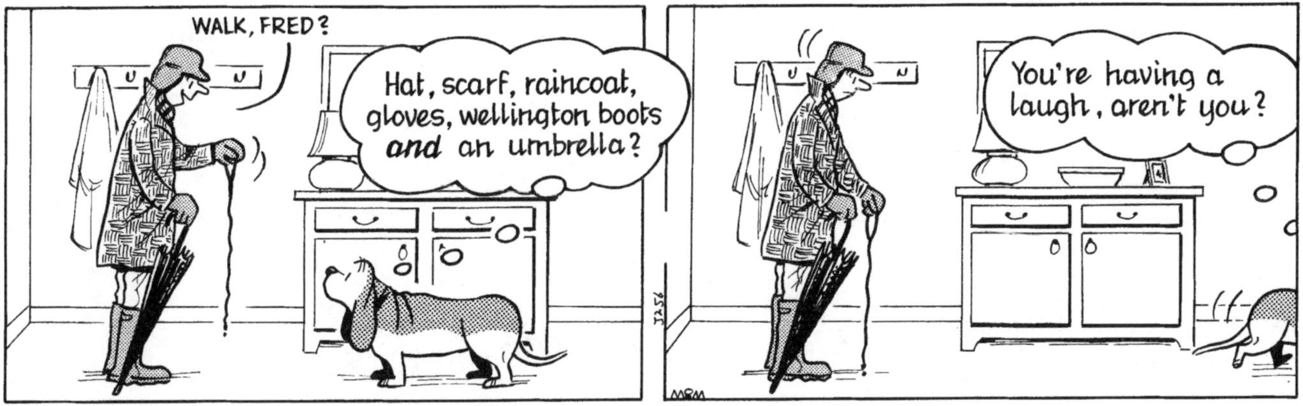
WALK, FRED?
Hat, scarf, raincoat, gloves, wellington boots *and* an umbrella?
You're having a laugh, aren't you?

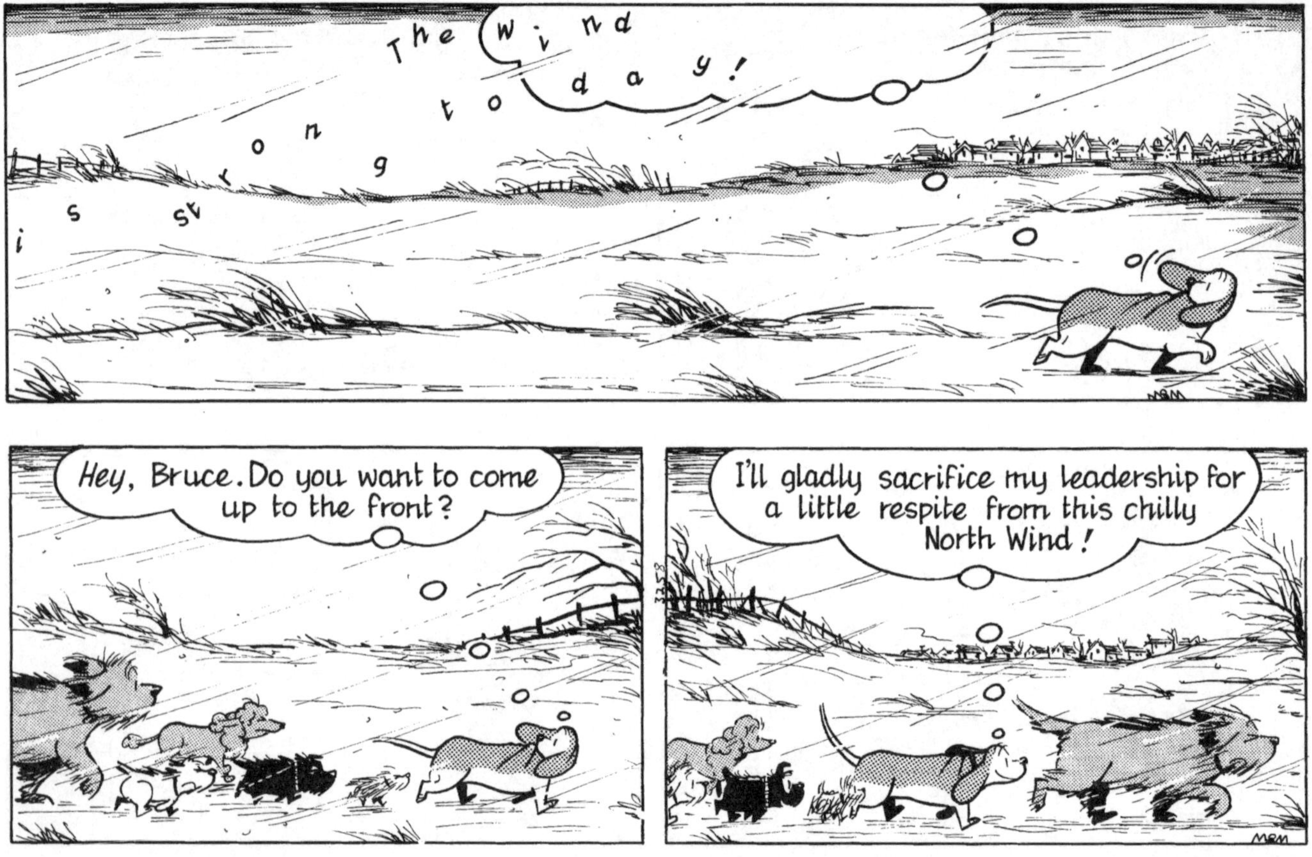
The wind is strong today!
Hey, Bruce. Do you want to come up to the front?
I'll gladly sacrifice my leadership for a little respite from this chilly North Wind!

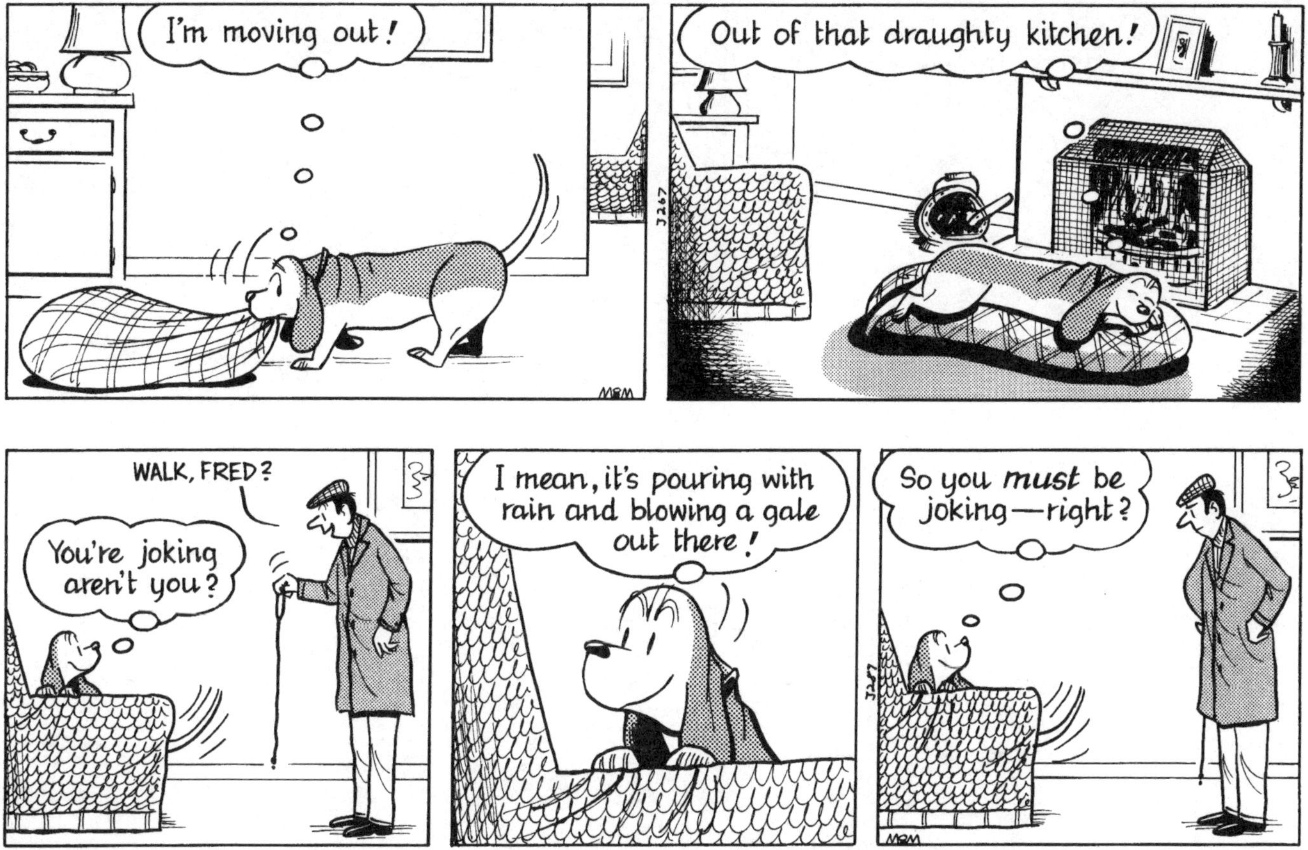

I'm moving out!
Out of that draughty kitchen!
WALK, FRED?
You're joking aren't you?
I mean, it's pouring with rain and blowing a gale out there!
So you *must* be joking—right?

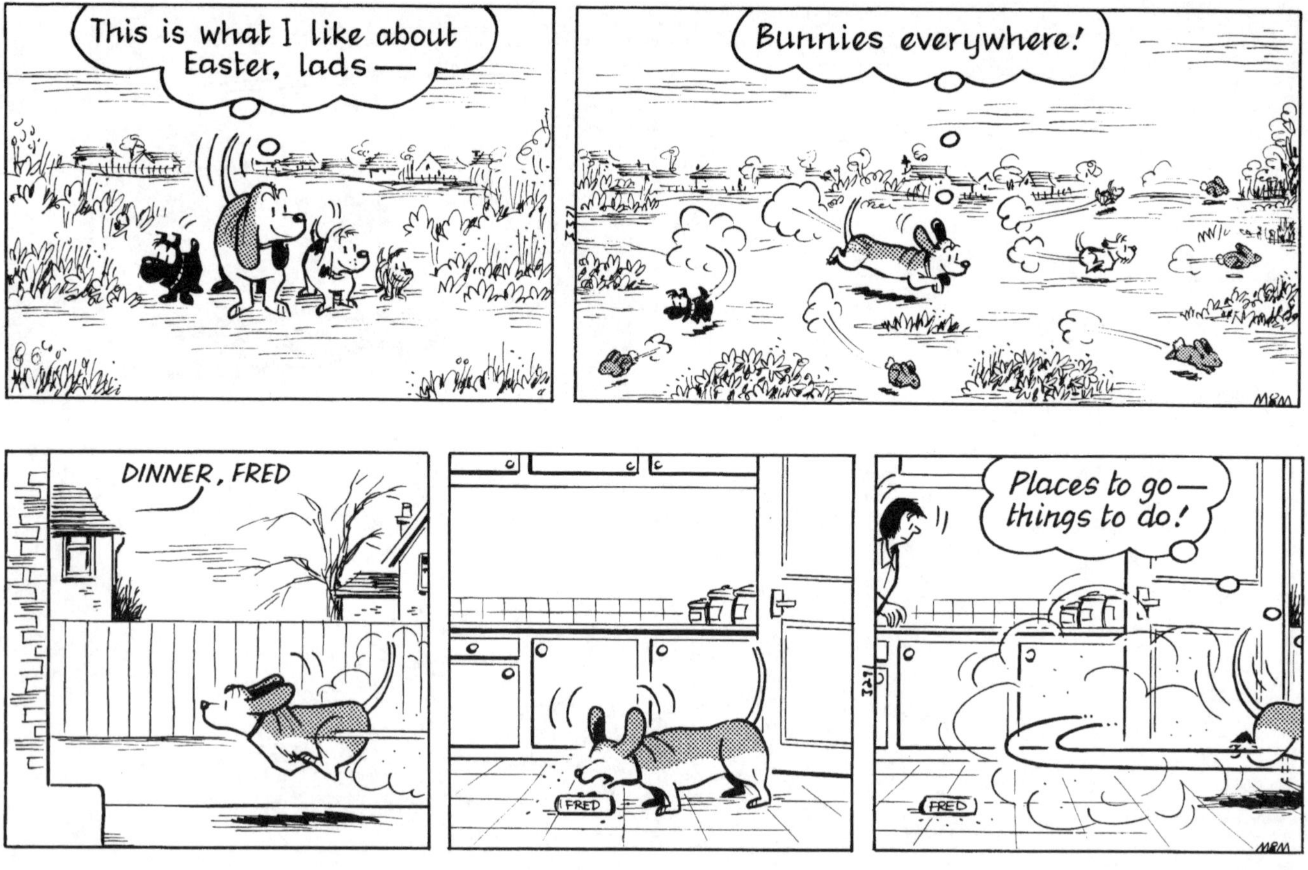

This is what I like about Easter, lads —
Bunnies everywhere!
MRM
DINNER, FRED
FRED
Places to go— things to do!
FRED
MRM

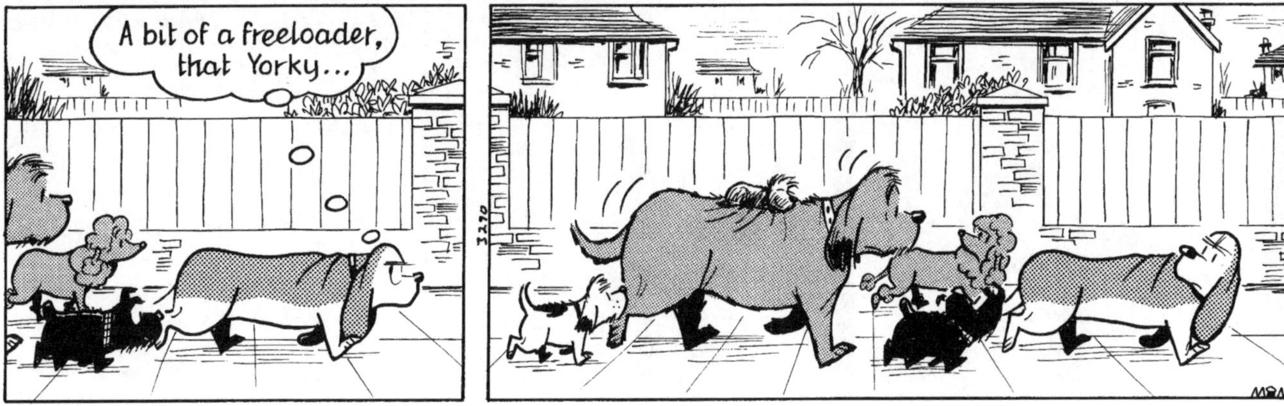
A bit of a freeloader, that Yorky...

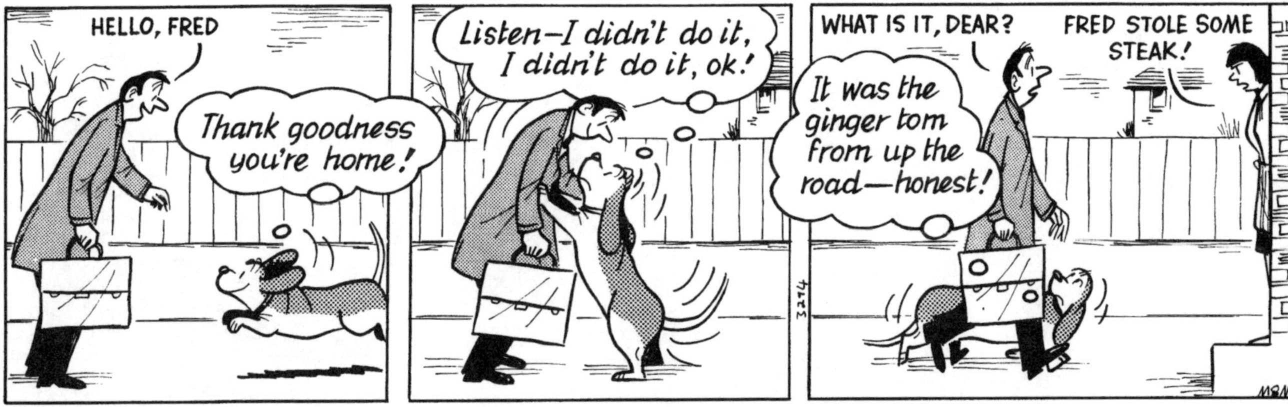
HELLO, FRED
Thank goodness you're home!
Listen–I didn't do it, I didn't do it, ok!
WHAT IS IT, DEAR?
FRED STOLE SOME STEAK!
It was the ginger tom from up the road—honest!

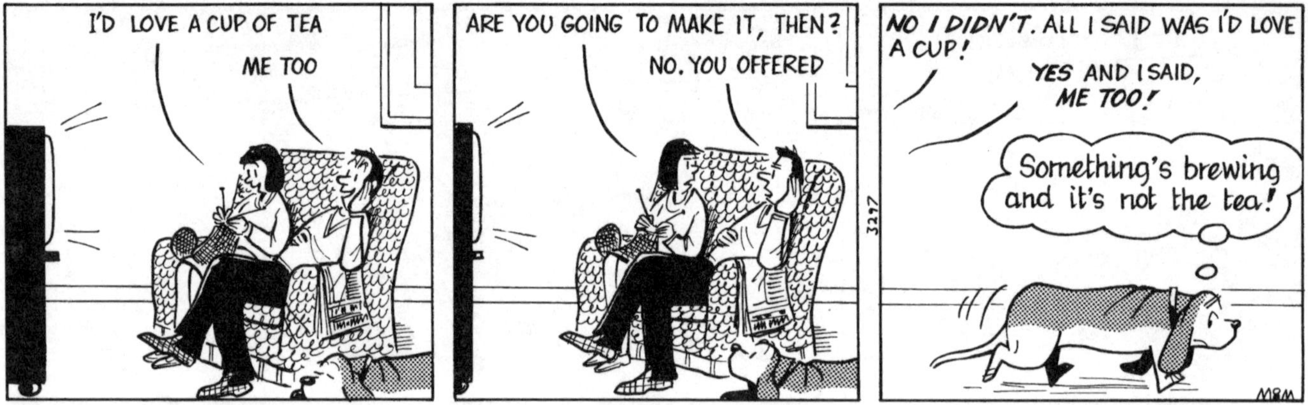
I'D LOVE A CUP OF TEA
ME TOO
ARE YOU GOING TO MAKE IT, THEN?
NO. YOU OFFERED
NO I DIDN'T. ALL I SAID WAS I'D LOVE A CUP!
YES AND I SAID, ME TOO!
Something's brewing and it's not the tea!

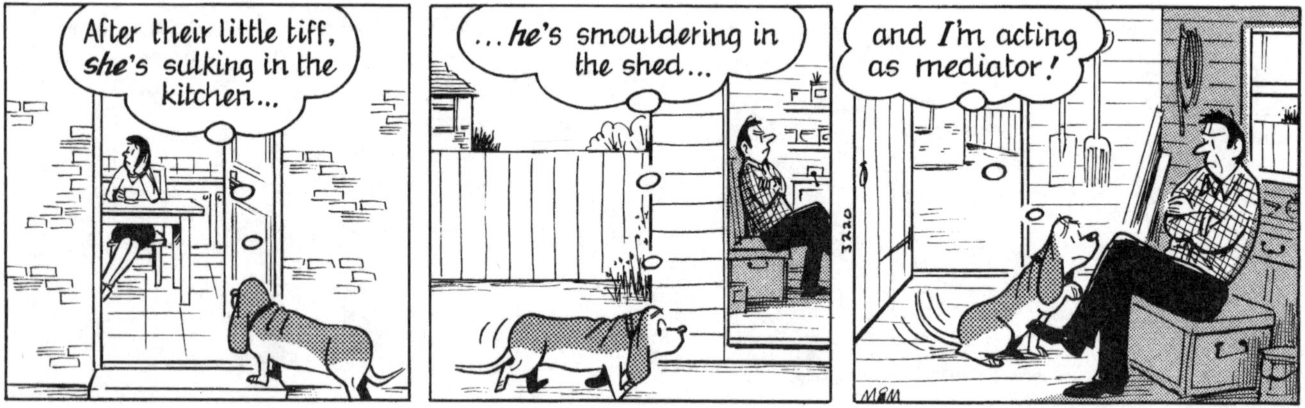
After their little tiff, she's sulking in the kitchen...
...he's smouldering in the shed...
and I'm acting as mediator!

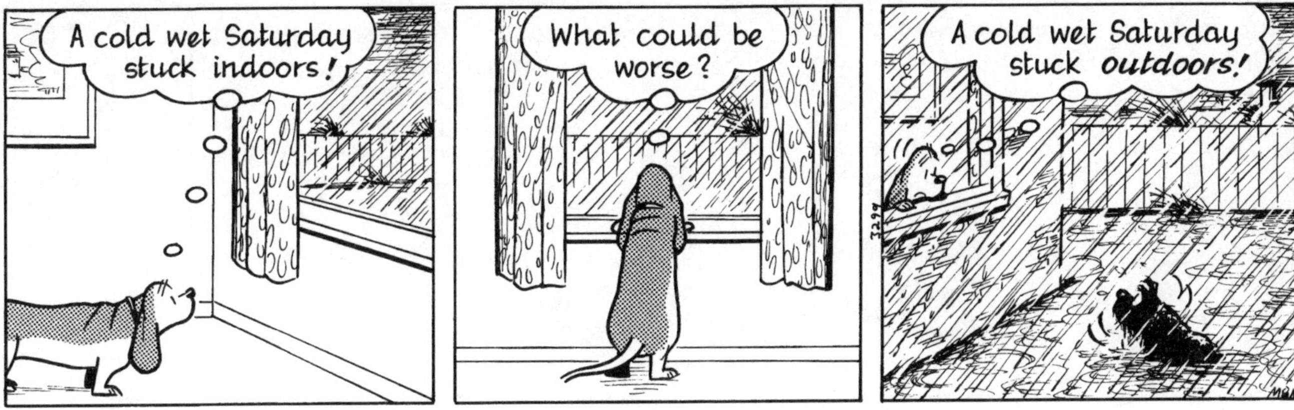
A cold wet Saturday stuck indoors!
What could be worse?
A cold wet Saturday stuck *outdoors!*

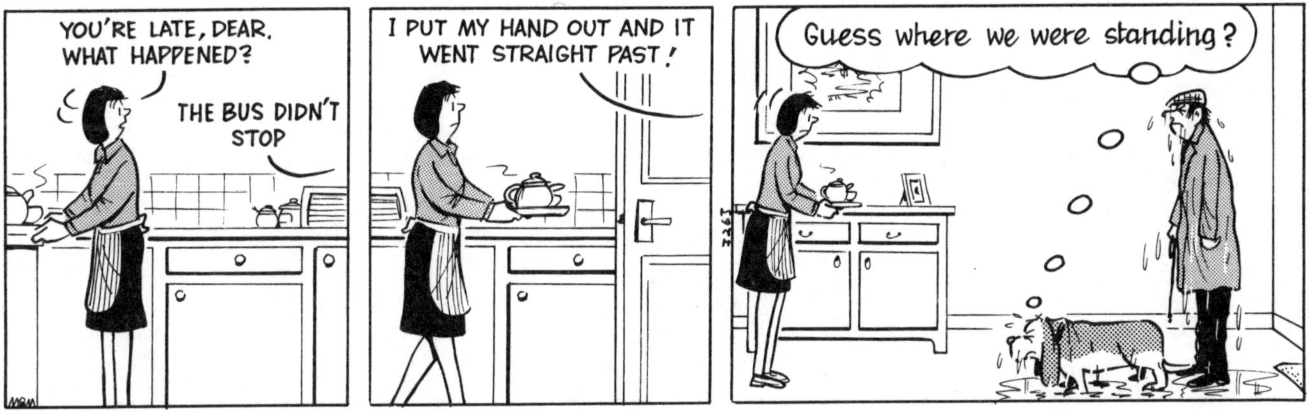
YOU'RE LATE, DEAR. WHAT HAPPENED?
THE BUS DIDN'T STOP
I PUT MY HAND OUT AND IT WENT STRAIGHT PAST!
Guess where we were standing?

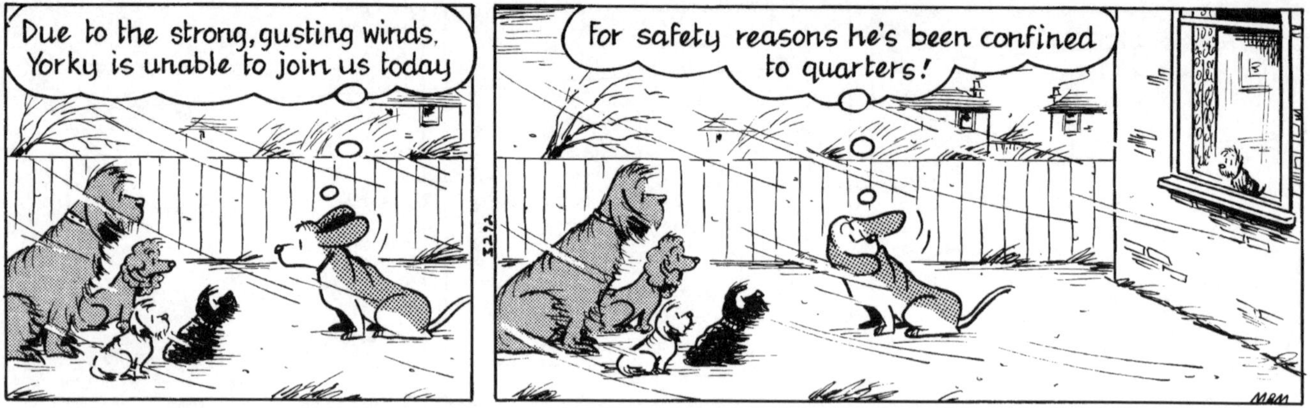
Due to the strong, gusting winds. Yorky is unable to join us today
For safety reasons he's been confined to quarters!

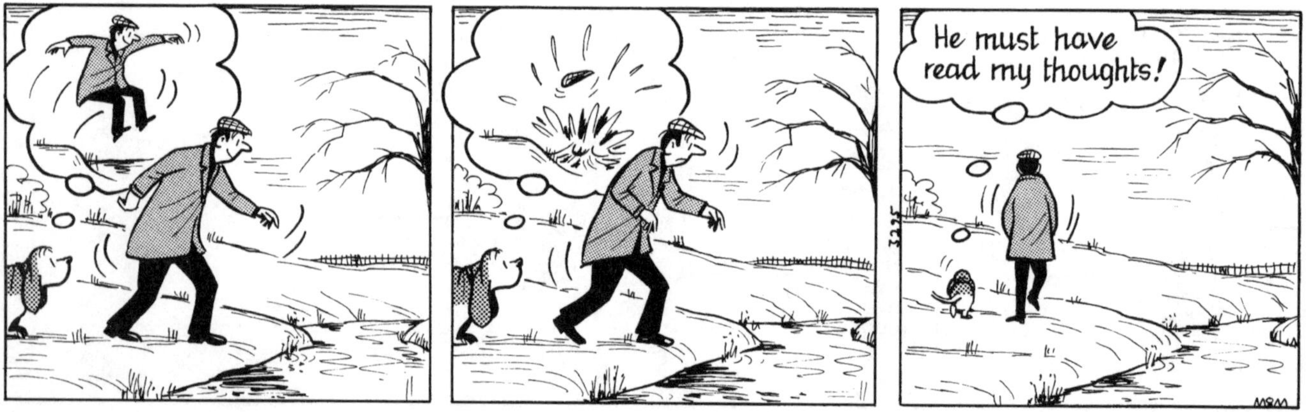
He must have read my thoughts!

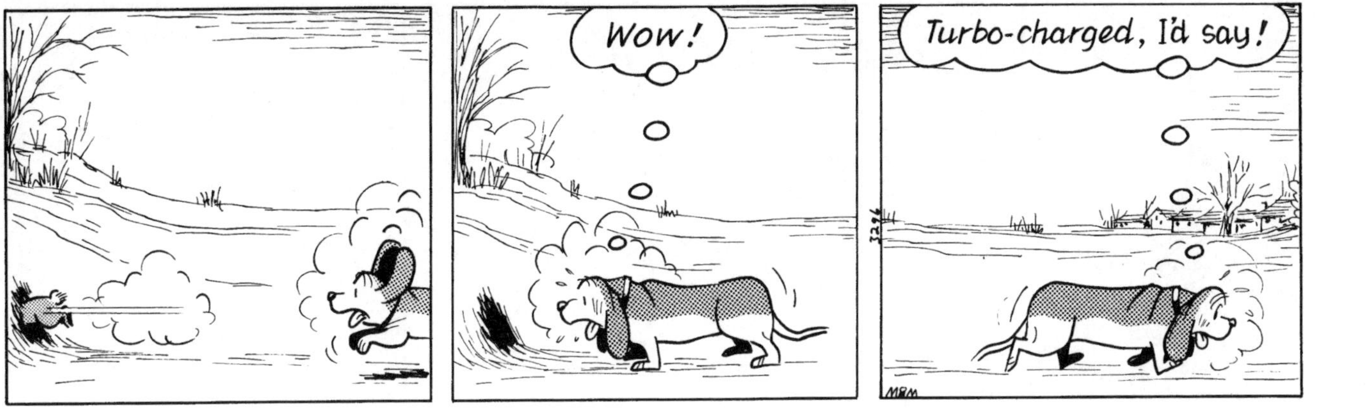
Wow!
Turbo-charged, I'd say!

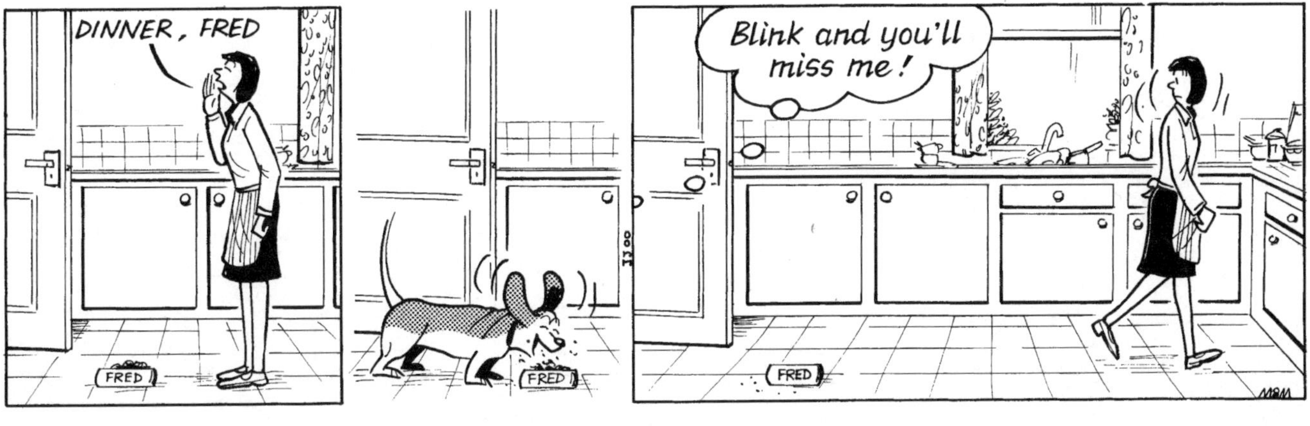
DINNER, FRED
FRED
FRED
Blink and you'll miss me!
FRED

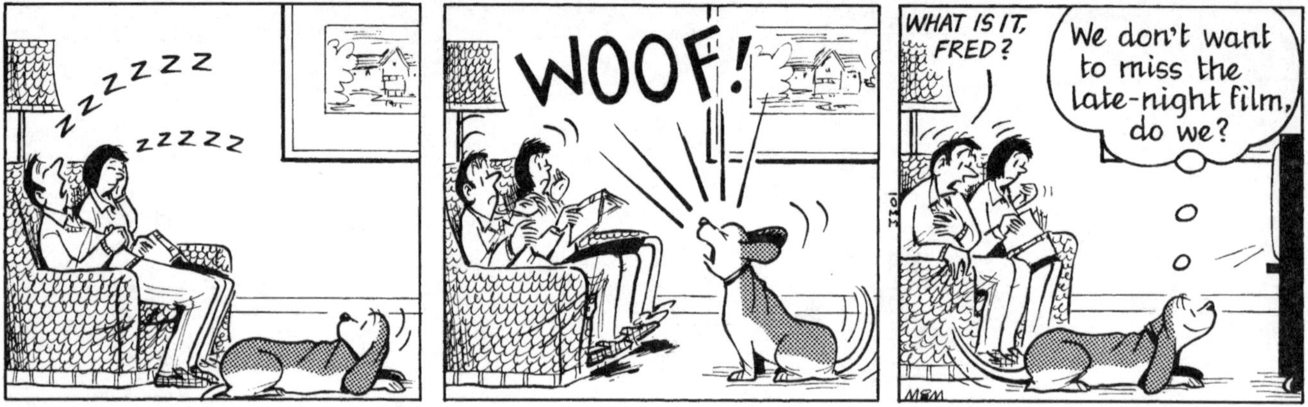
ZZZZZZZ
ZZZZZ
WOOF!
WHAT IS IT, FRED?
We don't want to miss the late-night film, do we?

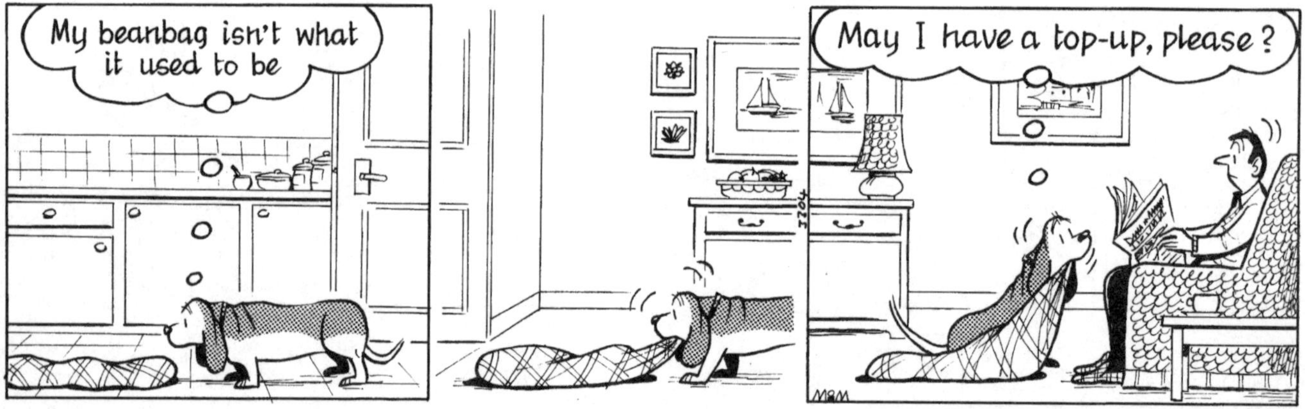
My beanbag isn't what it used to be
May I have a top-up, please?

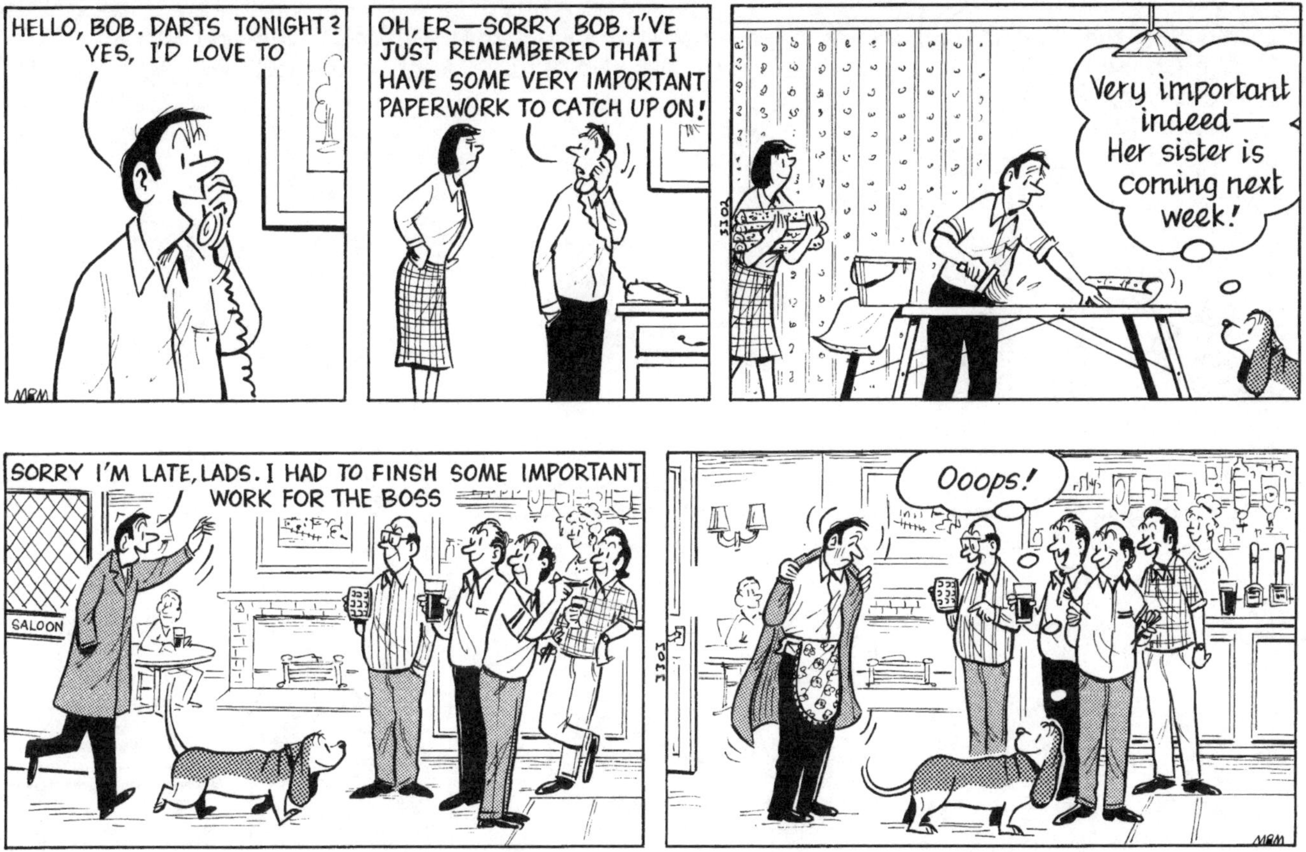
HELLO, BOB. DARTS TONIGHT? YES, I'D LOVE TO
OH, ER—SORRY BOB. I'VE JUST REMEMBERED THAT I HAVE SOME VERY IMPORTANT PAPERWORK TO CATCH UP ON!
Very important indeed— Her sister is coming next week!
SORRY I'M LATE, LADS. I HAD TO FINSH SOME IMPORTANT WORK FOR THE BOSS
SALOON
Ooops!

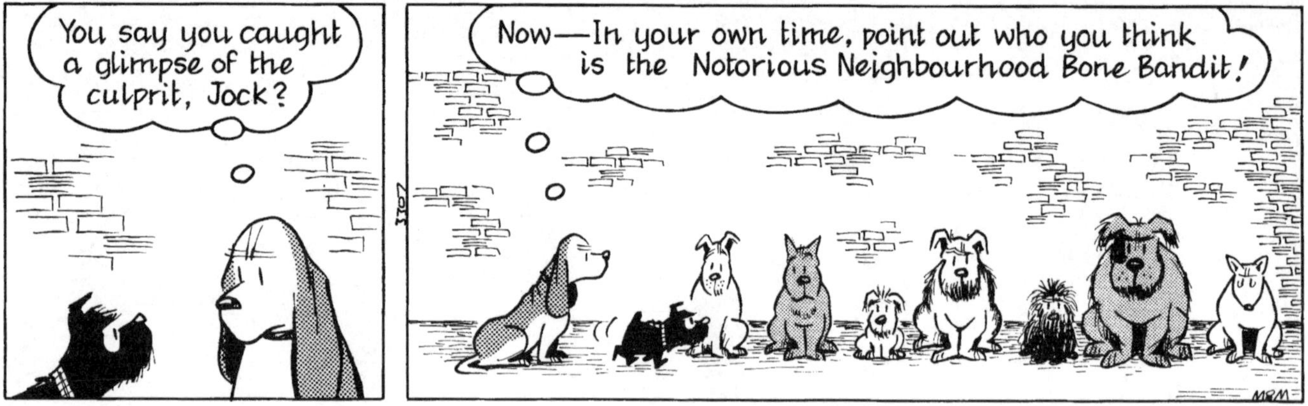
You say you caught a glimpse of the culprit, Jock?
Now—In your own time, point out who you think is the Notorious Neighbourhood Bone Bandit!

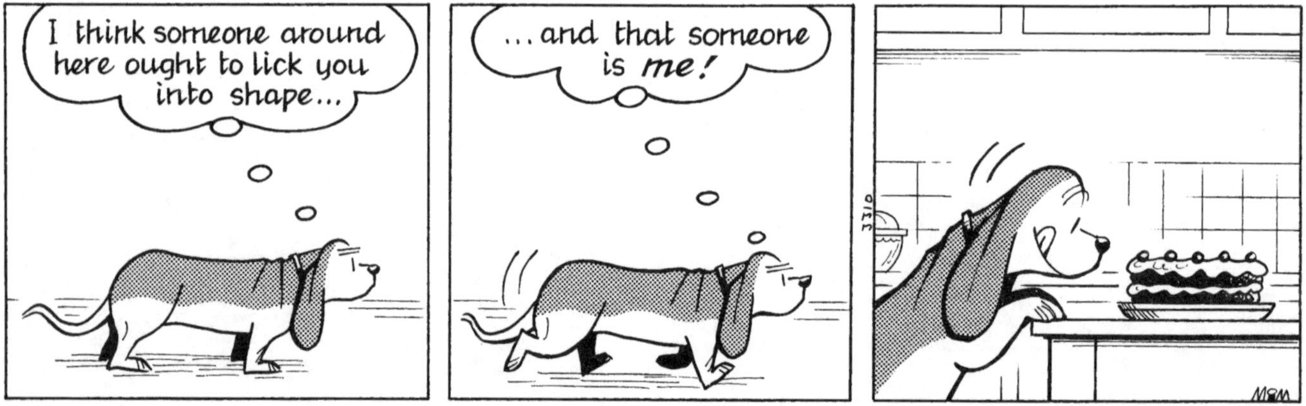
I think someone around here ought to lick you into shape...
...and that someone is *me!*

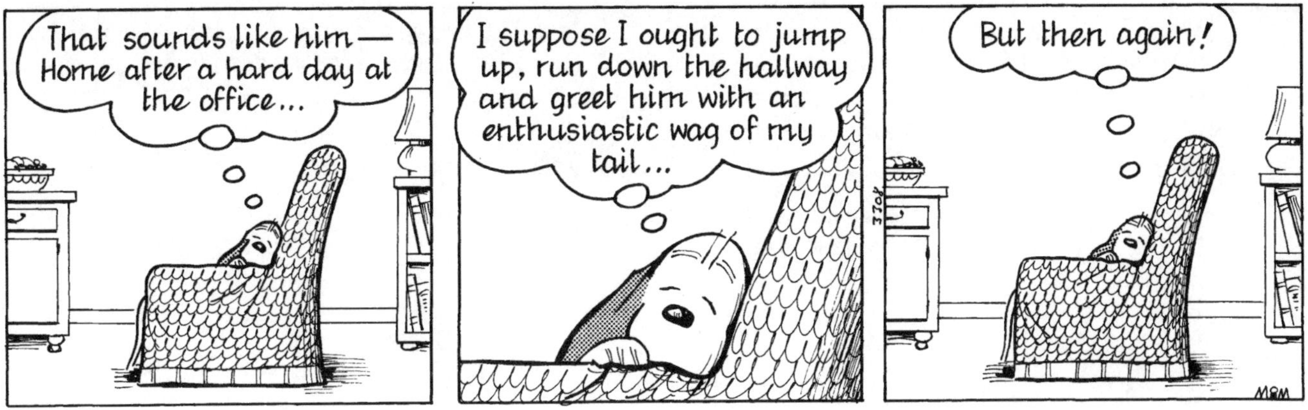
That sounds like him—
Home after a hard day at
the office...
I suppose I ought to jump
up, run down the hallway
and greet him with an
enthusiastic wag of my
tail...
But then again!

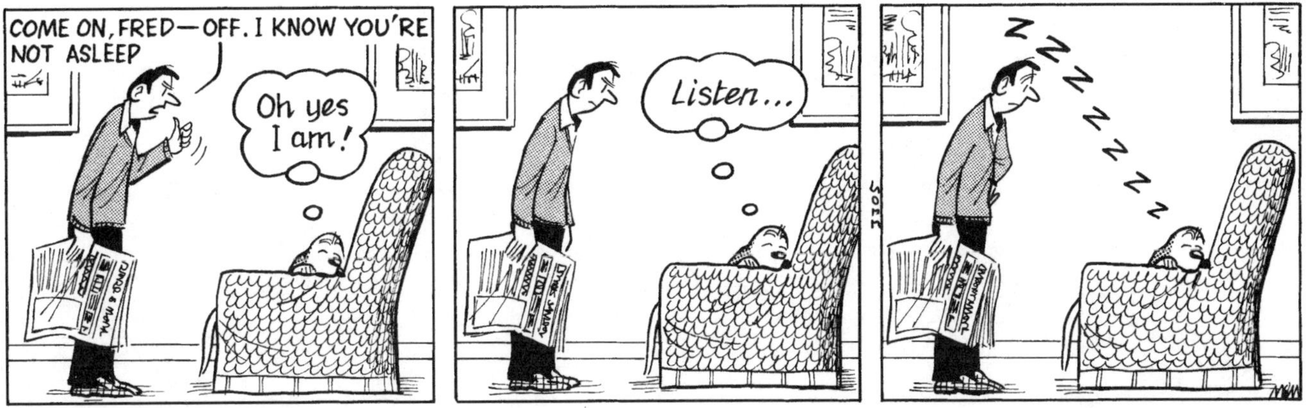
COME ON, FRED—OFF. I KNOW YOU'RE
NOT ASLEEP
Oh yes
I am!
Listen...
Z Z Z Z Z Z Z Z

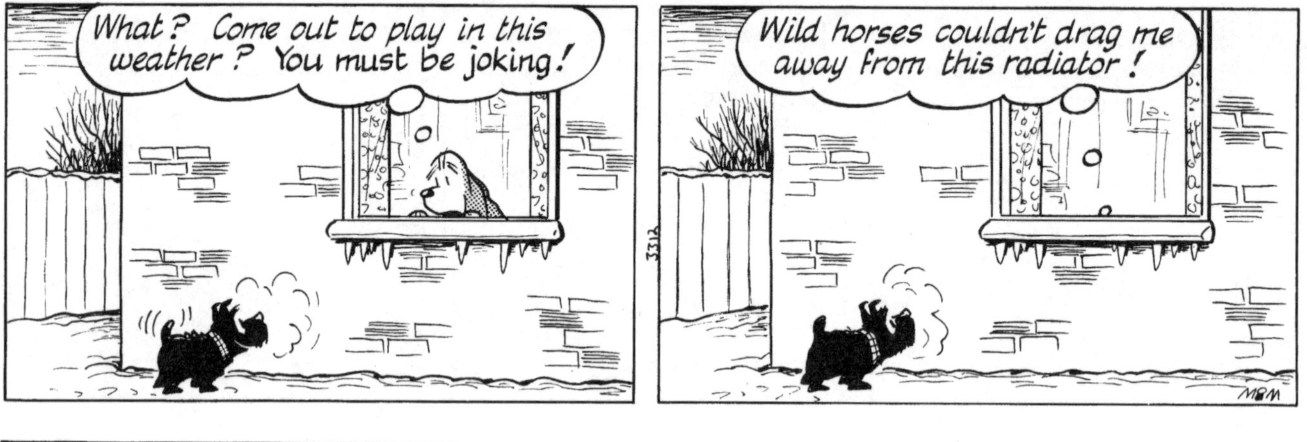
What? Come out to play in this weather? You must be joking!
Wild horses couldn't drag me away from this radiator!

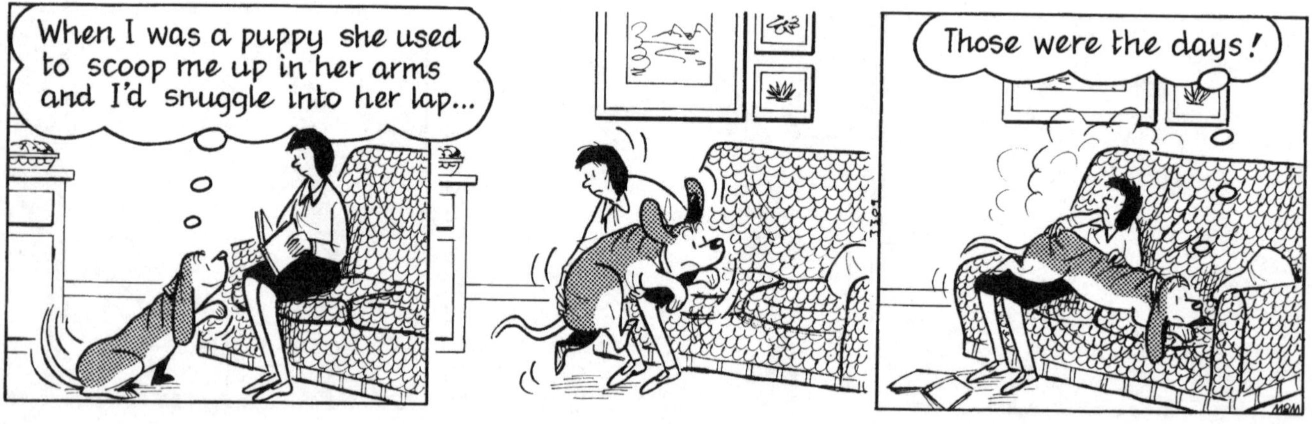
When I was a puppy she used to scoop me up in her arms and I'd snuggle into her lap...
Those were the days!

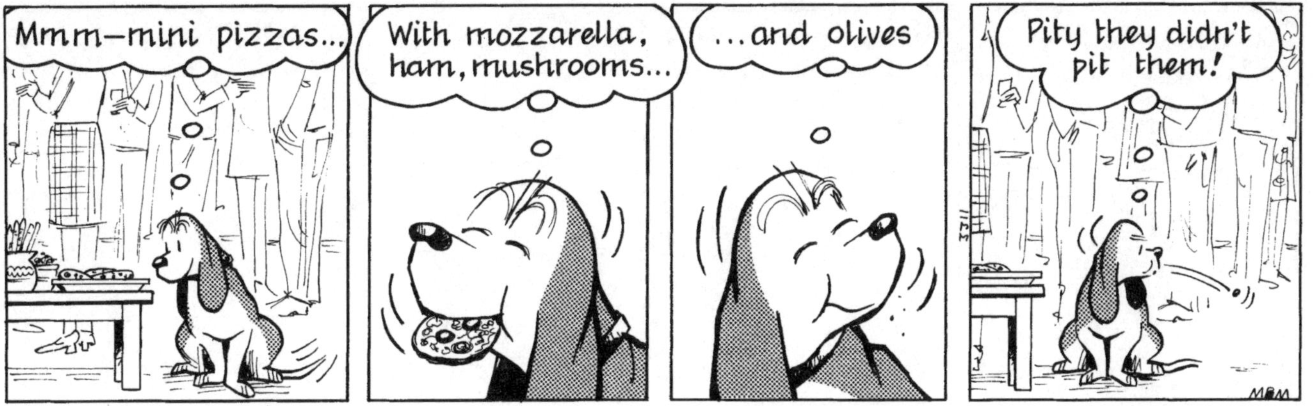
Mmm—mini pizzas...
With mozzarella, ham, mushrooms...
...and olives
Pity they didn't pit them!
MBM

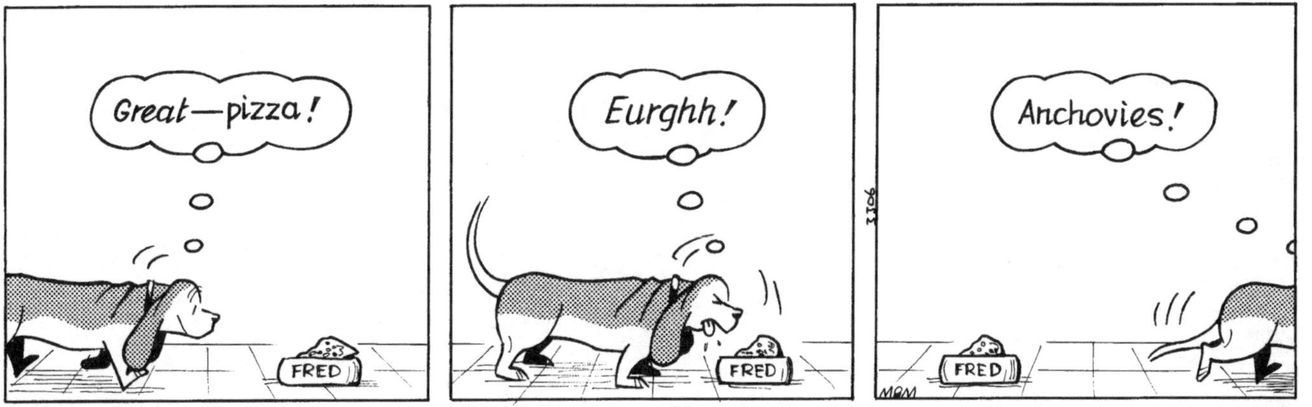
Great—pizza!
FRED
Eurghh!
FRED
Anchovies!
FRED
MBM

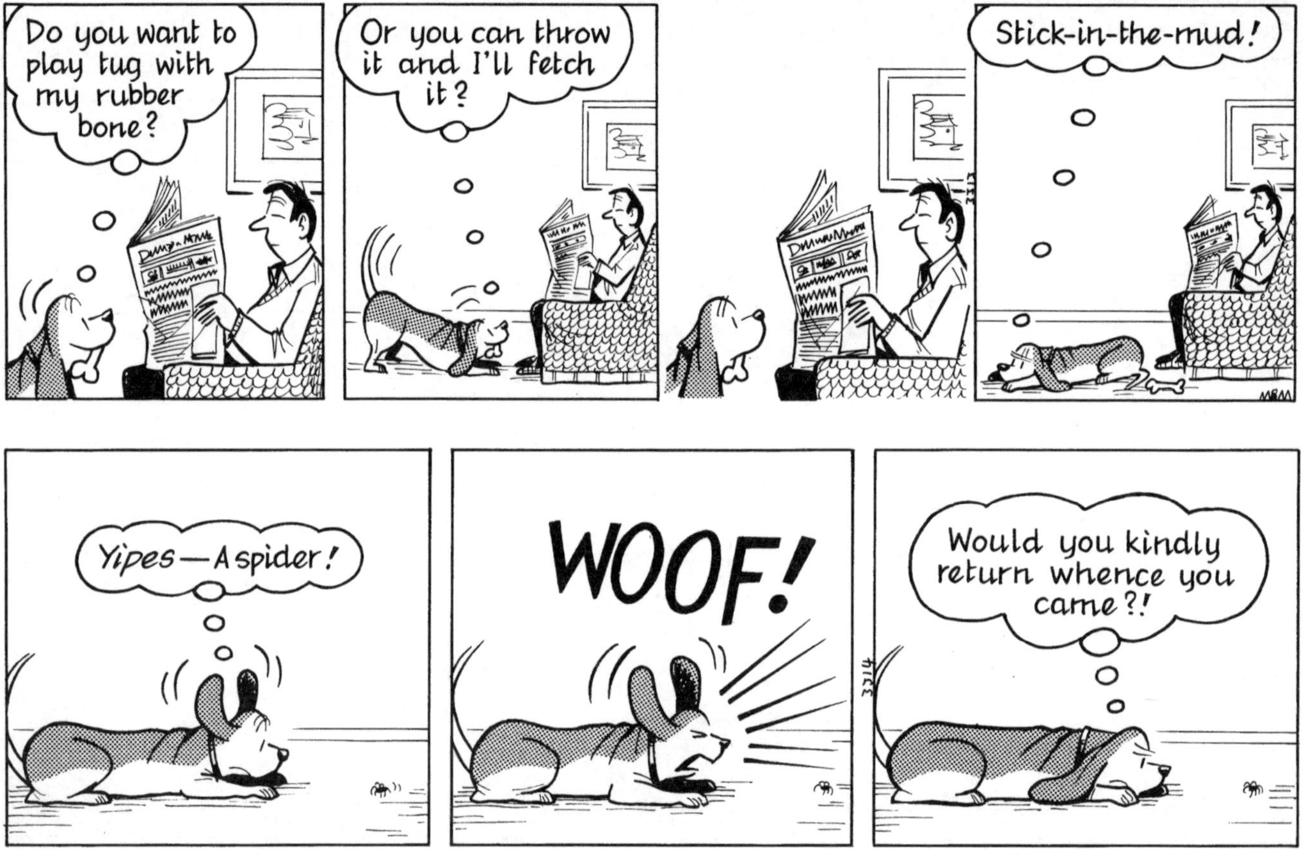
Do you want to play tug with my rubber bone?
Or you can throw it and I'll fetch it?
Stick-in-the-mud!
Yipes—A spider!
WOOF!
Would you kindly return whence you came?!

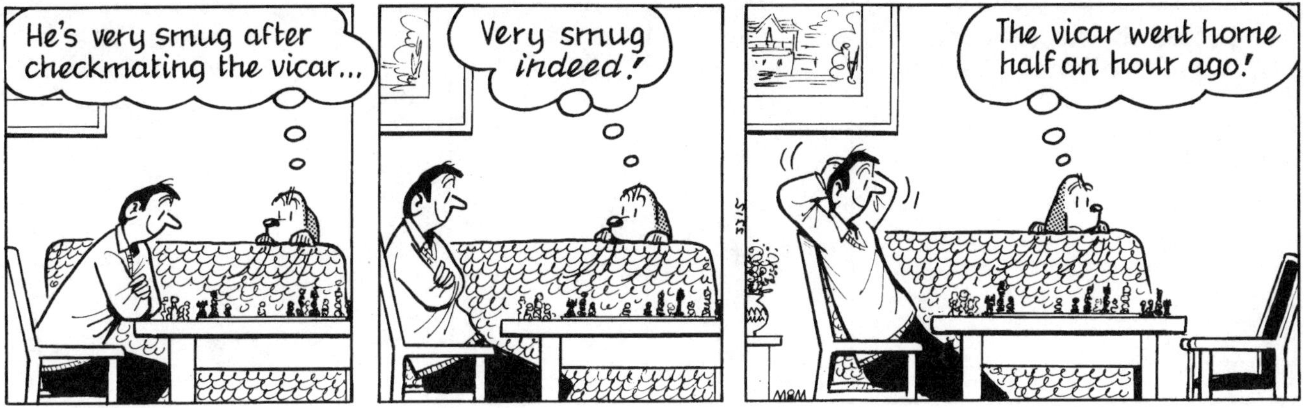
He's very smug after checkmating the vicar...
Very smug *indeed*!
The vicar went home half an hour ago!

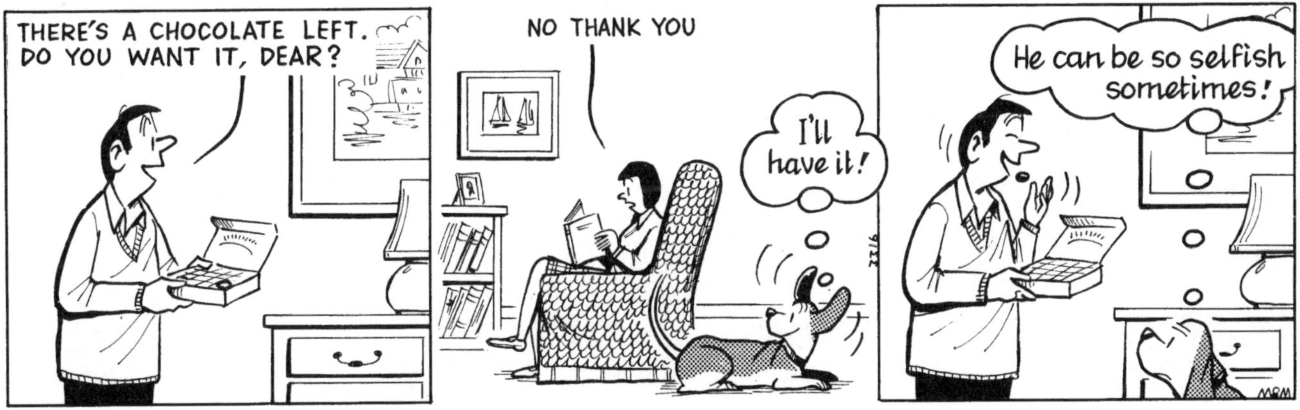
THERE'S A CHOCOLATE LEFT. DO YOU WANT IT, DEAR?
NO THANK YOU
I'll have it!
He can be so selfish sometimes!

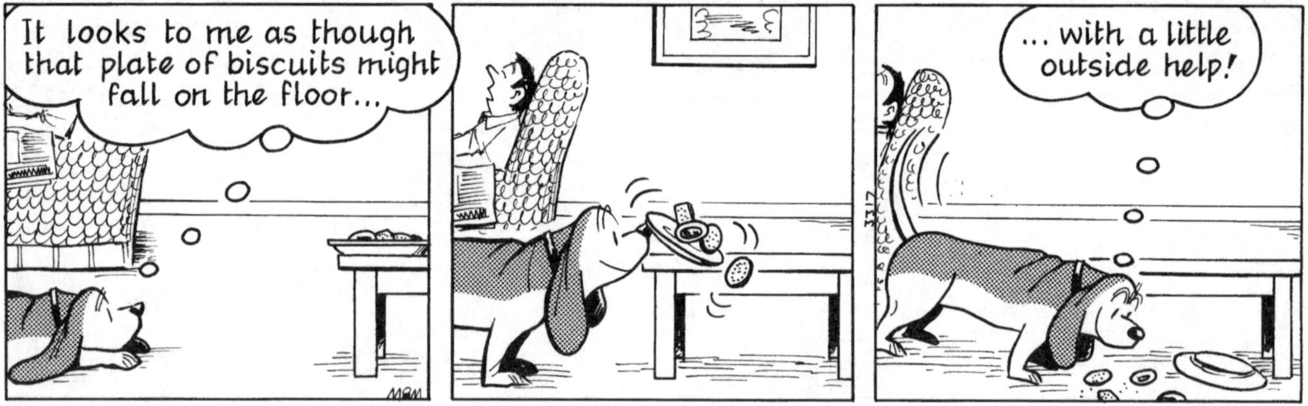
It looks to me as though that plate of biscuits might fall on the floor...
... with a little outside help!

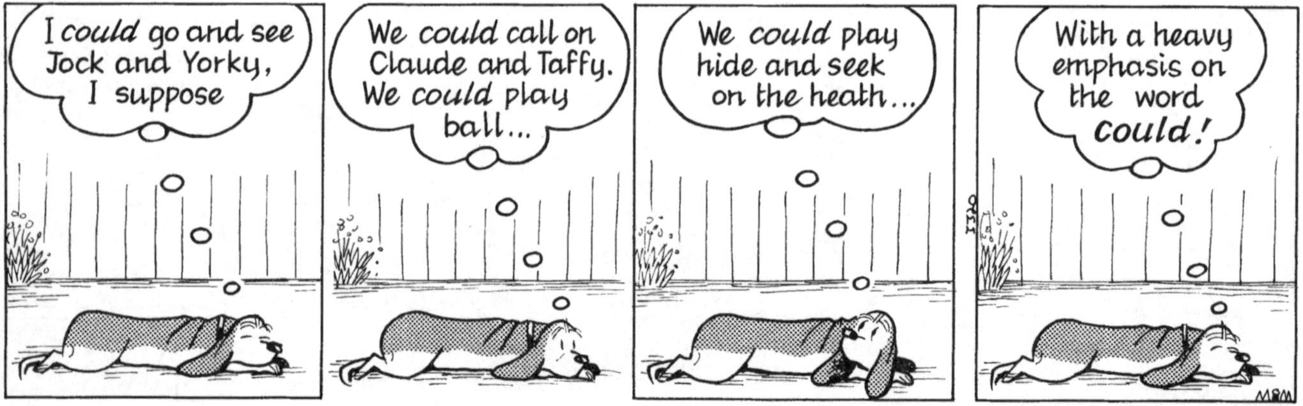
I *could* go and see Jock and Yorky, I suppose
We *could* call on Claude and Taffy. We *could* play ball...
We *could* play hide and seek on the heath...
With a heavy emphasis on the word **could**!

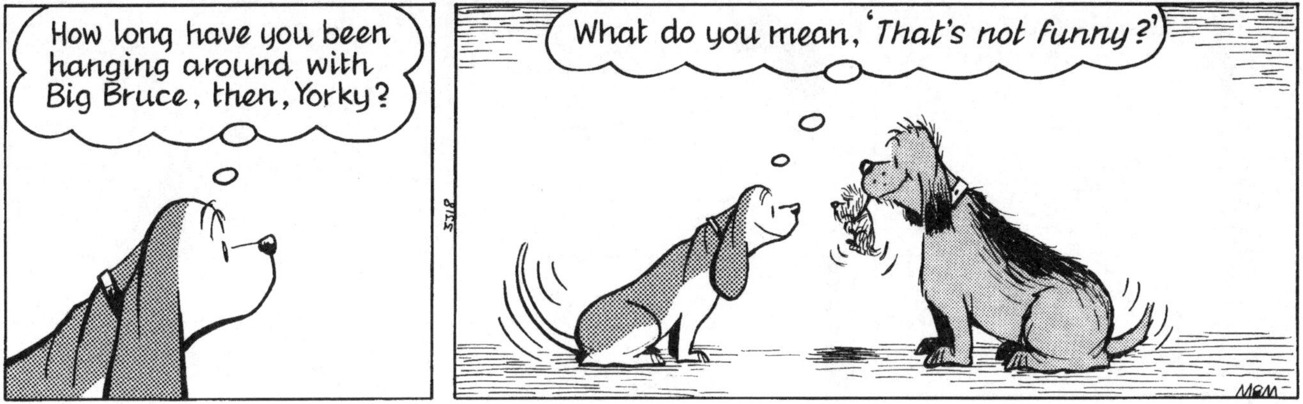
How long have you been hanging around with Big Bruce, then, Yorky?
What do you mean, 'That's not funny?'
3318
M&M

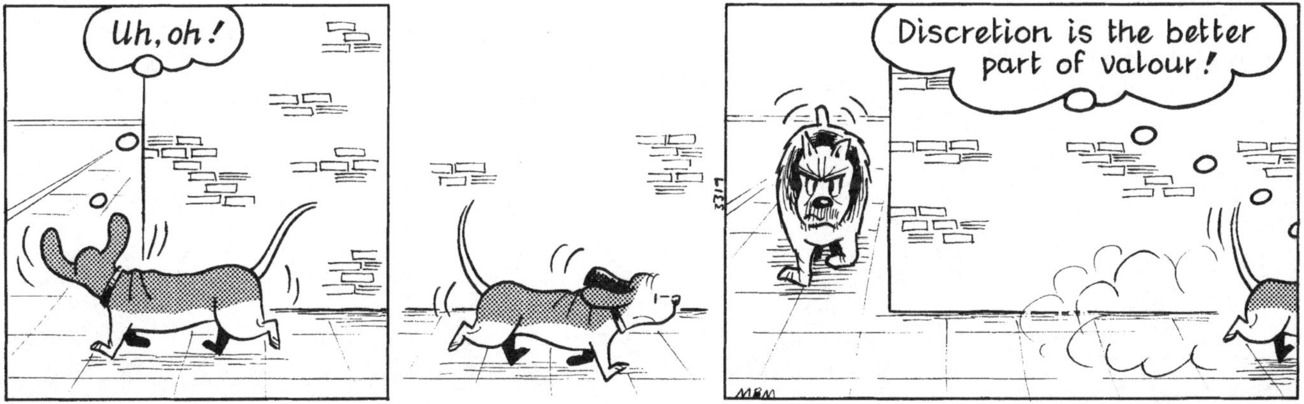
Uh, oh!
Discretion is the better part of valour!
3319
M&M

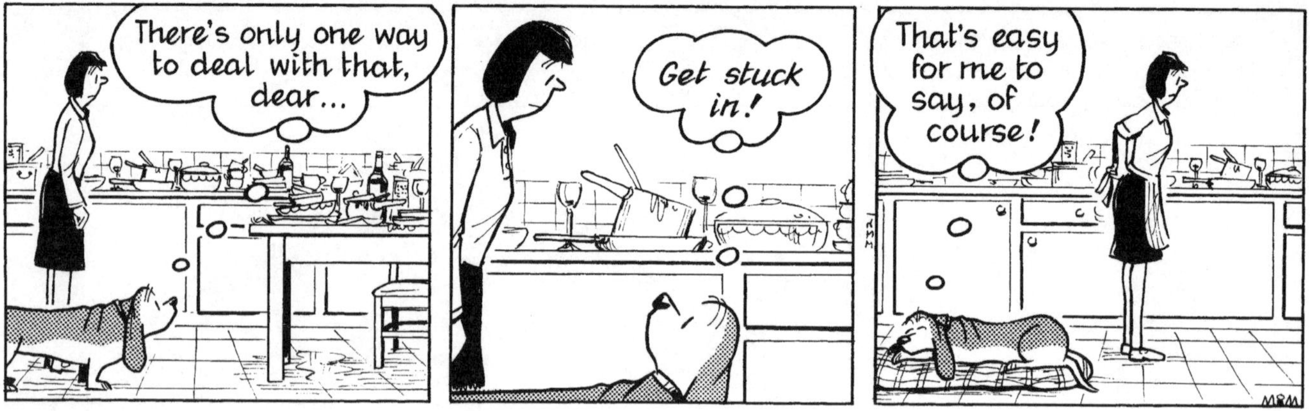
There's only one way to deal with that, dear...
Get stuck in!
That's easy for me to say, of course!

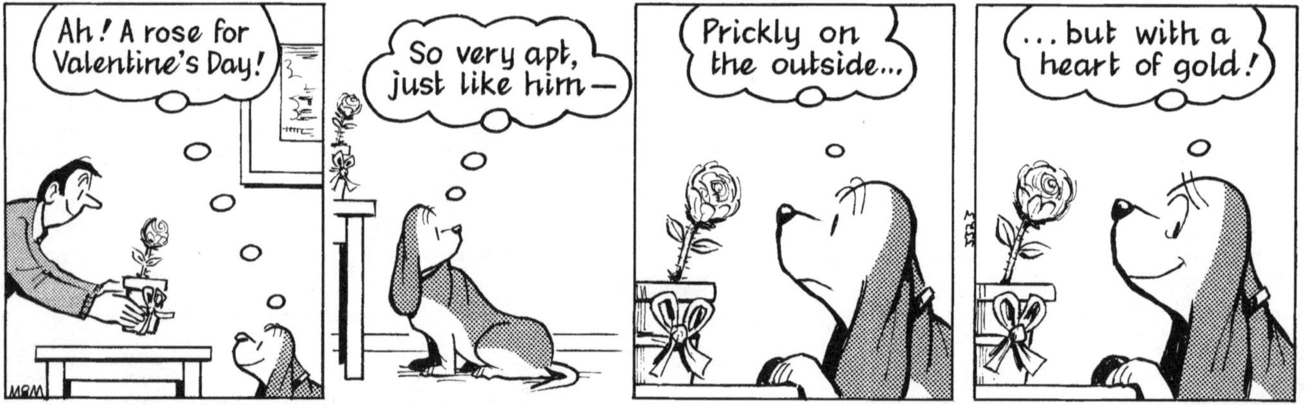
Ah! A rose for Valentine's Day!
So very apt, just like him —
Prickly on the outside...
... but with a heart of gold!

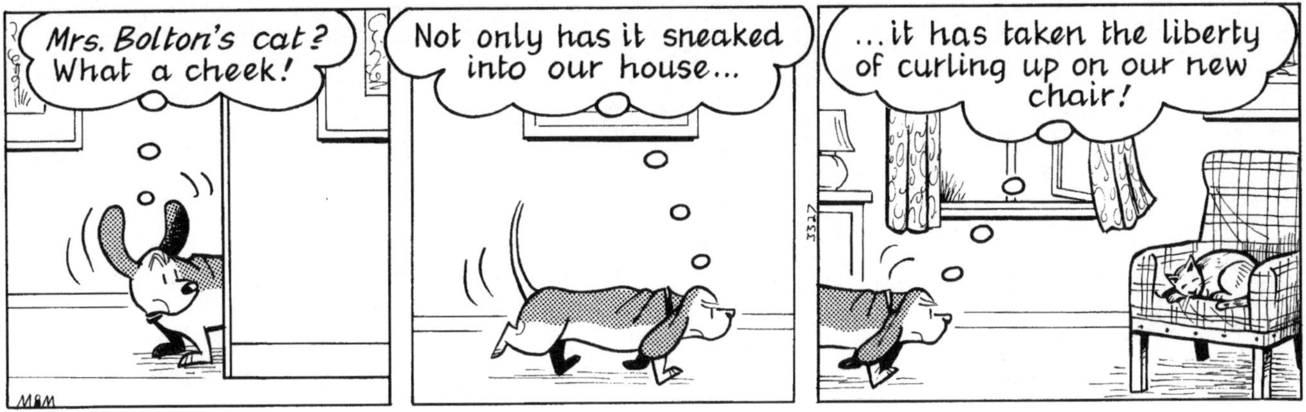
Mrs. Bolton's cat? What a cheek!
Not only has it sneaked into our house...
...it has taken the liberty of curling up on our new chair!

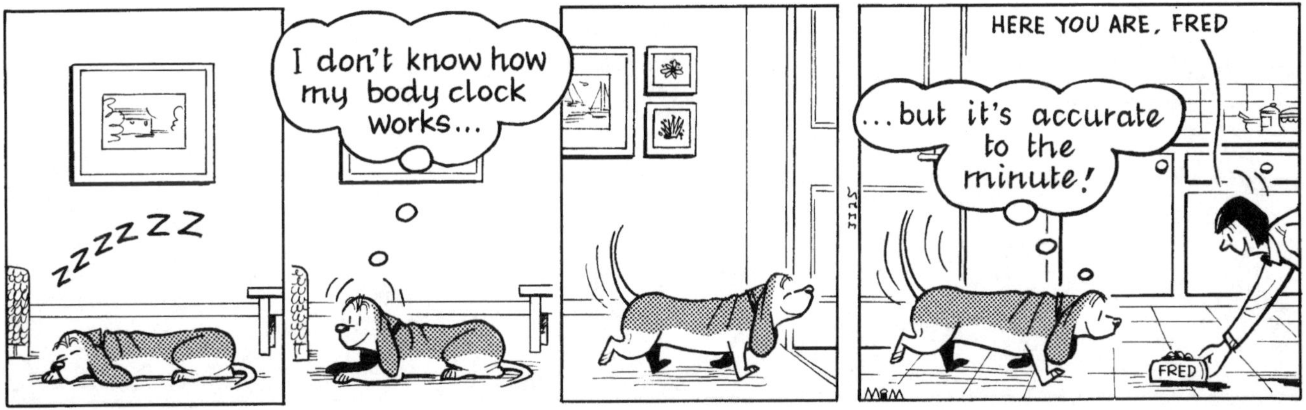
zzzzZZ
I don't know how my body clock works...
HERE YOU ARE, FRED
...but it's accurate to the minute!
FRED

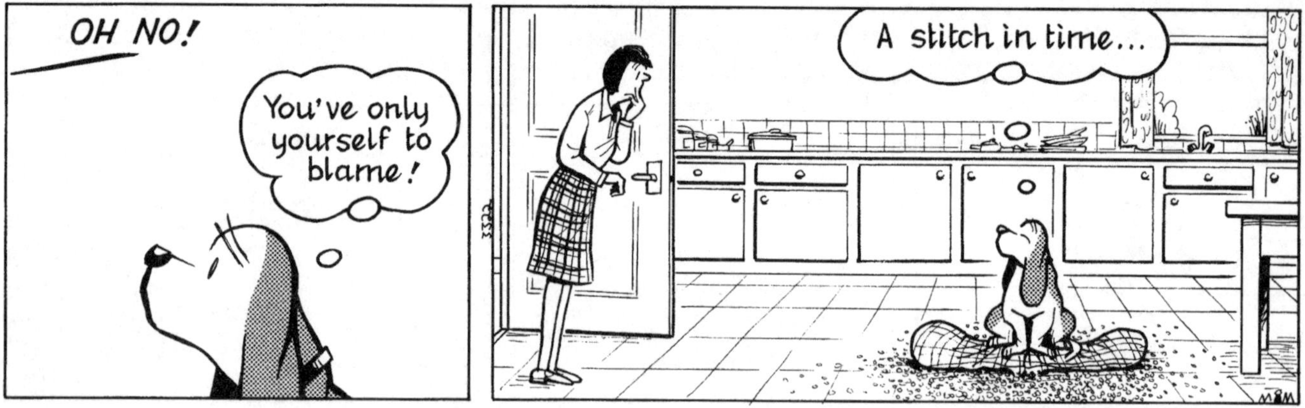
OH NO!
You've only yourself to blame!
A stitch in time...
3322
M&M

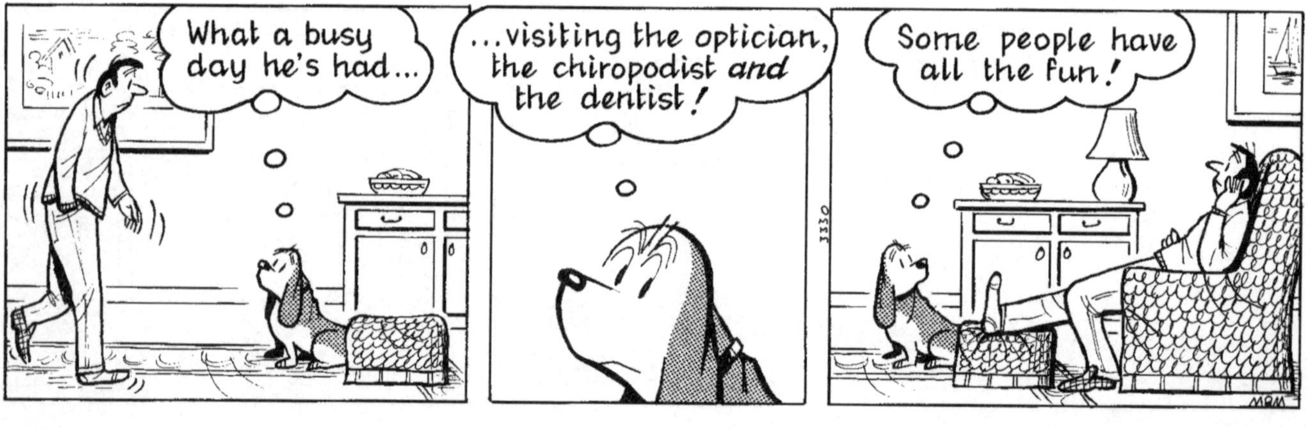
What a busy day he's had...
...visiting the optician, the chiropodist *and* the dentist!
Some people have all the fun!
3330
M&M

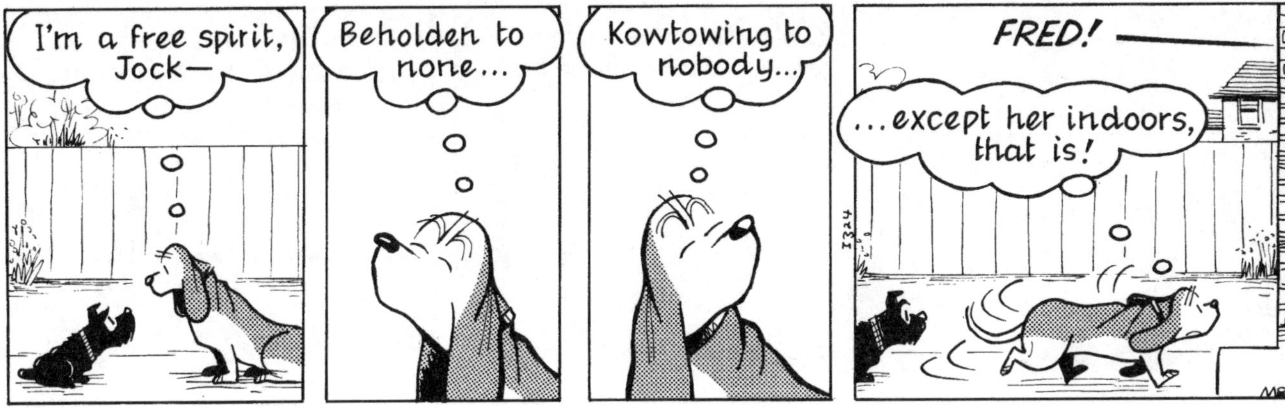
I'm a free spirit, Jock—
Beholden to none...
Kowtowing to nobody...
FRED!
...except her indoors, that is!
MBM

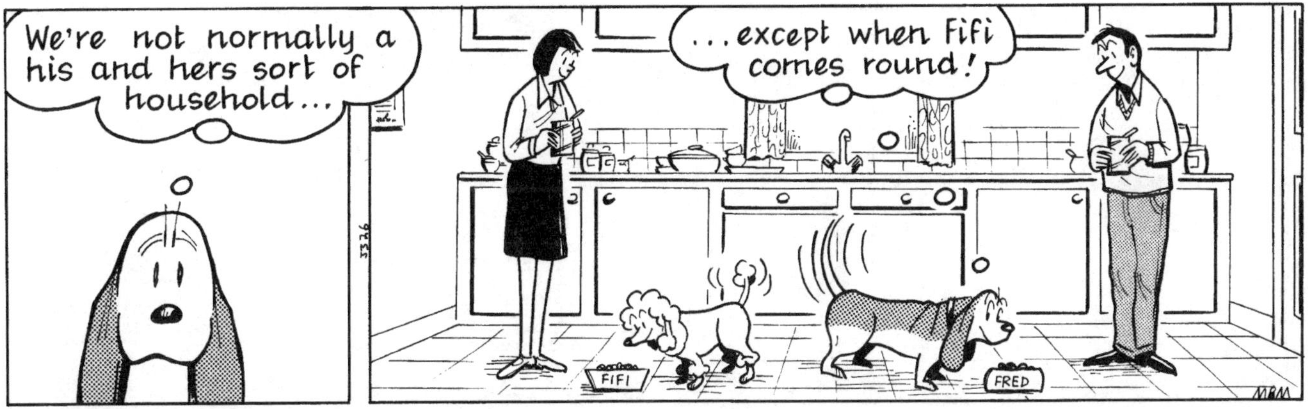
We're not normally a his and hers sort of household...
...except when Fifi comes round!
FIFI
FRED
MBM

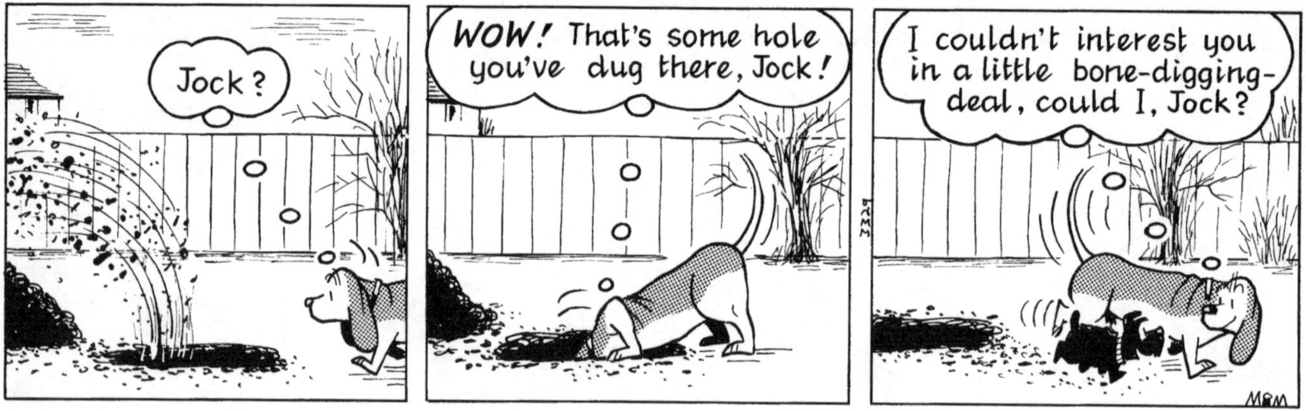
Jock?
WOW! That's some hole you've dug there, Jock!
I couldn't interest you in a little bone-digging-deal, could I, Jock?
M&M

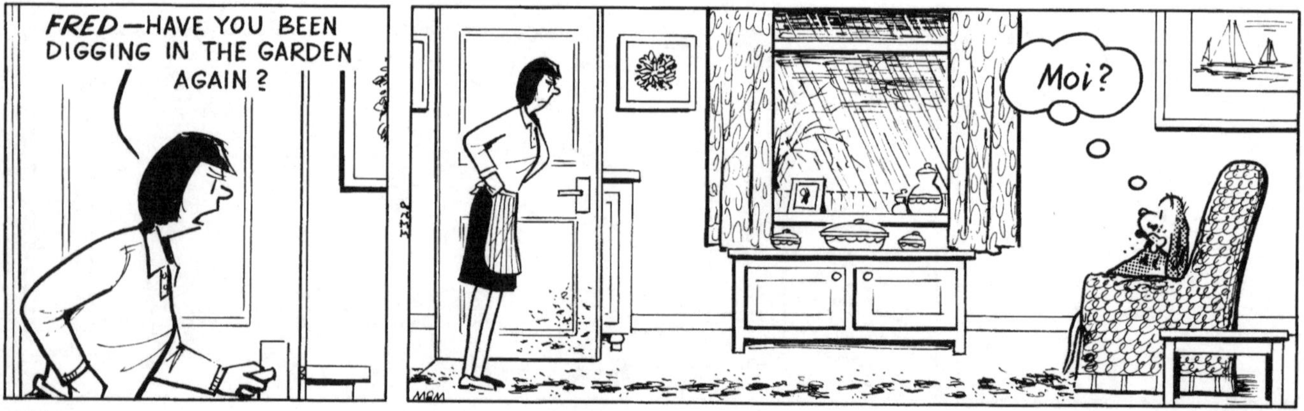
FRED—HAVE YOU BEEN DIGGING IN THE GARDEN AGAIN?
Moi?
M&M

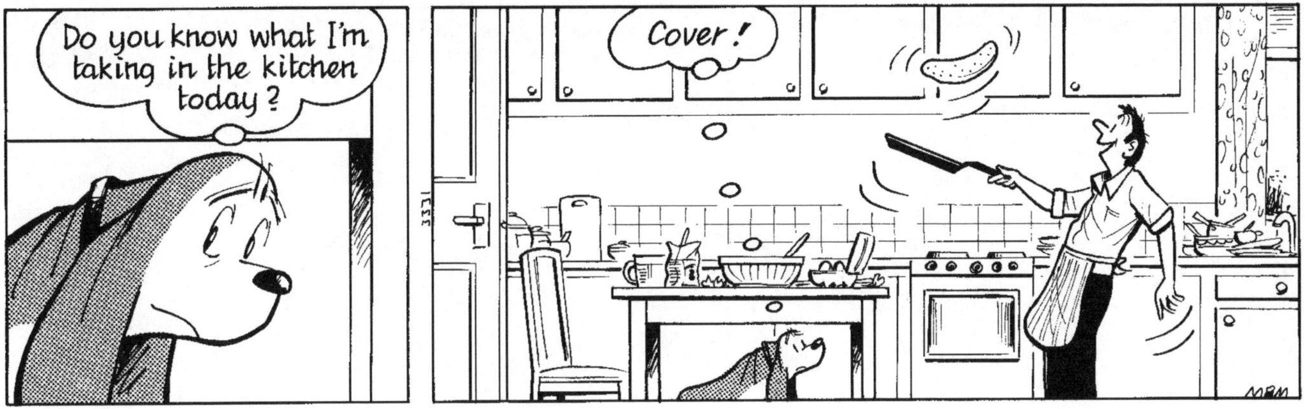
Do you know what I'm taking in the kitchen today?
Cover!
MBM

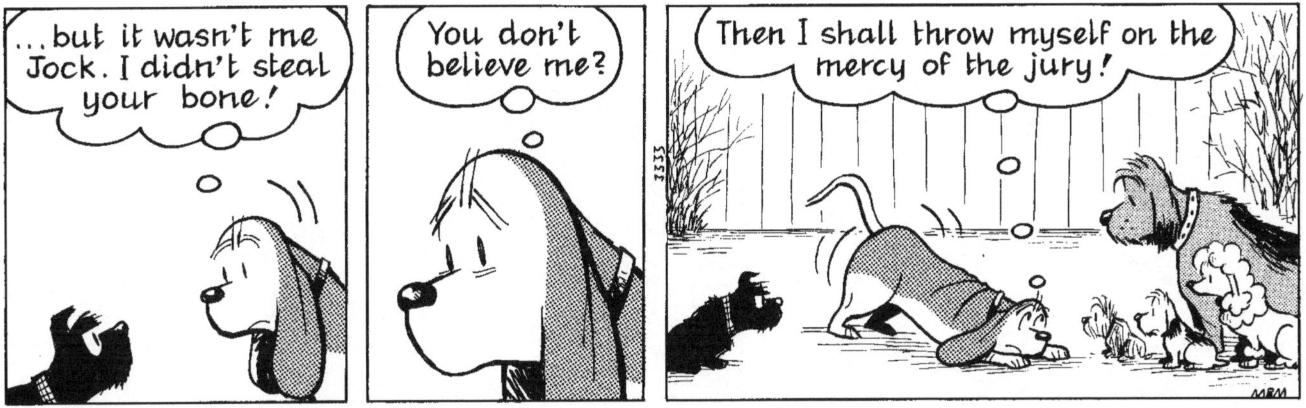
...but it wasn't me Jock. I didn't steal your bone!
You don't believe me?
Then I shall throw myself on the mercy of the jury!
MBM

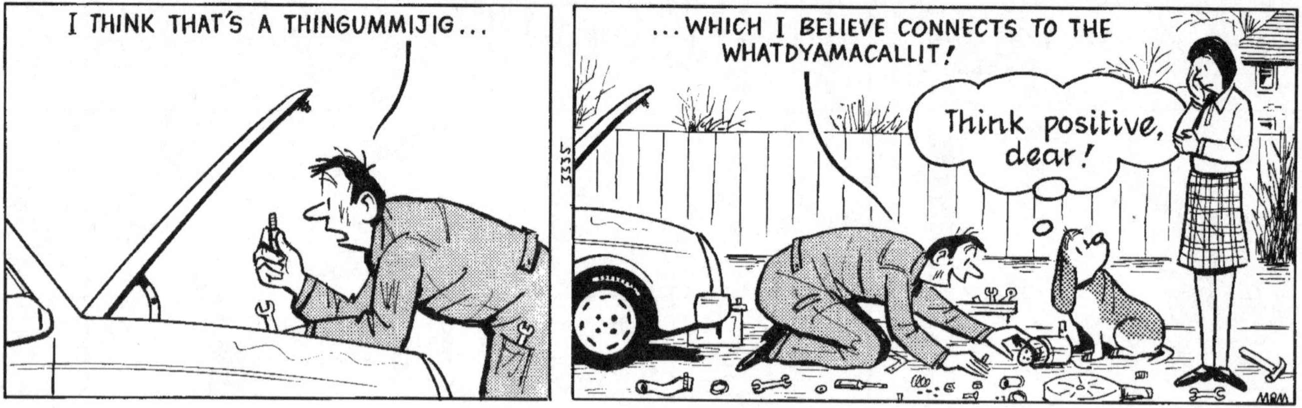
I THINK THAT'S A THINGUMMIJIG...
...WHICH I BELIEVE CONNECTS TO THE WHATDYAMACALLIT!
Think positive, dear!

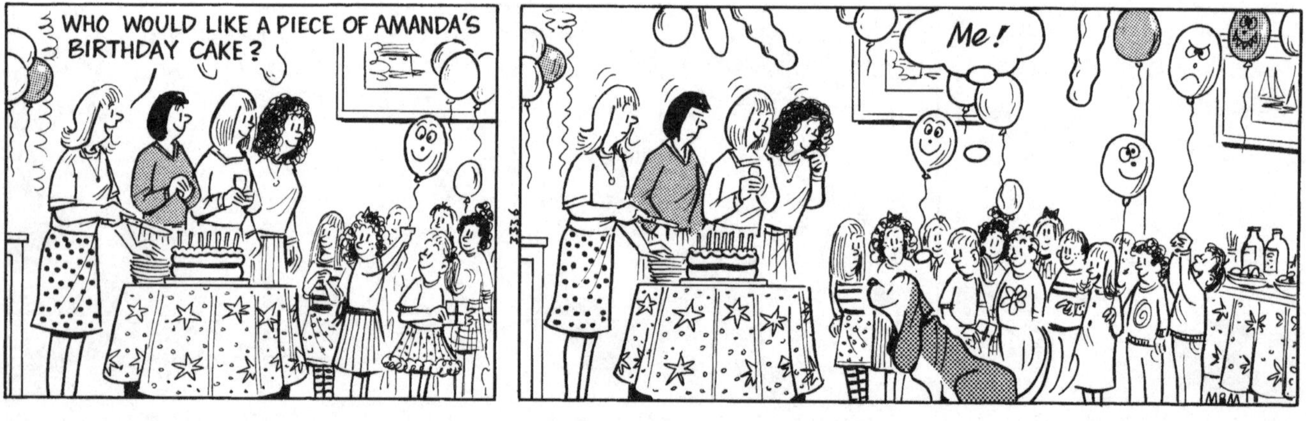
WHO WOULD LIKE A PIECE OF AMANDA'S BIRTHDAY CAKE?
Me!

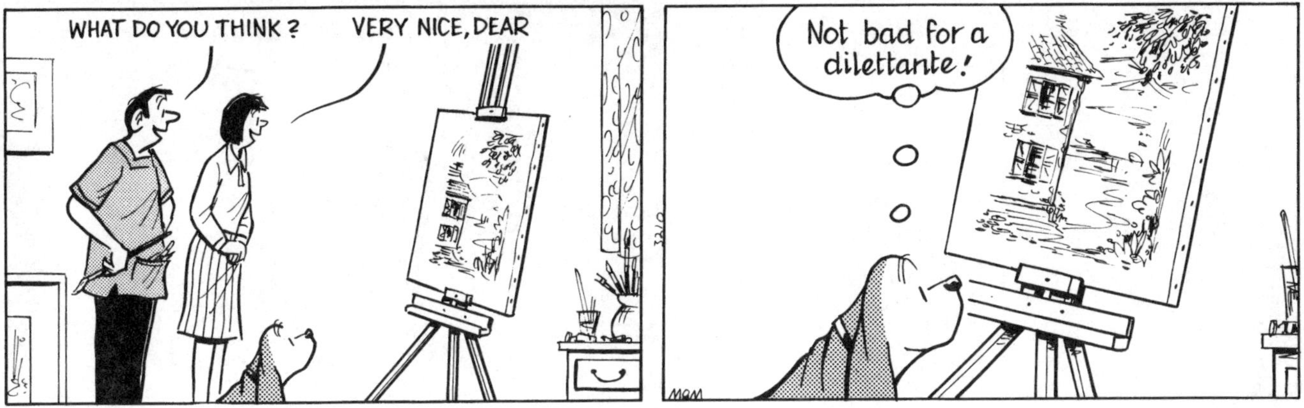
WHAT DO YOU THINK ?
VERY NICE, DEAR
Not bad for a dilettante !

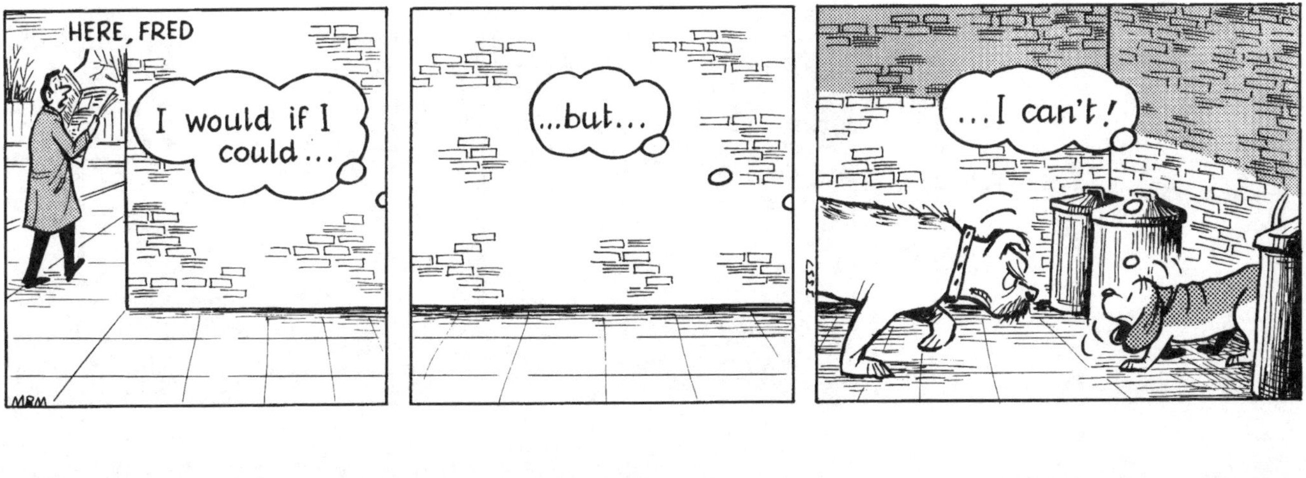
HERE, FRED
I would if I could ...
...but...
...I can't !

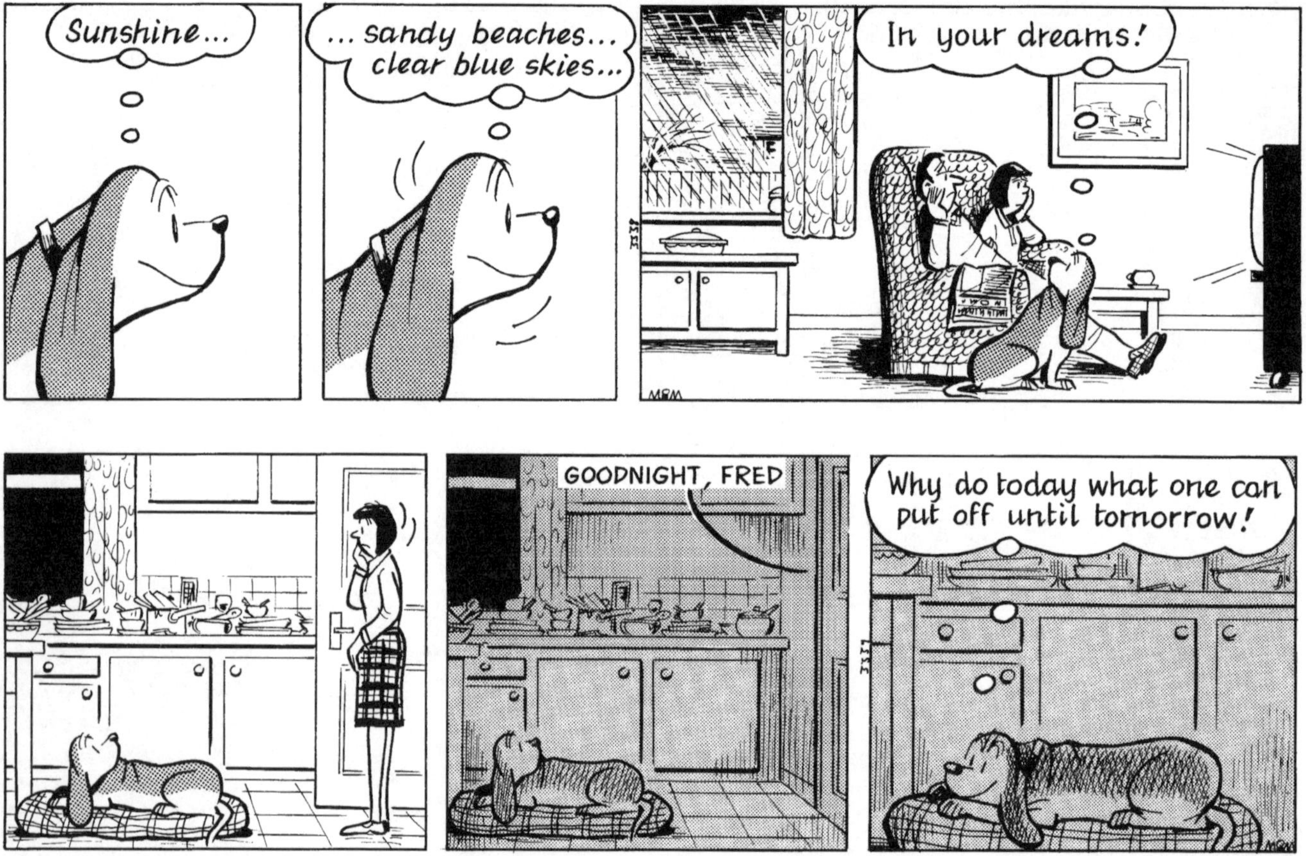
Sunshine...
... sandy beaches... clear blue skies...
In your dreams!
GOODNIGHT, FRED
Why do today what one can put off until tomorrow!

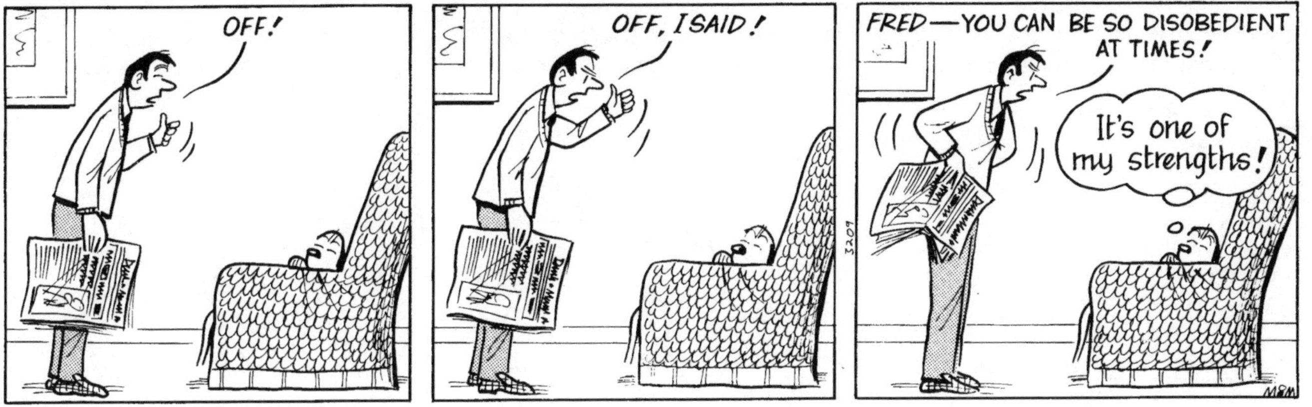
OFF!
OFF, I SAID!
FRED—YOU CAN BE SO DISOBEDIENT AT TIMES!
It's one of my strengths!
M&M

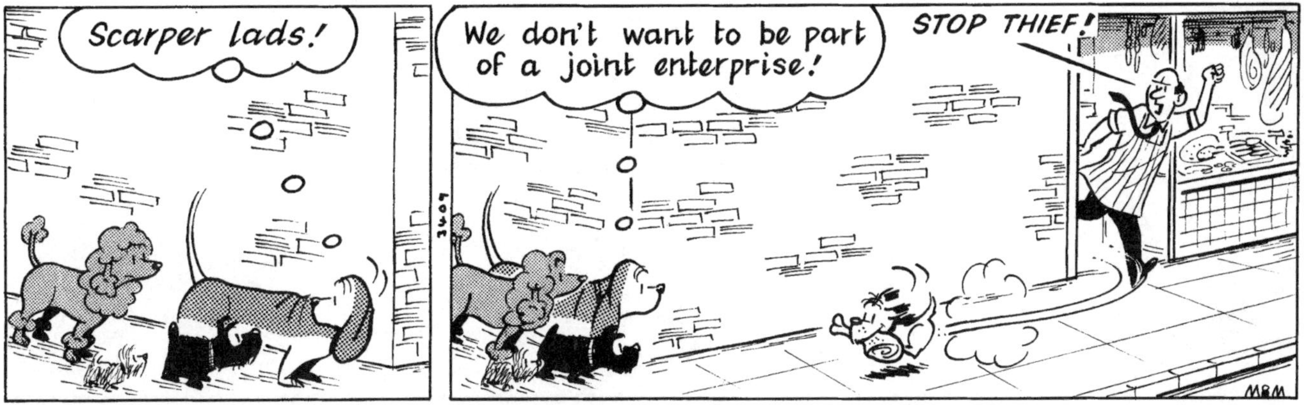
Scarper lads!
We don't want to be part of a joint enterprise!
STOP THIEF!
M&M

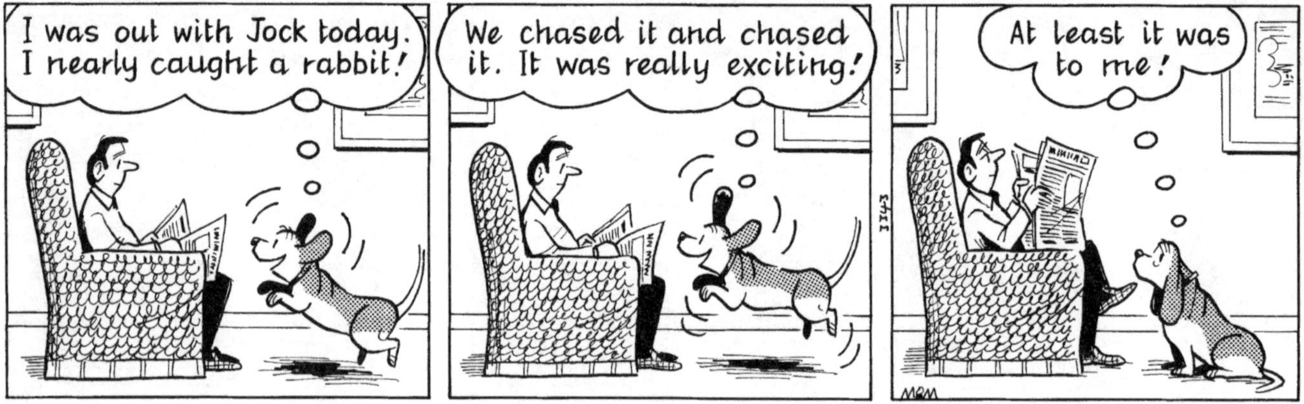
I was out with Jock today. I nearly caught a rabbit!
We chased it and chased it. It was really exciting!
At least it was to me!

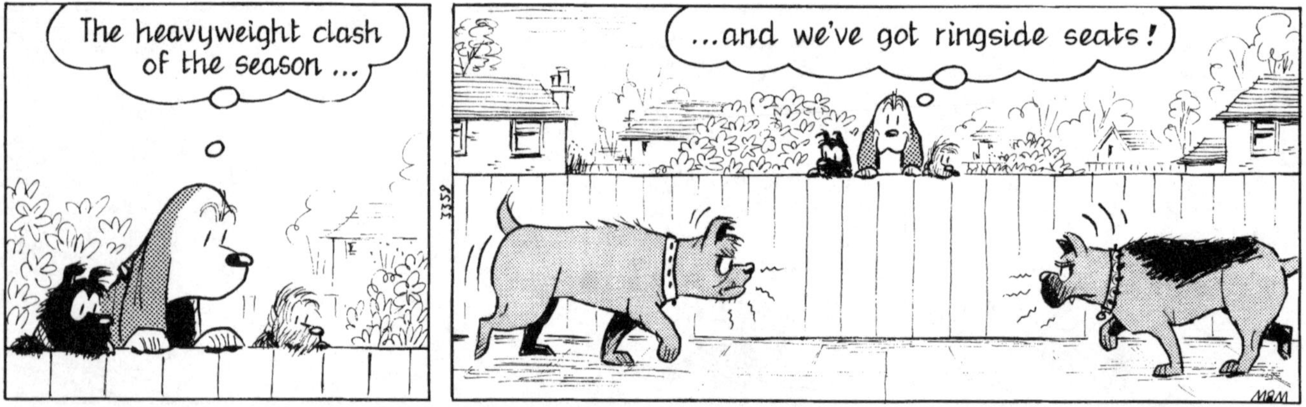
The heavyweight clash of the season ...
...and we've got ringside seats!

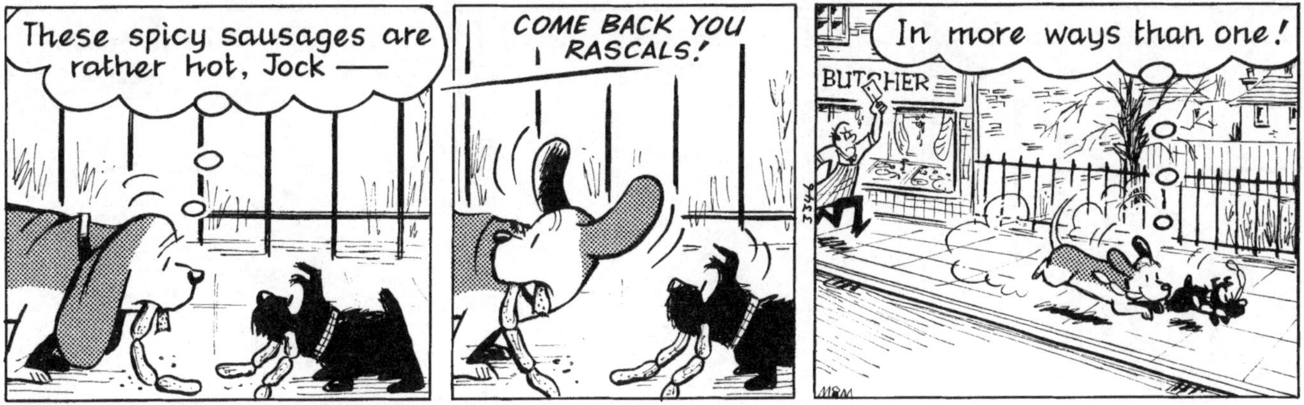
These spicy sausages are rather hot, Jock —
COME BACK YOU RASCALS!
BUTCHER
In more ways than one!
3346
M&M

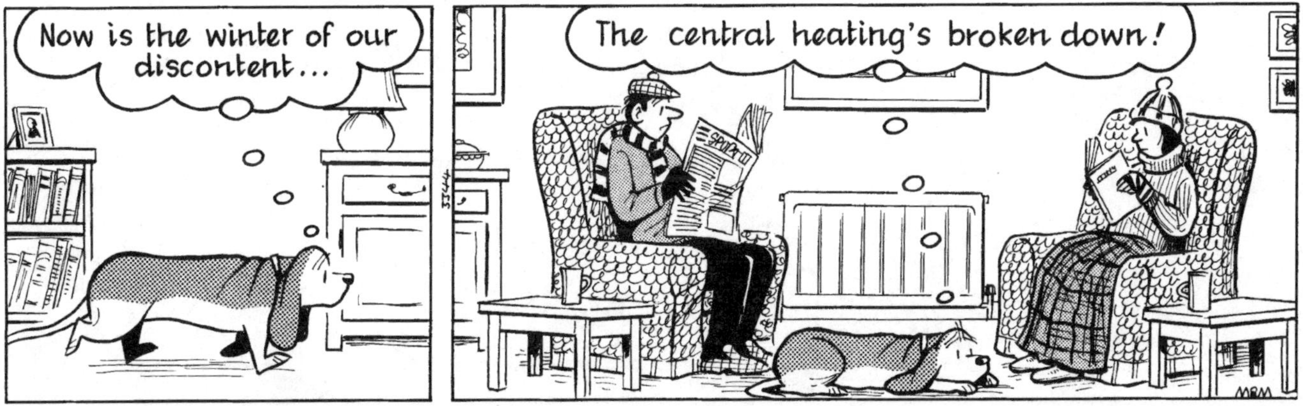
Now is the winter of our discontent...
The central heating's broken down!
3344
M&M

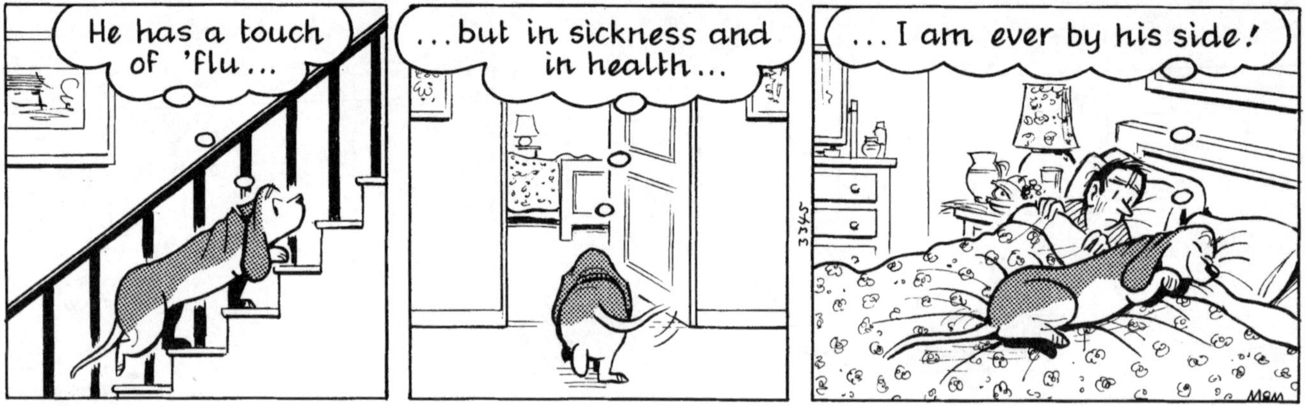
He has a touch of 'flu...
...but in sickness and in health...
...I am ever by his side!

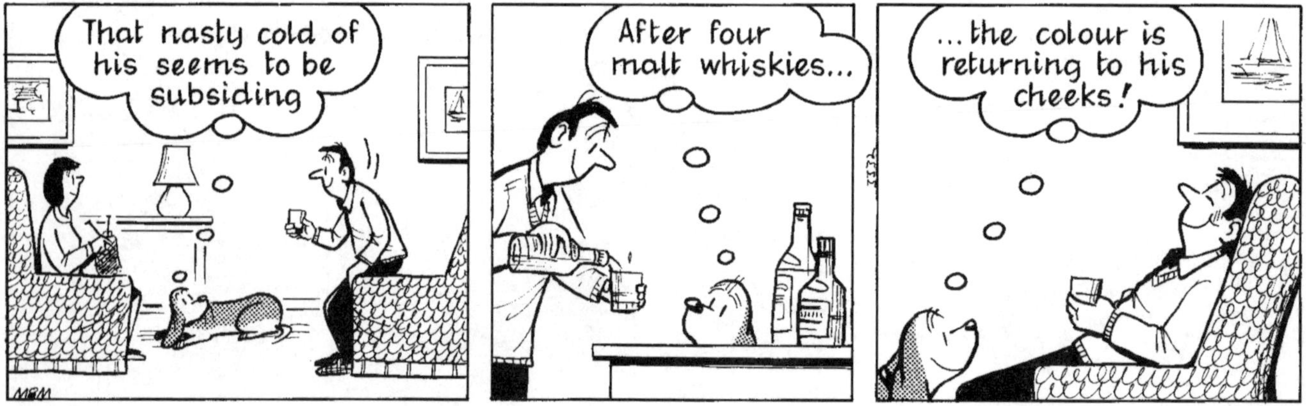
That nasty cold of his seems to be subsiding
After four malt whiskies...
...the colour is returning to his cheeks!

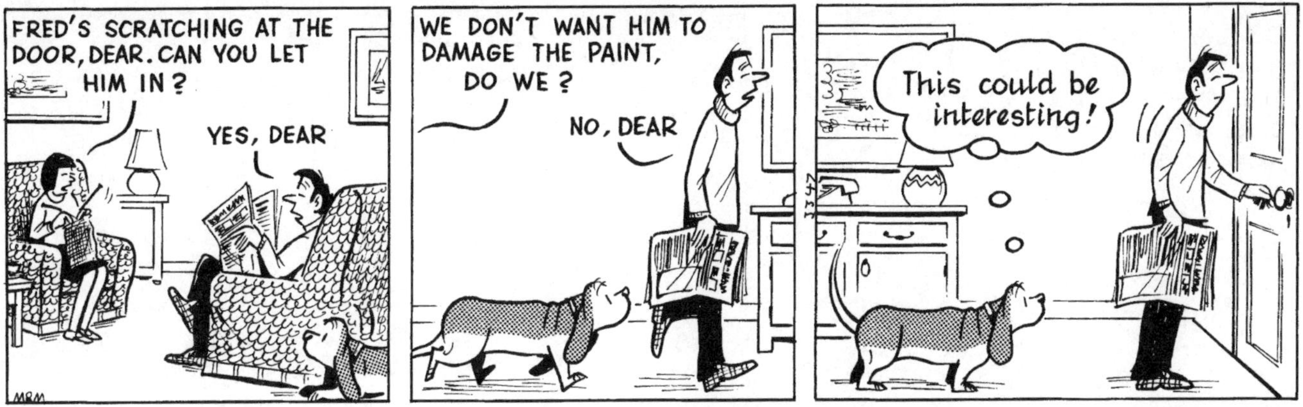
FRED'S SCRATCHING AT THE DOOR, DEAR. CAN YOU LET HIM IN?
YES, DEAR
WE DON'T WANT HIM TO DAMAGE THE PAINT, DO WE?
NO, DEAR
This could be interesting!

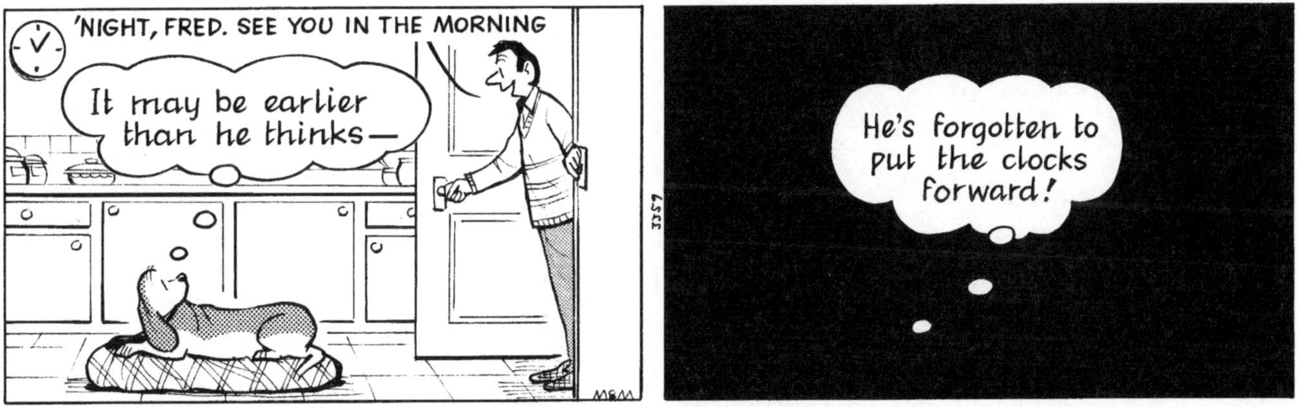
'NIGHT, FRED. SEE YOU IN THE MORNING
It may be earlier than he thinks—
He's forgotten to put the clocks forward!

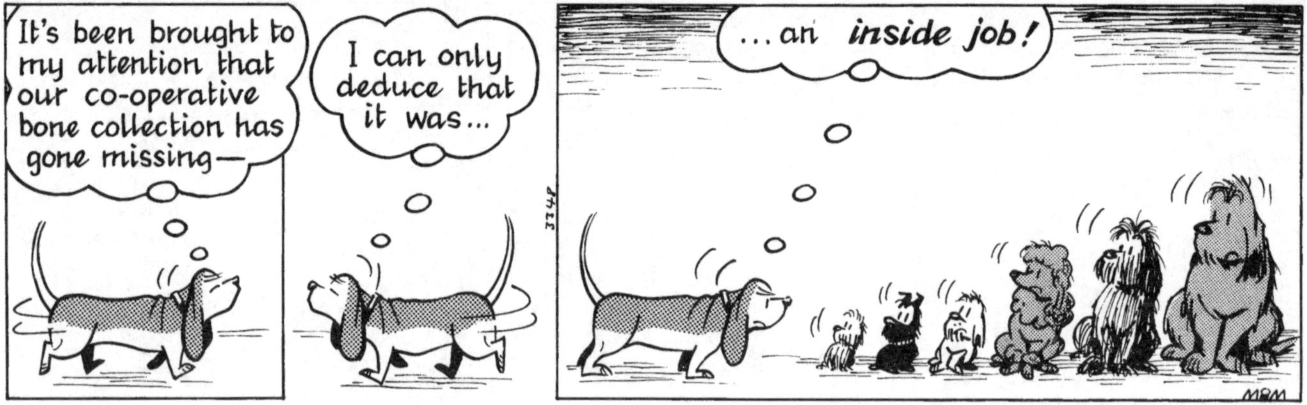
It's been brought to my attention that our co-operative bone collection has gone missing—
I can only deduce that it was...
... an *inside job!*

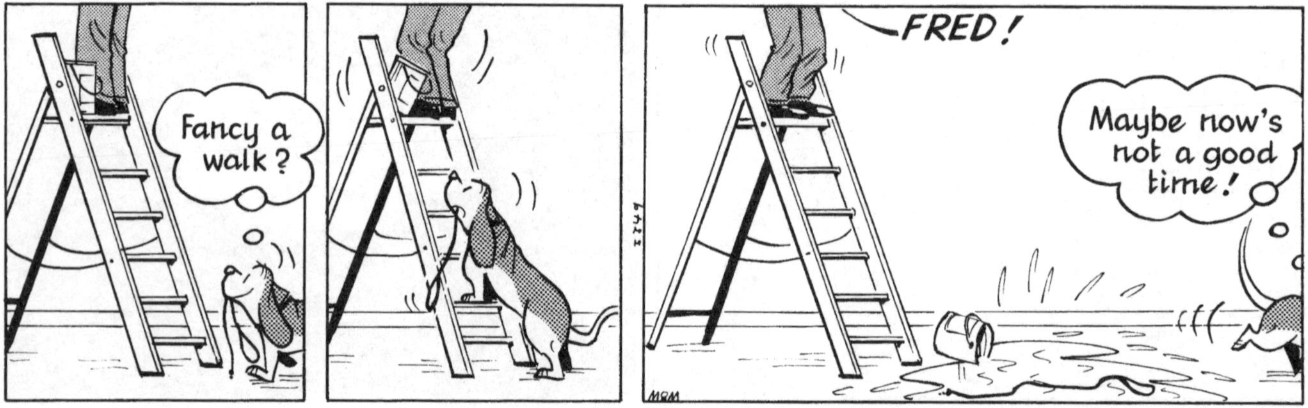
Fancy a walk?
FRED!
Maybe now's not a good time!

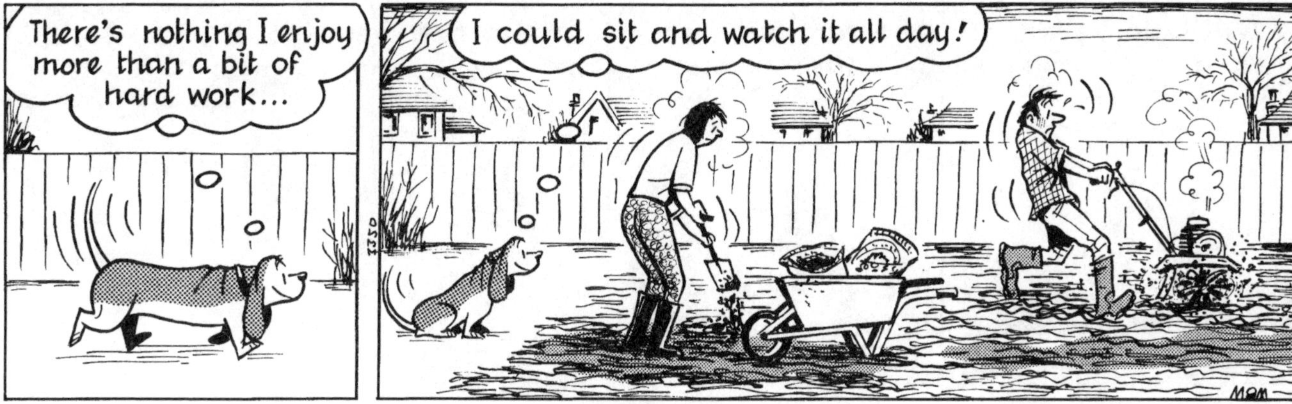
There's nothing I enjoy more than a bit of hard work...
I could sit and watch it all day!

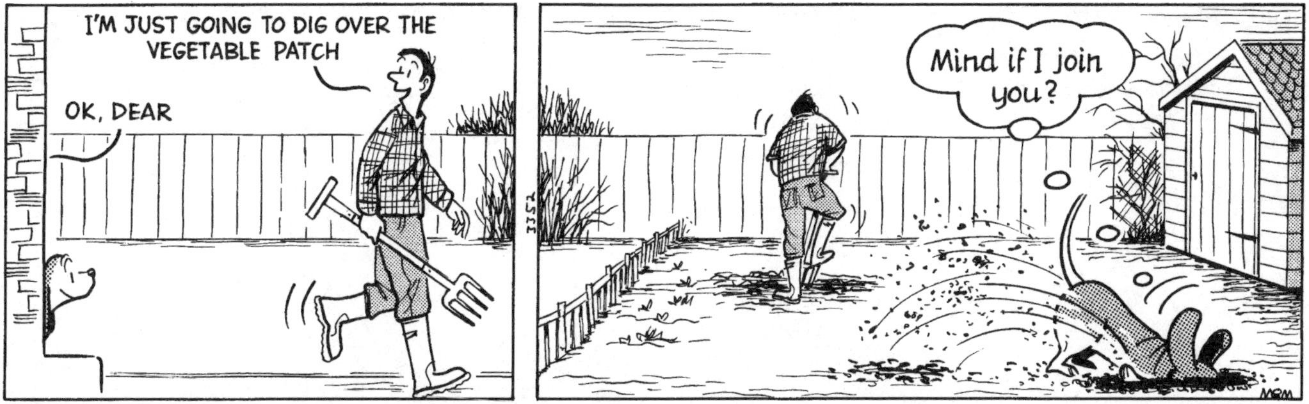
I'M JUST GOING TO DIG OVER THE VEGETABLE PATCH
OK, DEAR
Mind if I join you?

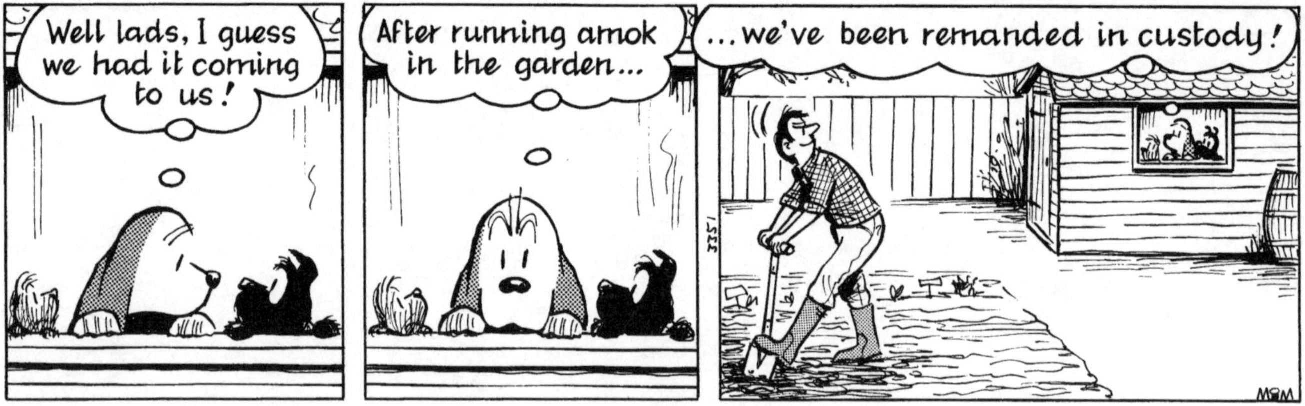
Well lads, I guess we had it coming to us!
After running amok in the garden...
...we've been remanded in custody!

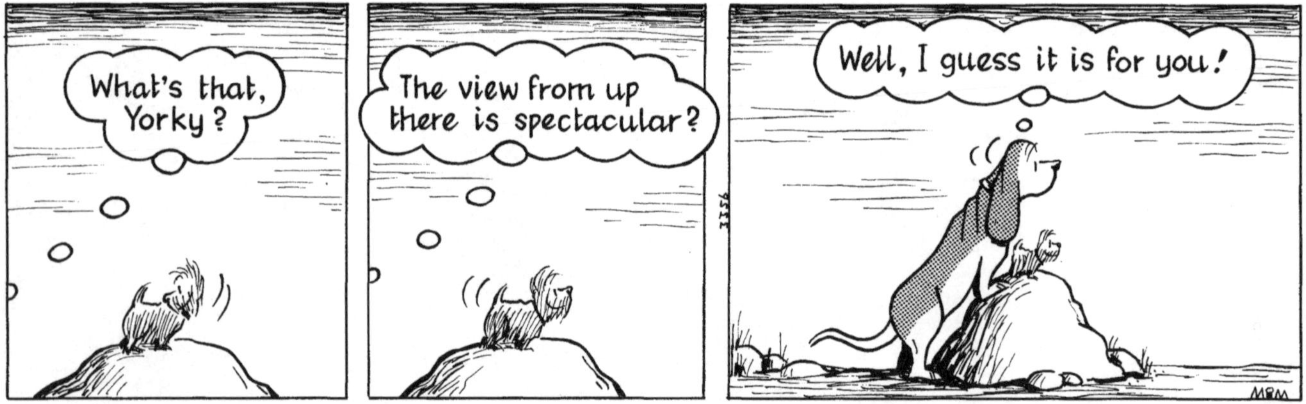
What's that, Yorky?
The view from up there is spectacular?
Well, I guess it is for you!

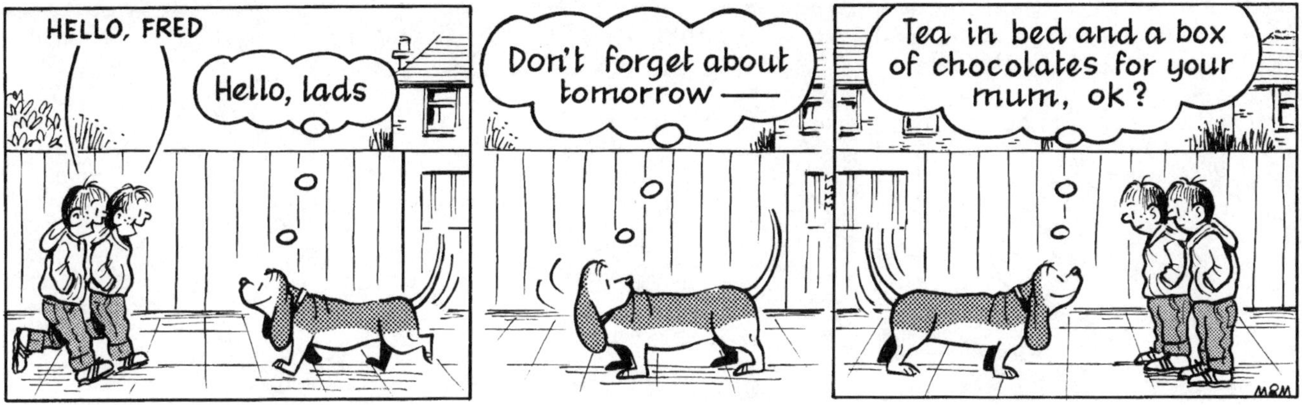
HELLO, FRED
Hello, lads
Don't forget about tomorrow —
Tea in bed and a box of chocolates for your mum, ok?
MRM

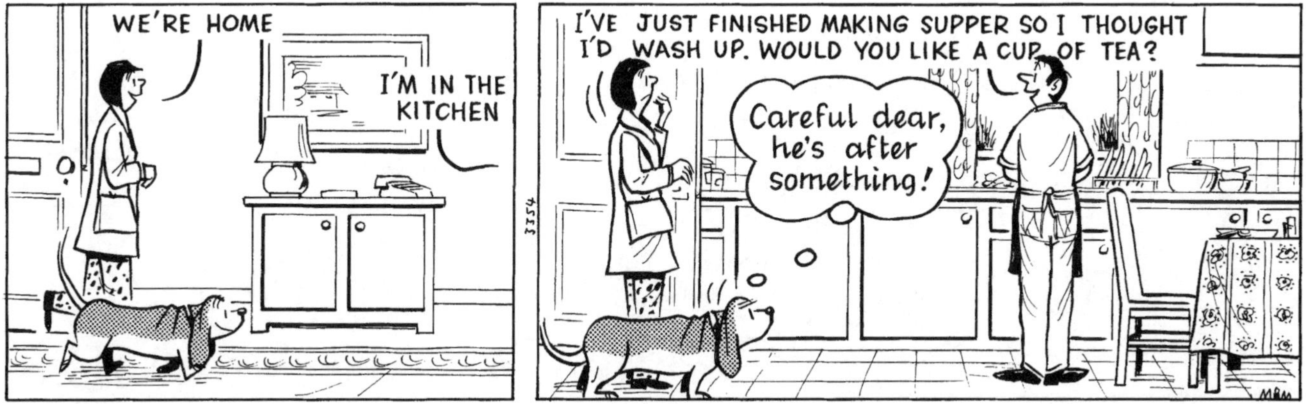
WE'RE HOME
I'M IN THE KITCHEN
I'VE JUST FINISHED MAKING SUPPER SO I THOUGHT I'D WASH UP. WOULD YOU LIKE A CUP OF TEA?
Careful dear, he's after something!
MRM

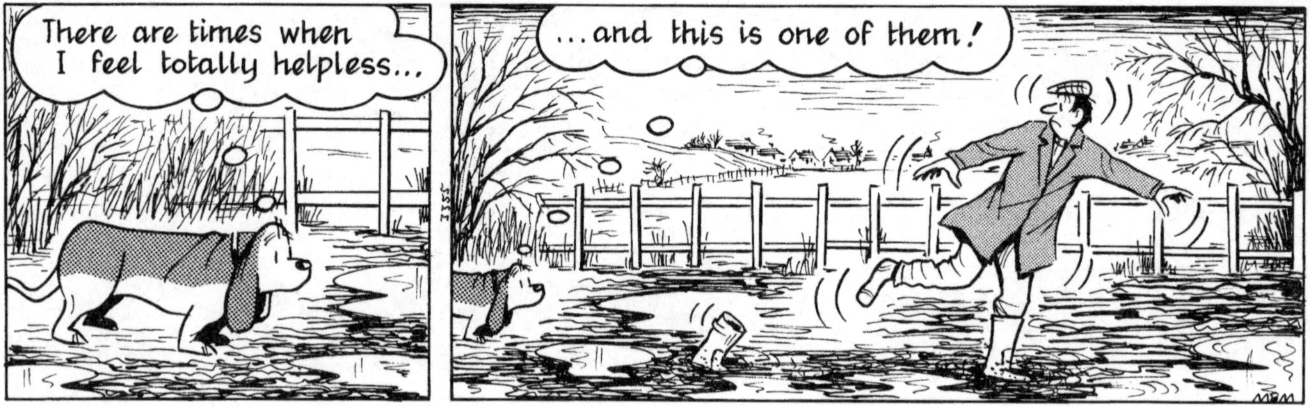
There are times when I feel totally helpless...
...and this is one of them!

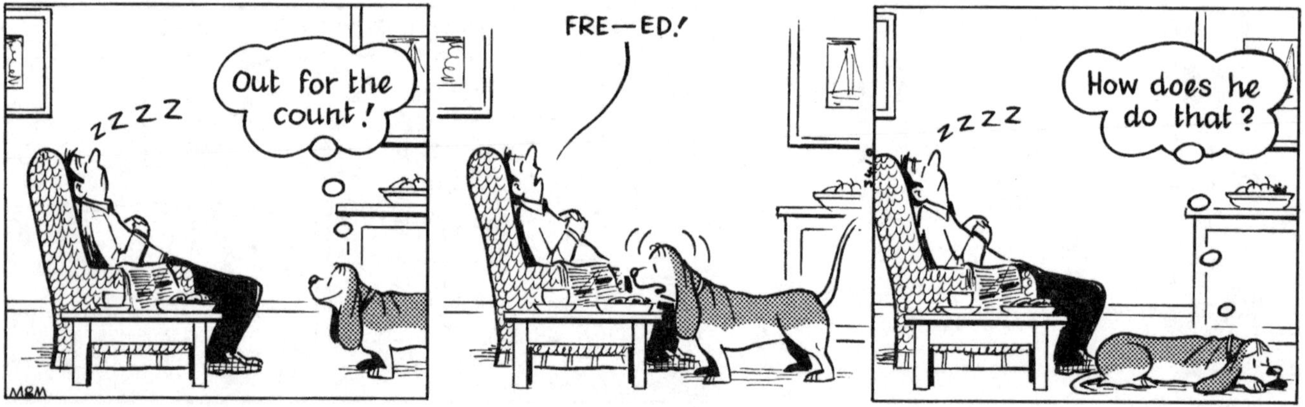
ZZZZ
Out for the count!
FRE—ED!
ZZZZ
How does he do that?

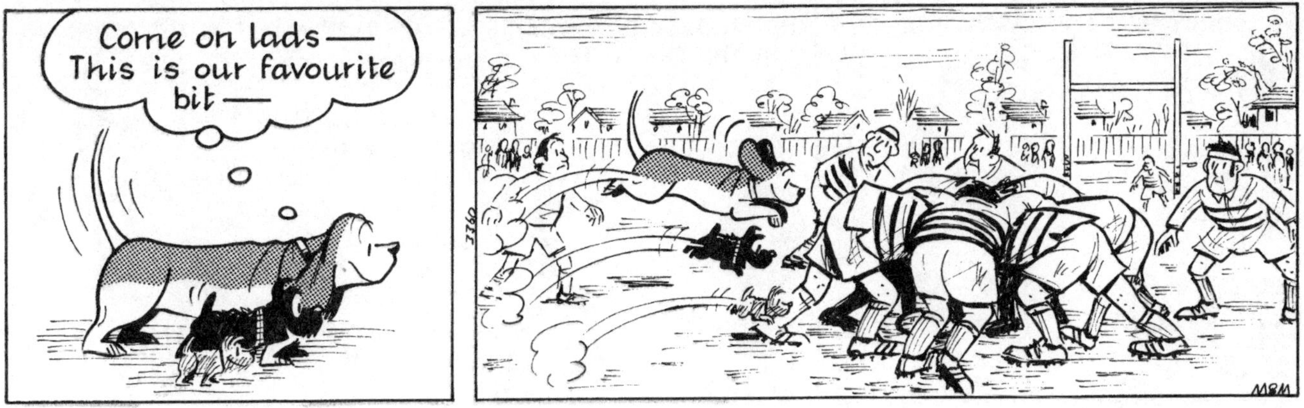
Come on lads—
This is our favourite bit—
3360
M&M

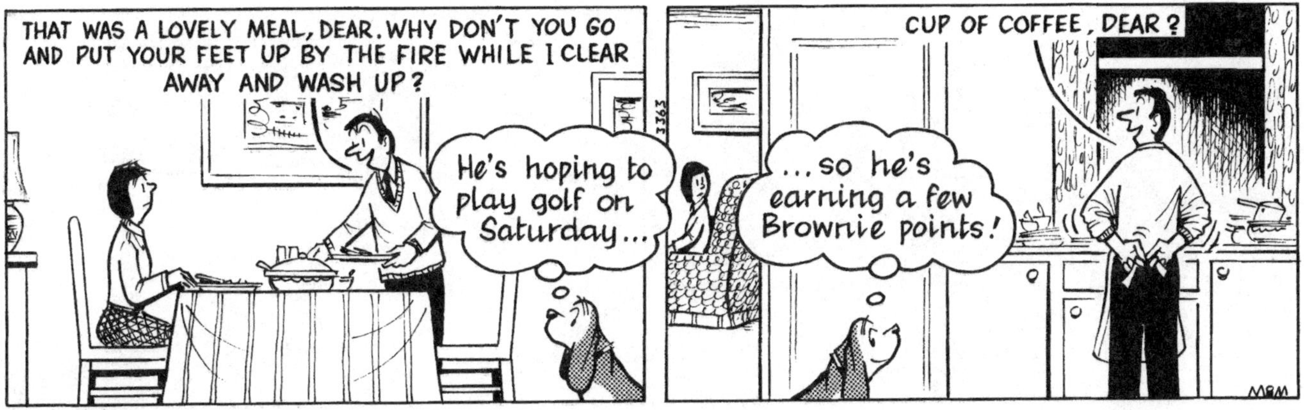
THAT WAS A LOVELY MEAL, DEAR. WHY DON'T YOU GO AND PUT YOUR FEET UP BY THE FIRE WHILE I CLEAR AWAY AND WASH UP?
He's hoping to play golf on Saturday...
3363
CUP OF COFFEE, DEAR?
...so he's earning a few Brownie points!
M&M

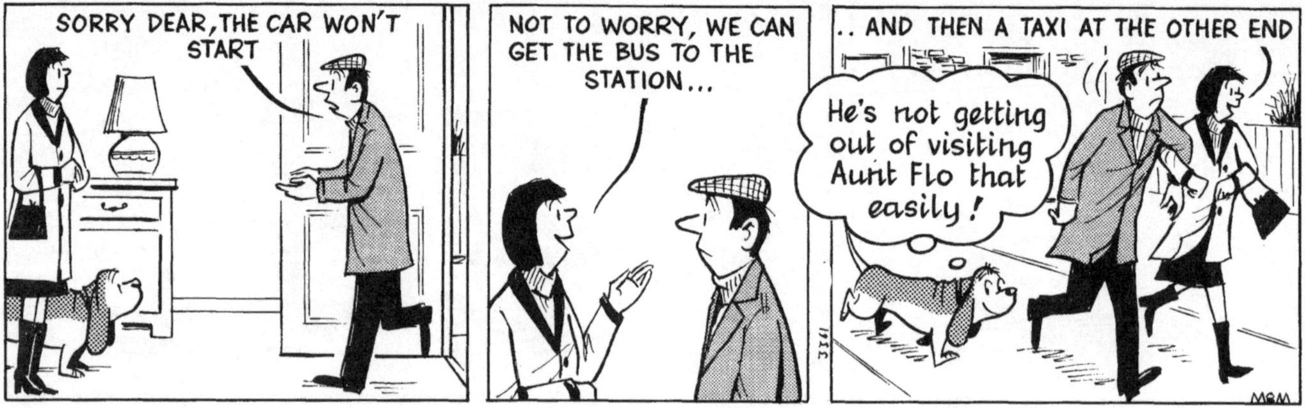
SORRY DEAR, THE CAR WON'T START
NOT TO WORRY, WE CAN GET THE BUS TO THE STATION...
.. AND THEN A TAXI AT THE OTHER END
He's not getting out of visiting Aunt Flo that easily!

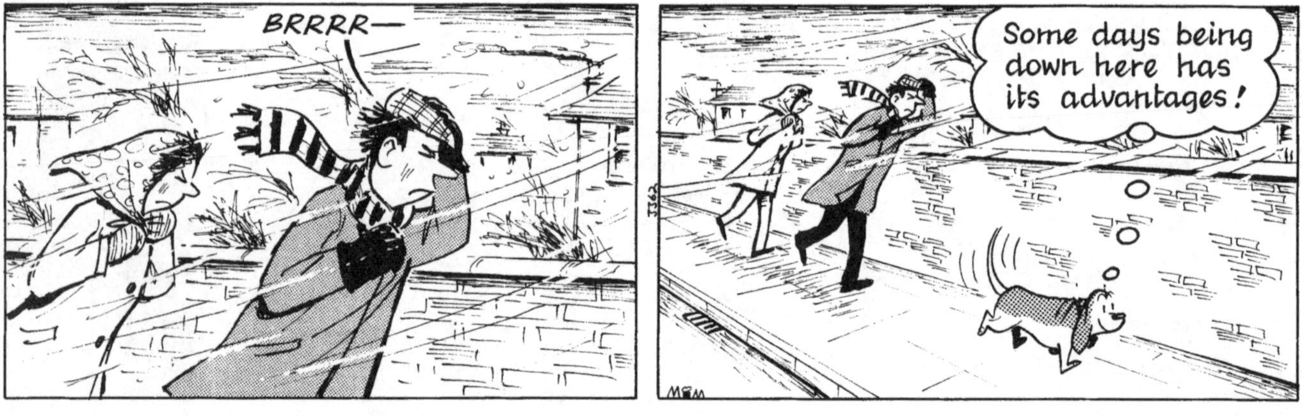
BRRRR—
Some days being down here has its advantages!

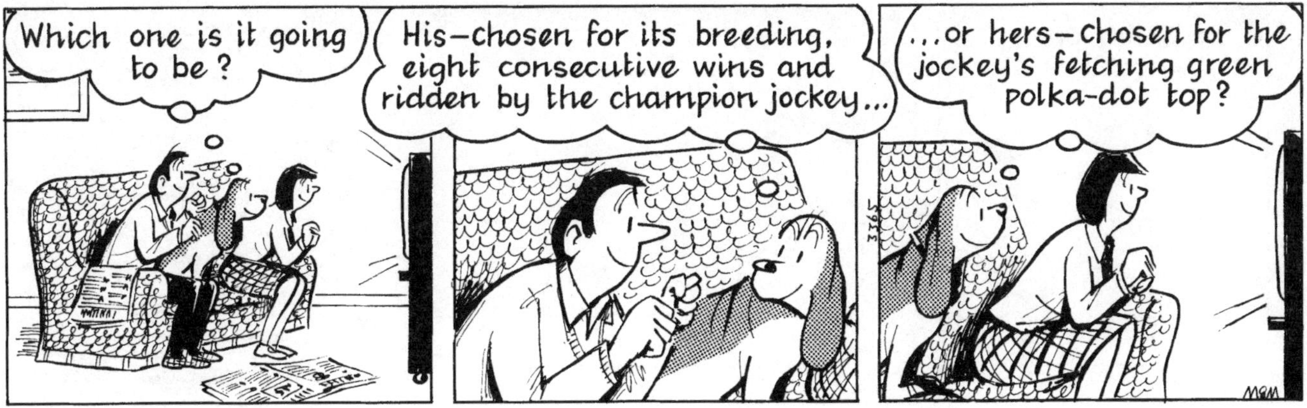
Which one is it going to be?
His–chosen for its breeding, eight consecutive wins and ridden by the champion jockey...
...or hers–chosen for the jockey's fetching green polka-dot top?

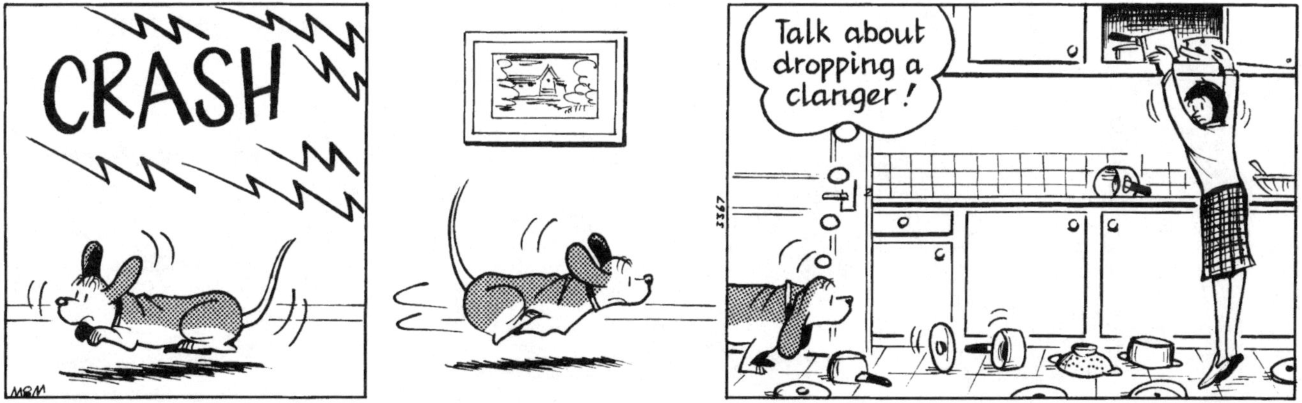
CRASH
Talk about dropping a clanger!

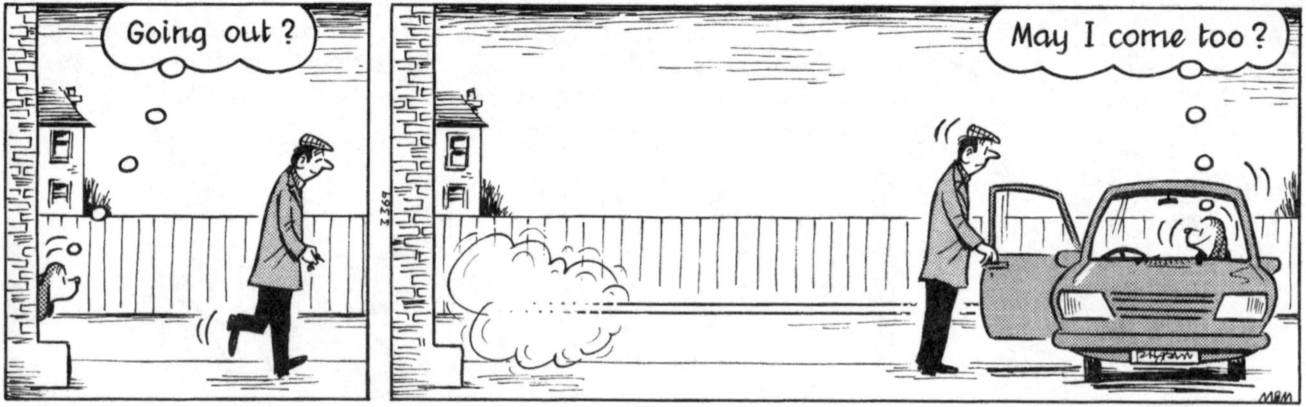
Going out ?
May I come too ?

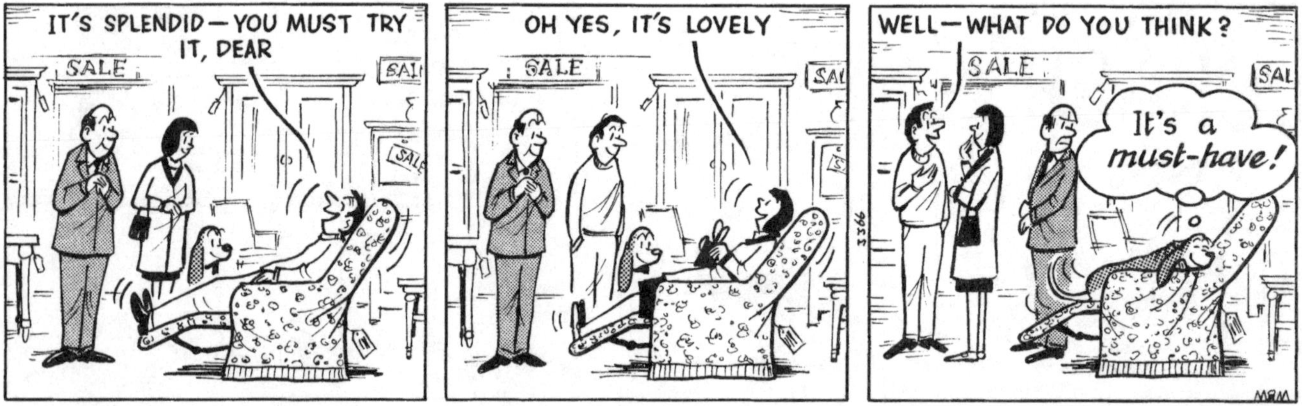
IT'S SPLENDID — YOU MUST TRY IT, DEAR
OH YES, IT'S LOVELY
WELL — WHAT DO YOU THINK ?
It's a *must-have!*

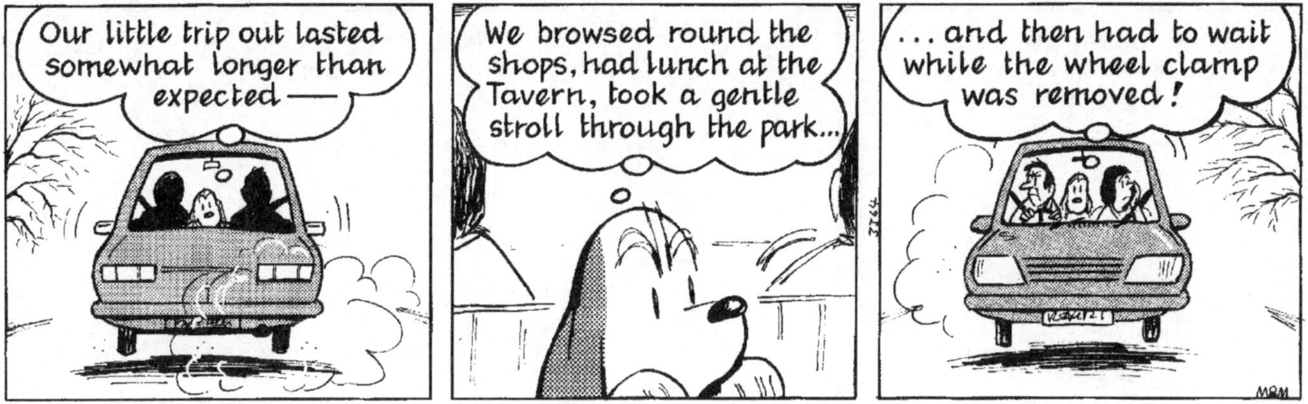
Our little trip out lasted somewhat longer than expected —
We browsed round the shops, had lunch at the Tavern, took a gentle stroll through the park...
... and then had to wait while the wheel clamp was removed!

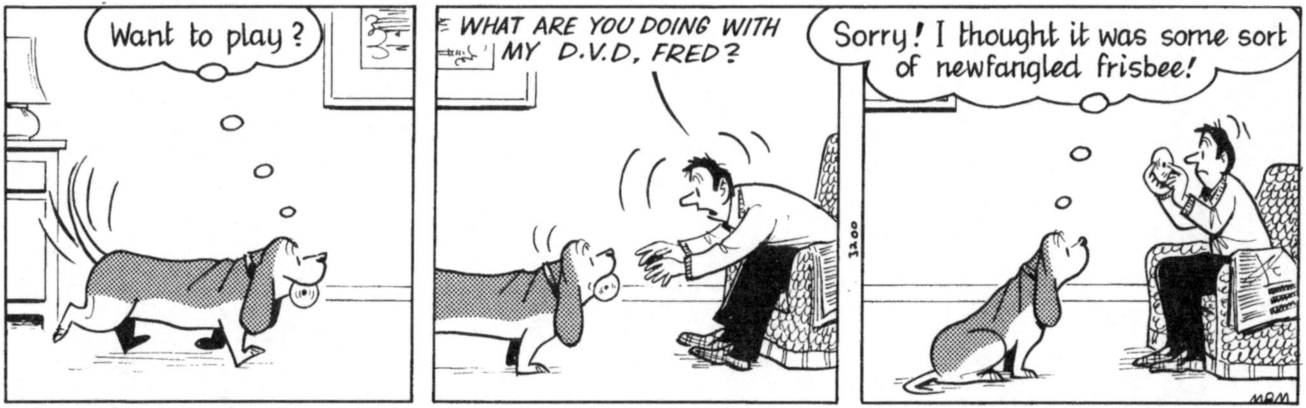
Want to play?
WHAT ARE YOU DOING WITH MY D.V.D, FRED?
Sorry! I thought it was some sort of newfangled frisbee!

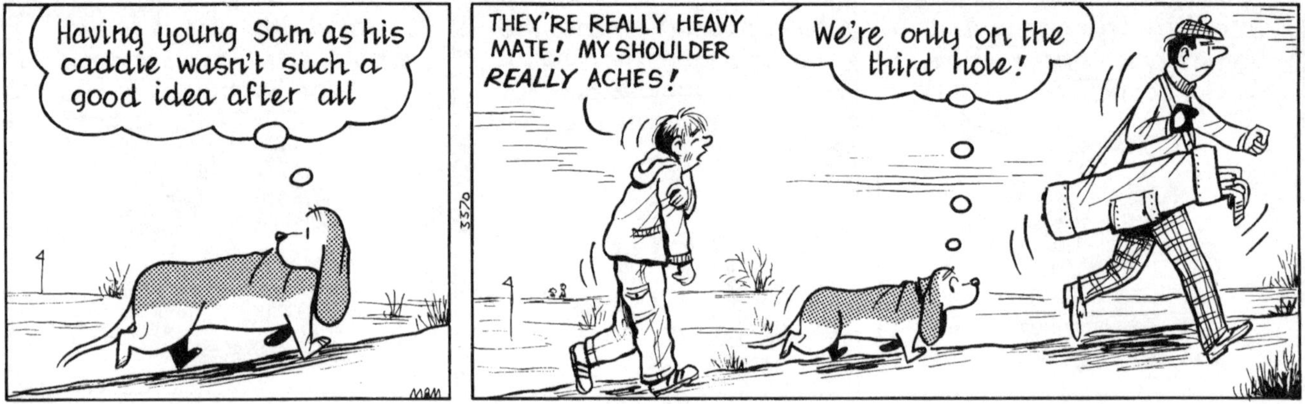
Having young Sam as his caddie wasn't such a good idea after all
3370
THEY'RE REALLY HEAVY MATE! MY SHOULDER REALLY ACHES!
We're only on the third hole!

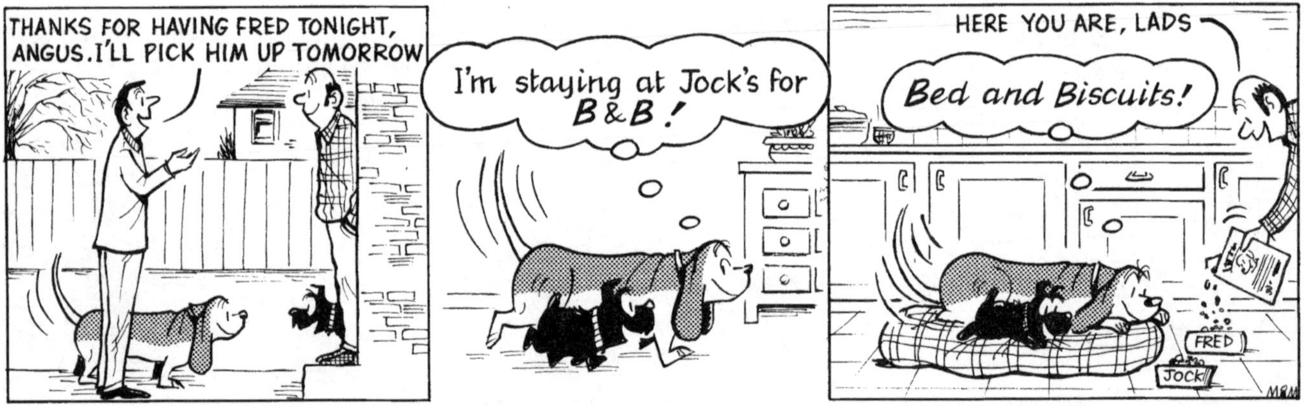
THANKS FOR HAVING FRED TONIGHT, ANGUS. I'LL PICK HIM UP TOMORROW
I'm staying at Jock's for B&B!
HERE YOU ARE, LADS
Bed and Biscuits!
FRED
JOCK

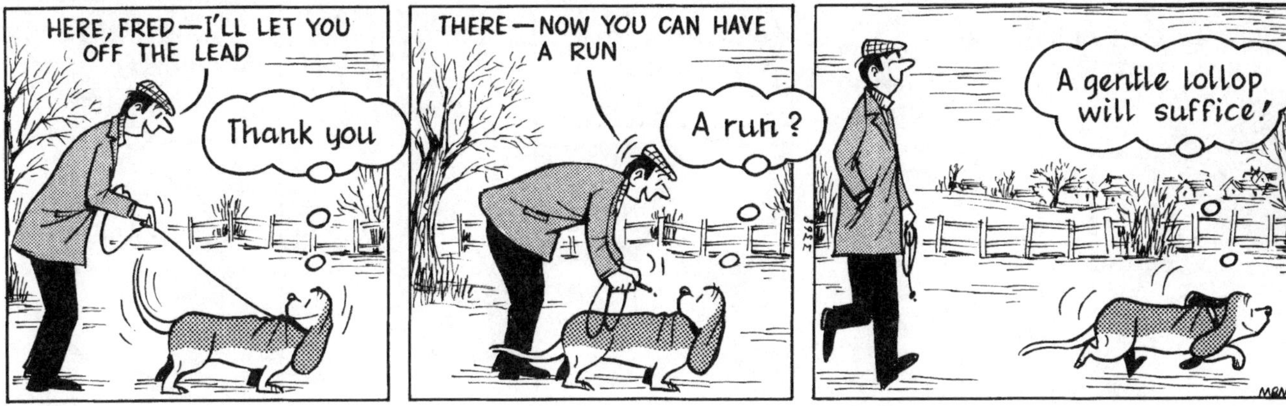
HERE, FRED—I'LL LET YOU OFF THE LEAD
Thank you
THERE—NOW YOU CAN HAVE A RUN
A run?
A gentle lollop will suffice!
MBM

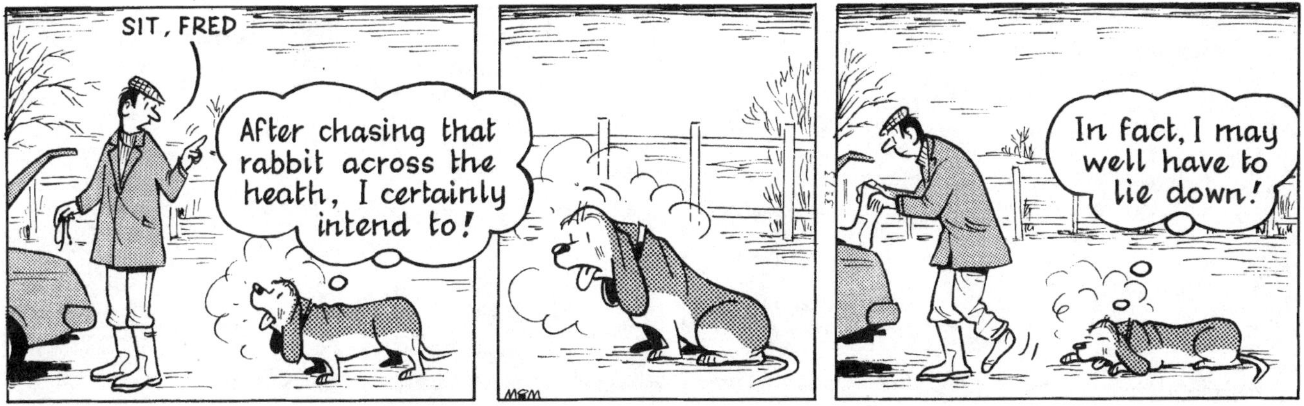
SIT, FRED
After chasing that rabbit across the heath, I certainly intend to!
MBM
In fact, I may well have to lie down!

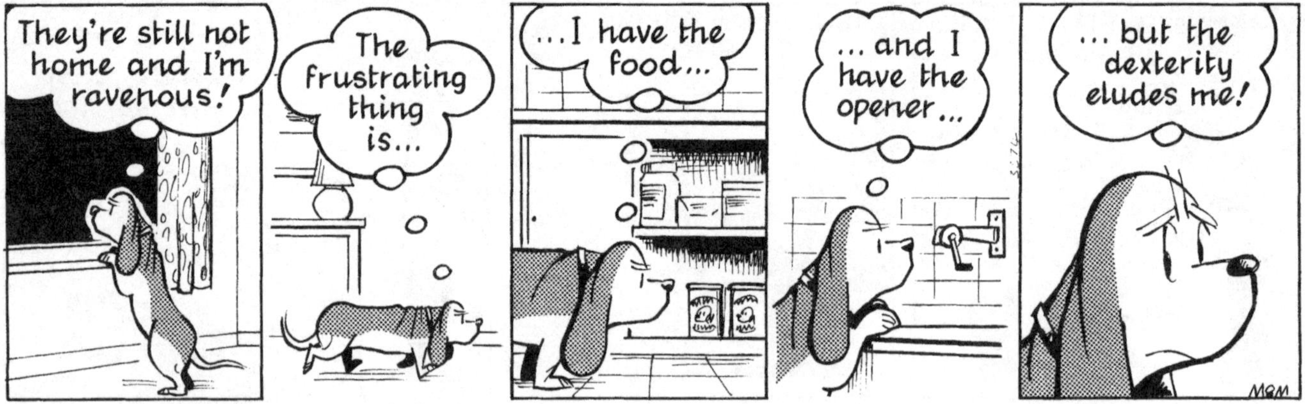
They're still not home and I'm ravenous!
The frustrating thing is...
...I have the food...
...and I have the opener...
...but the dexterity eludes me!

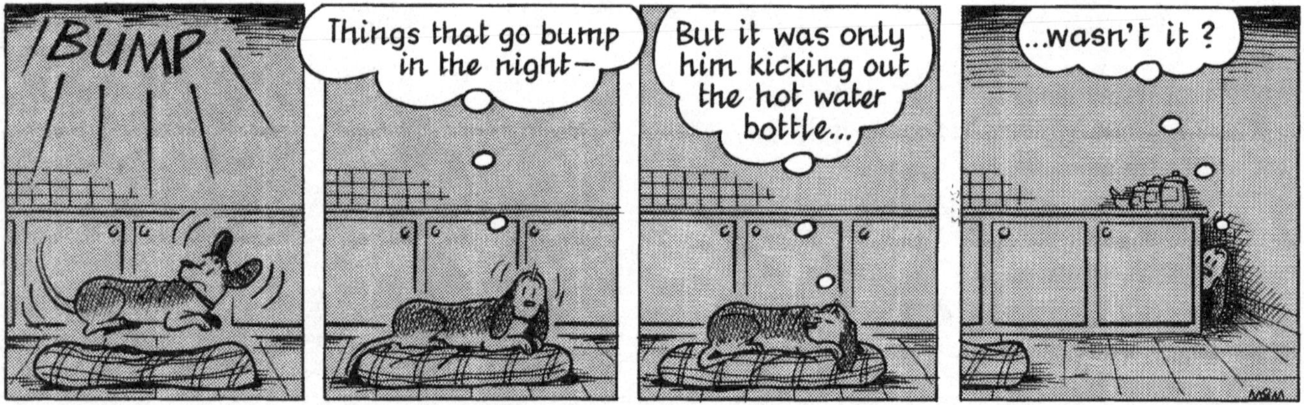
BUMP
Things that go bump in the night—
But it was only him kicking out the hot water bottle...
...wasn't it ?

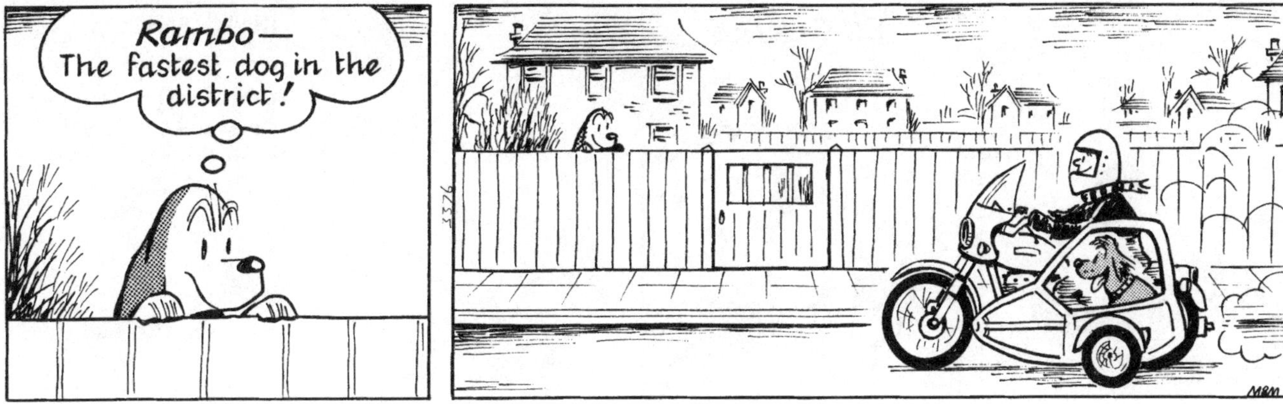
Rambo—
The fastest dog in the district!
3376
M&M

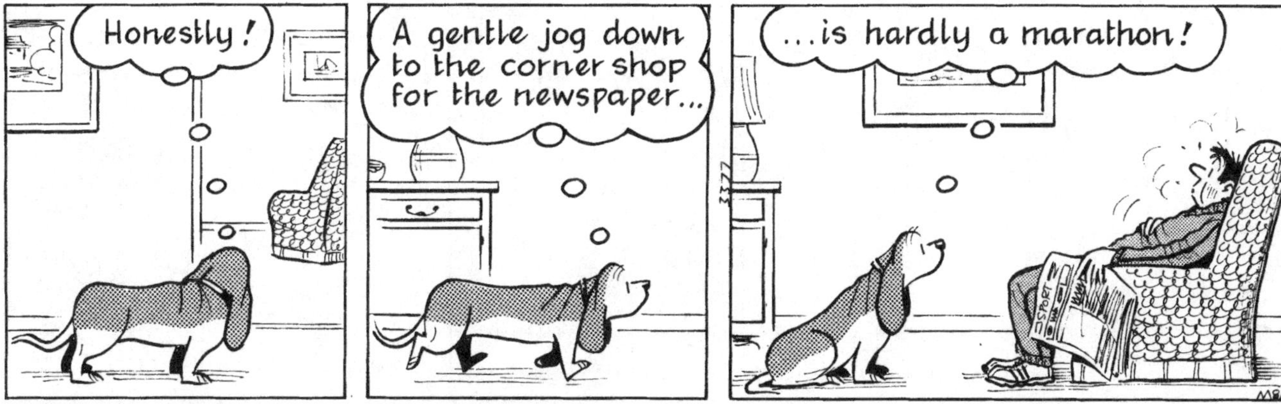
Honestly!
A gentle jog down to the corner shop for the newspaper...
...is hardly a marathon!
3377
SPORT
M&M

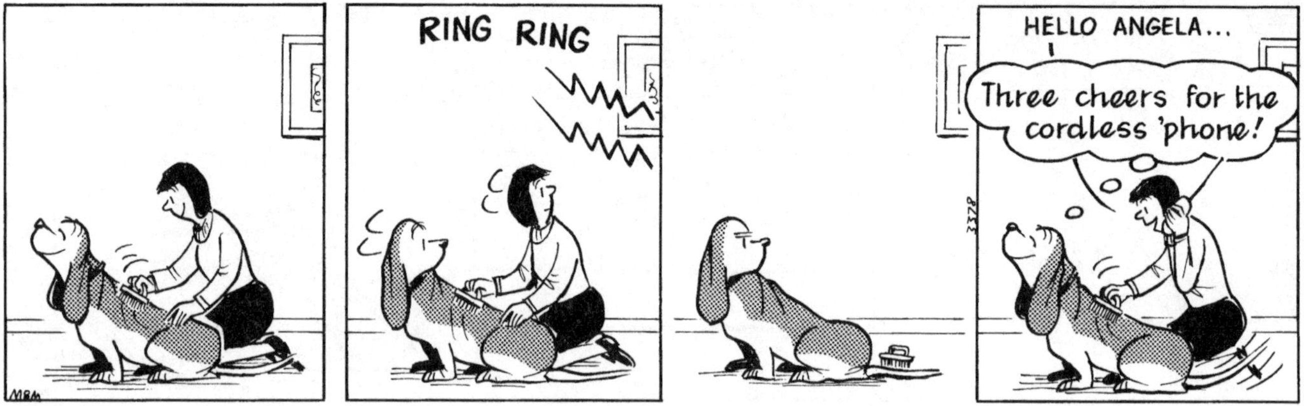
MBM
RING RING
3378
HELLO ANGELA...
Three cheers for the cordless 'phone!

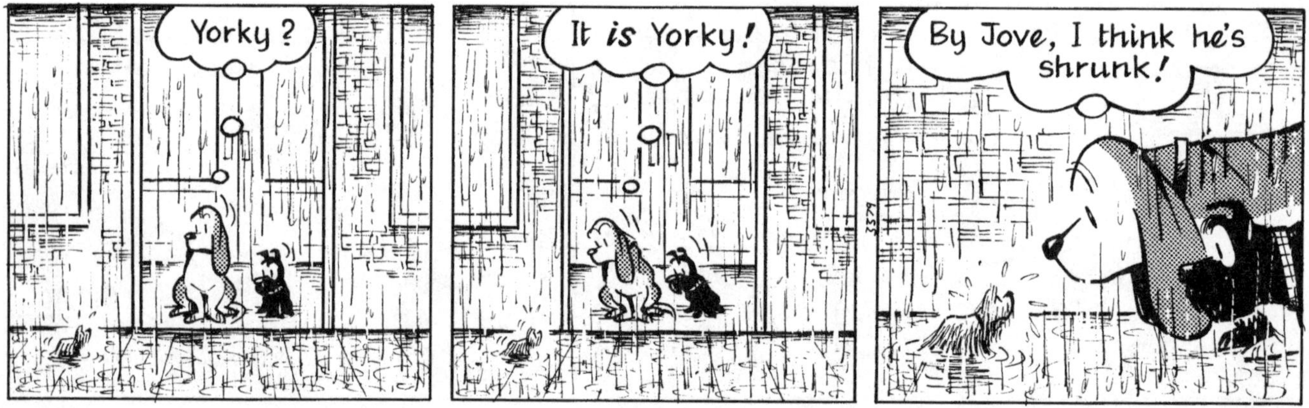
Yorky ?
3379
It *is* Yorky!
By Jove, I think he's shrunk!

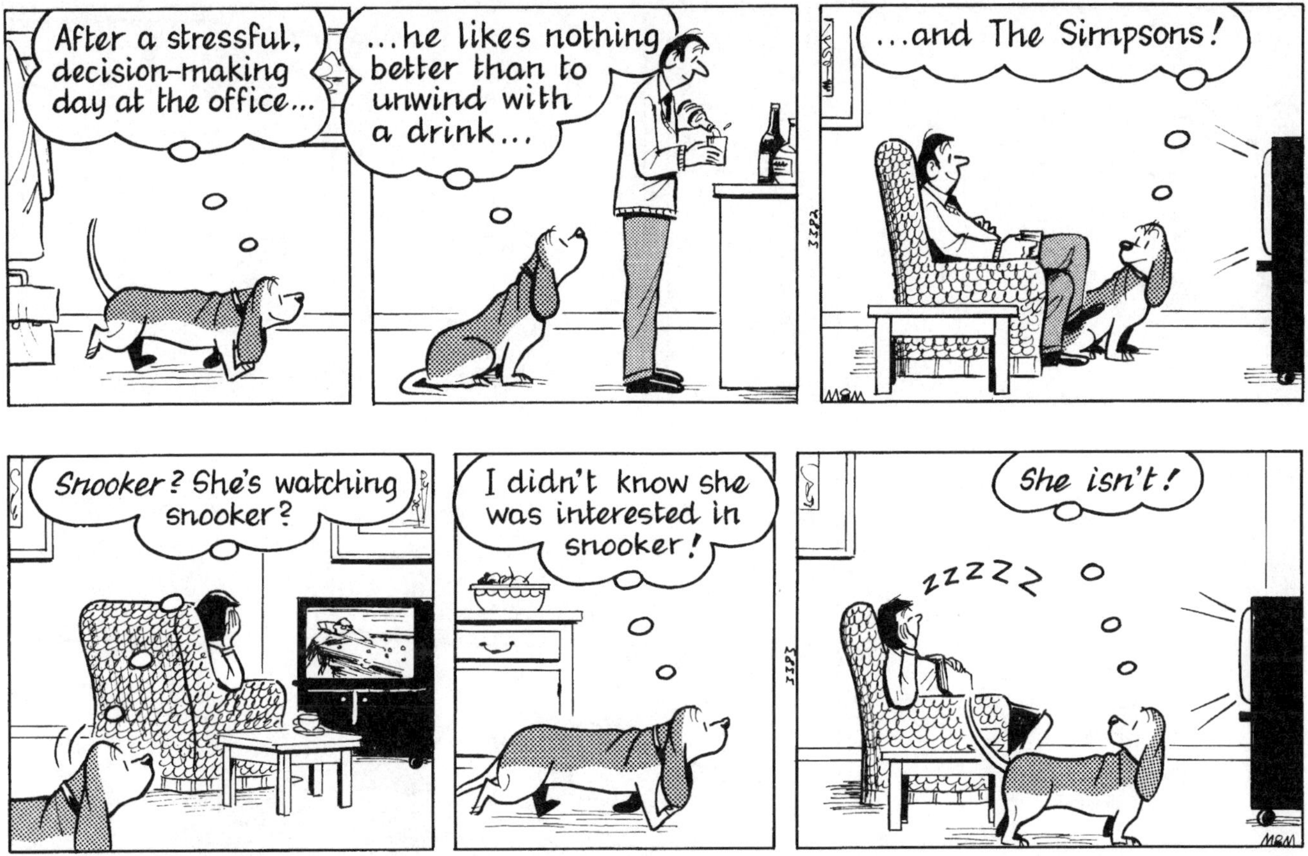
After a stressful, decision-making day at the office...
...he likes nothing better than to unwind with a drink...
...and The Simpsons!
Snooker? She's watching snooker?
I didn't know she was interested in snooker!
ZZZZZ
She isn't!

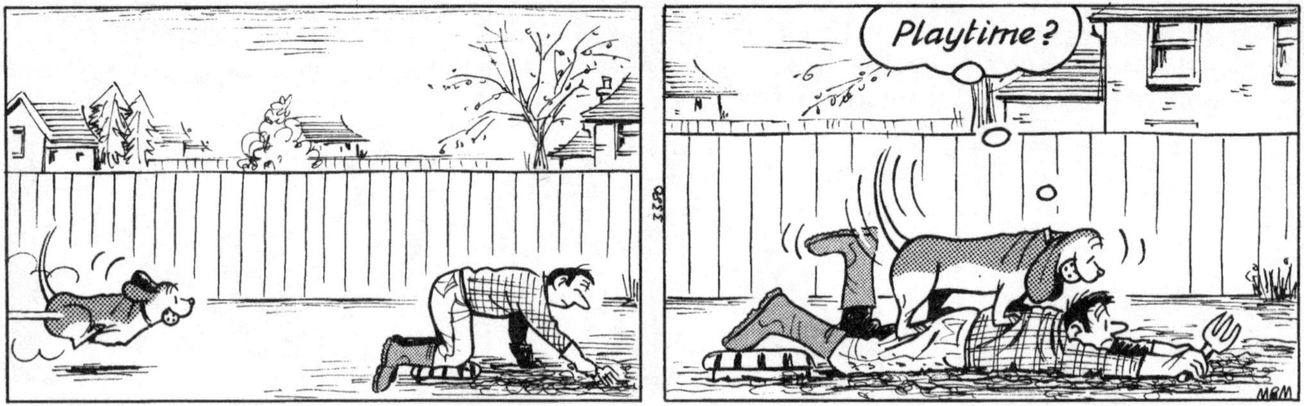
Playtime?

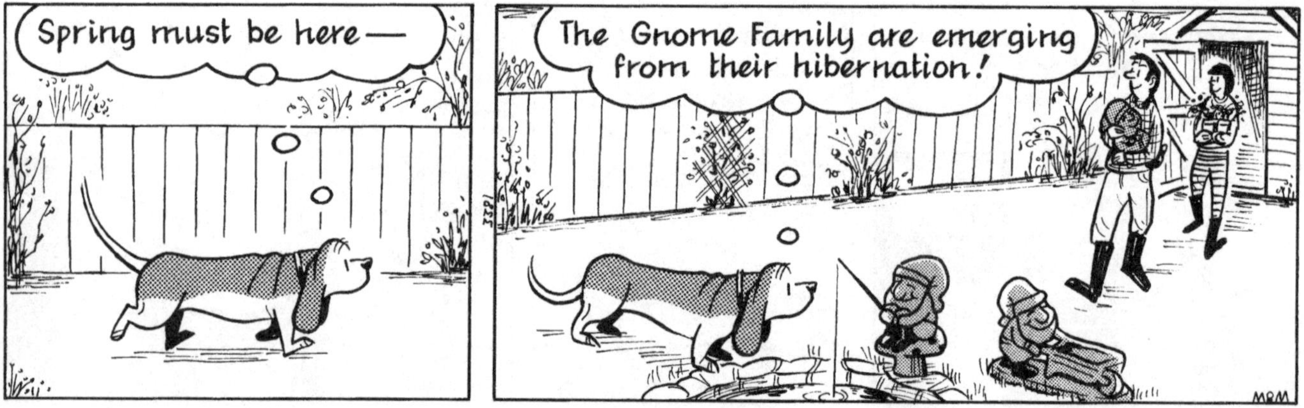
Spring must be here—
The Gnome Family are emerging from their hibernation!

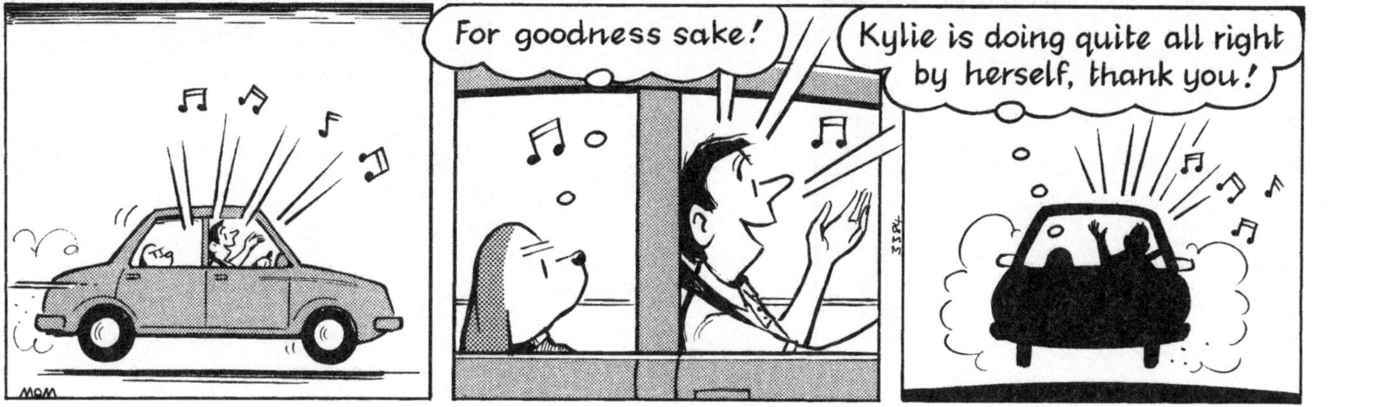
For goodness sake!
Kylie is doing quite all right by herself, thank you!

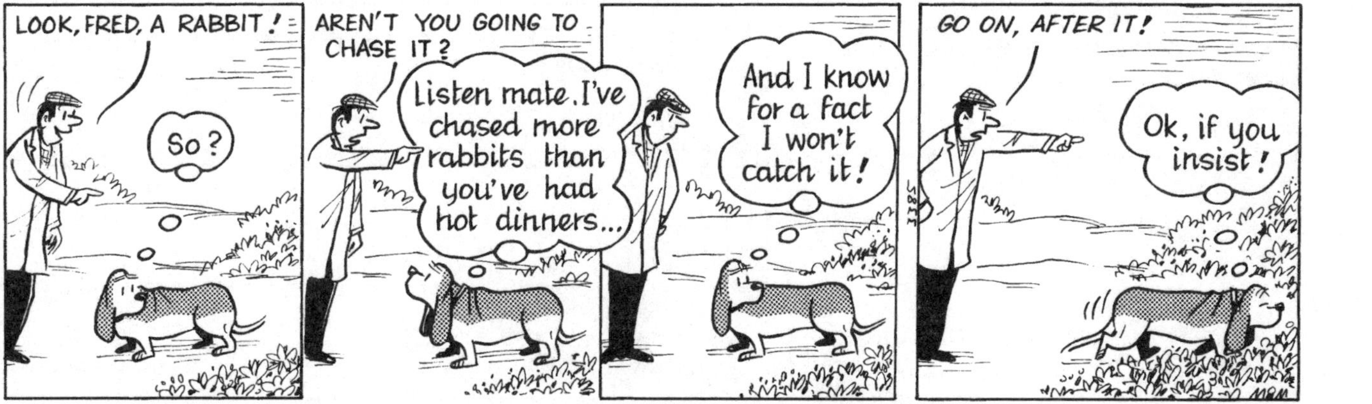
LOOK, FRED, A RABBIT!
So?
AREN'T YOU GOING TO CHASE IT?
Listen mate. I've chased more rabbits than you've had hot dinners...
And I know for a fact I won't catch it!
GO ON, AFTER IT!
Ok, if you insist!

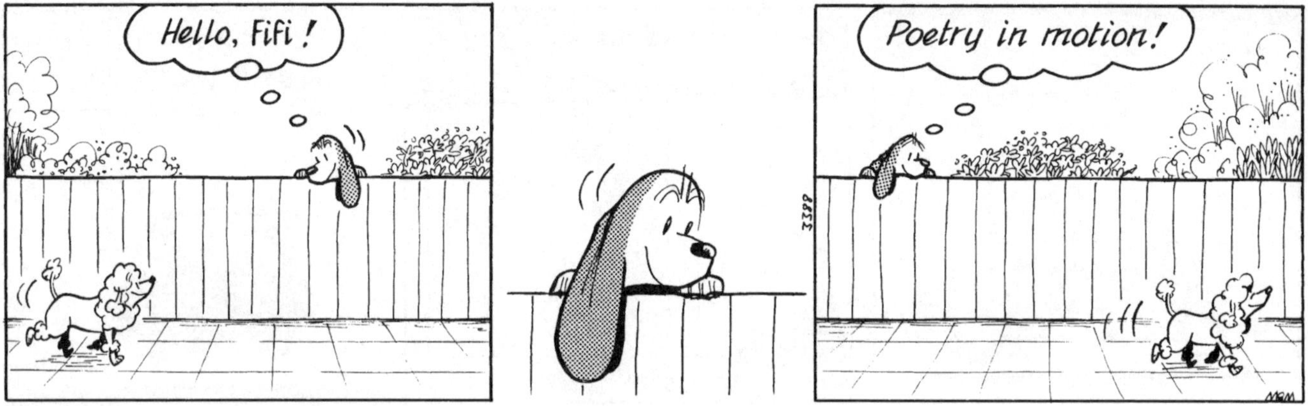
Hello, Fifi!
Poetry in motion!

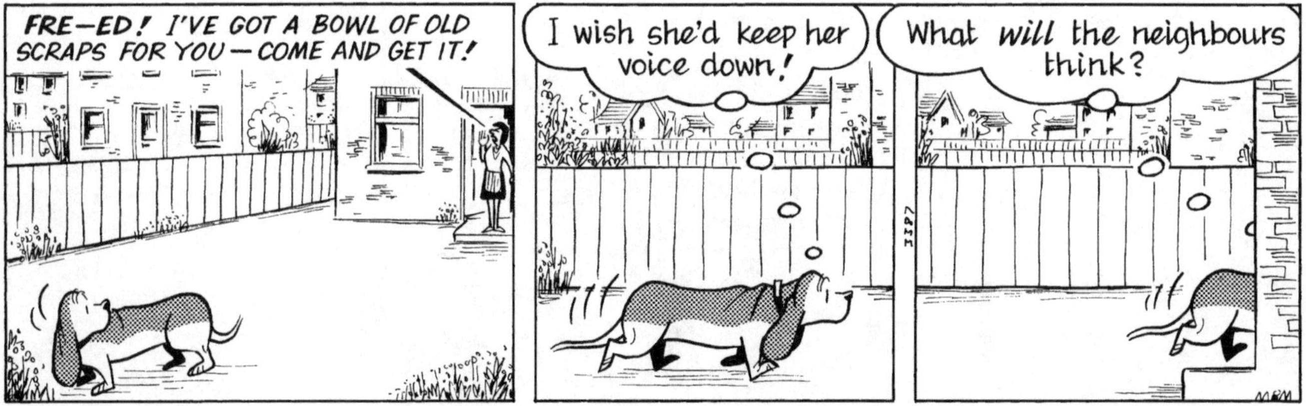
FRE—ED! I'VE GOT A BOWL OF OLD SCRAPS FOR YOU—COME AND GET IT!
I wish she'd keep her voice down!
What *will* the neighbours think?

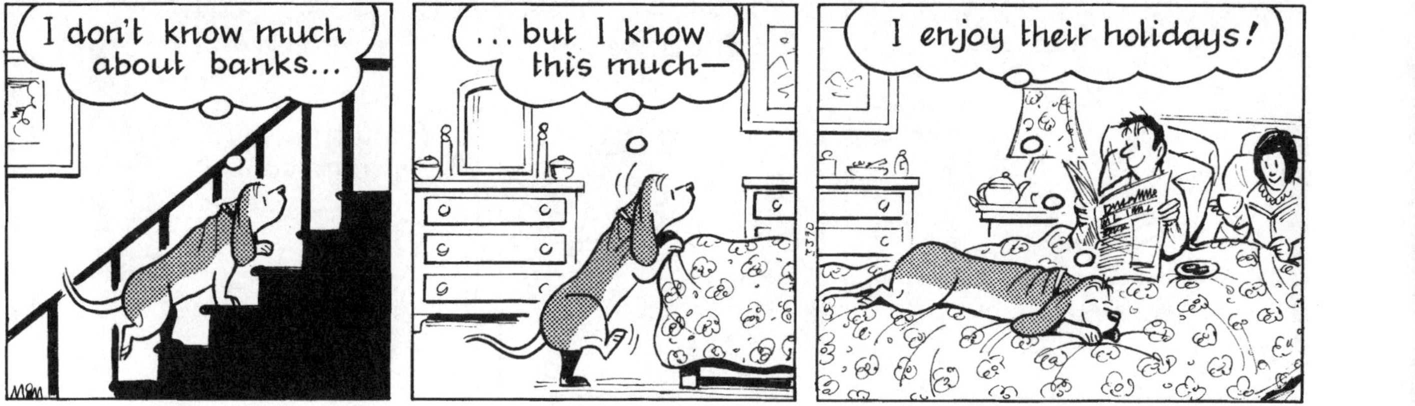
I don't know much about banks...
... but I know this much—
I enjoy their holidays!

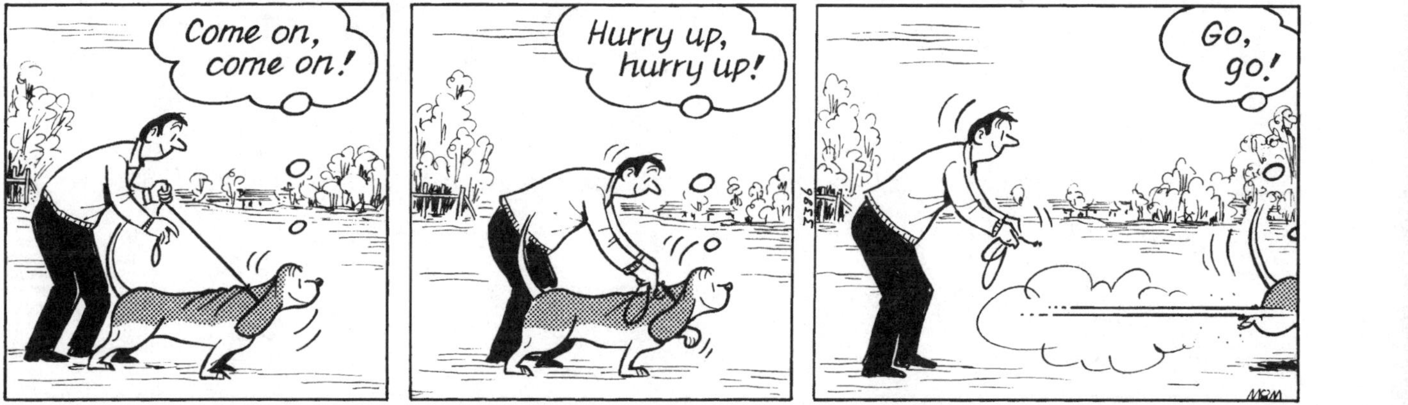
Come on, come on!
Hurry up, hurry up!
Go, go!

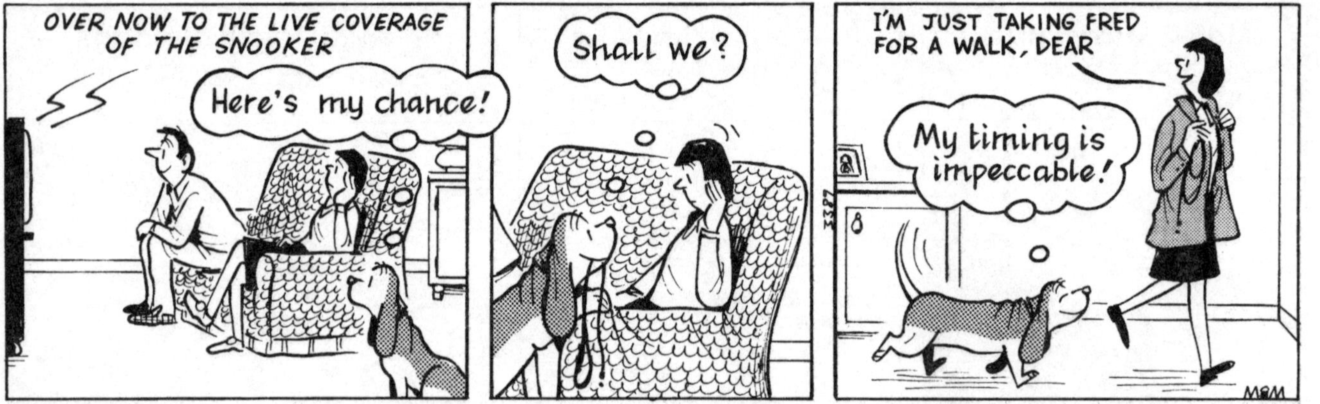
OVER NOW TO THE LIVE COVERAGE OF THE SNOOKER
Here's my chance!
Shall we?
I'M JUST TAKING FRED FOR A WALK, DEAR
My timing is impeccable!

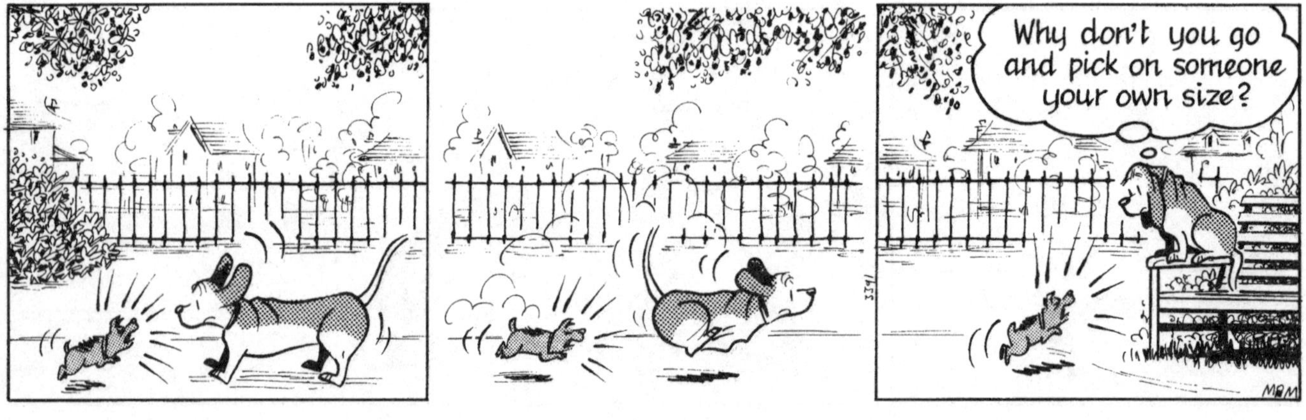
Why don't you go and pick on someone your own size?

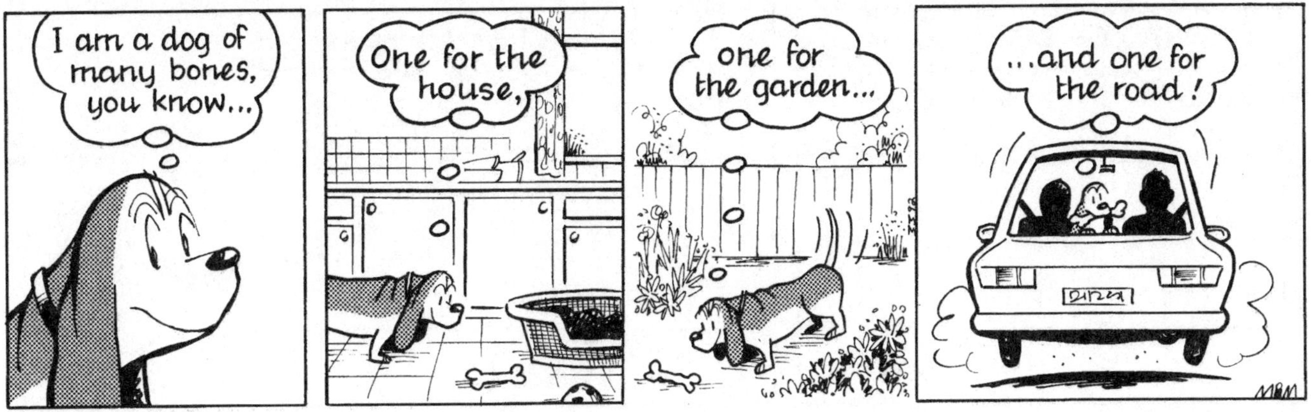

I am a dog of many bones, you know...
One for the house,
one for the garden...
...and one for the road!

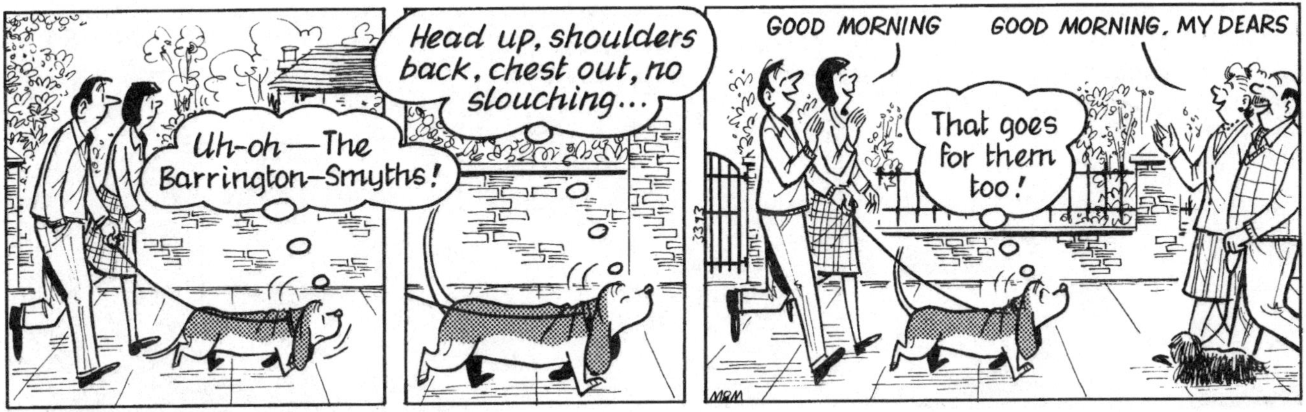

Uh-oh—The Barrington-Smyths!
Head up, shoulders back, chest out, no slouching...
GOOD MORNING
GOOD MORNING, MY DEARS
That goes for them too!

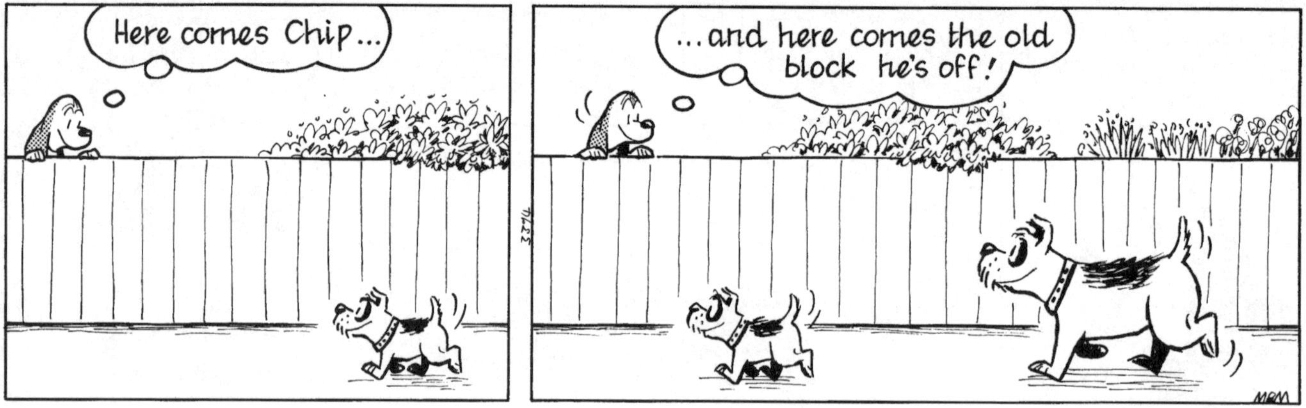
Here comes Chip...
...and here comes the old block he's off!

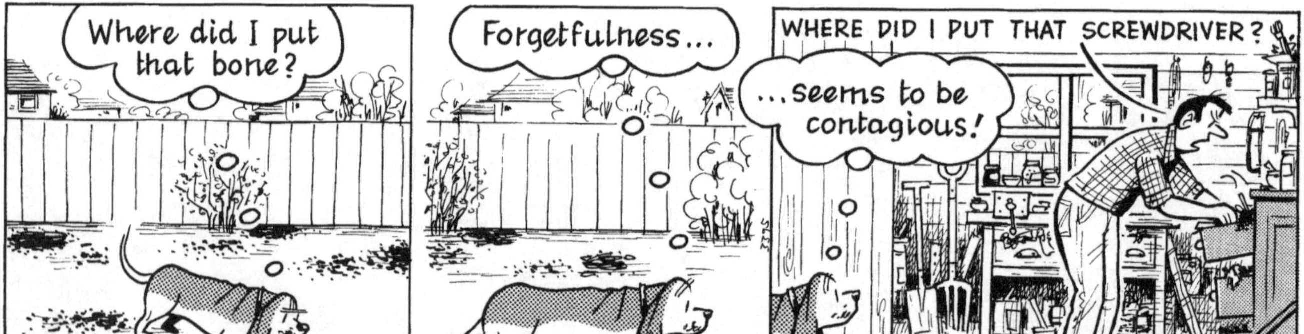
Where did I put that bone?
Forgetfulness...
WHERE DID I PUT THAT SCREWDRIVER?
...seems to be contagious!

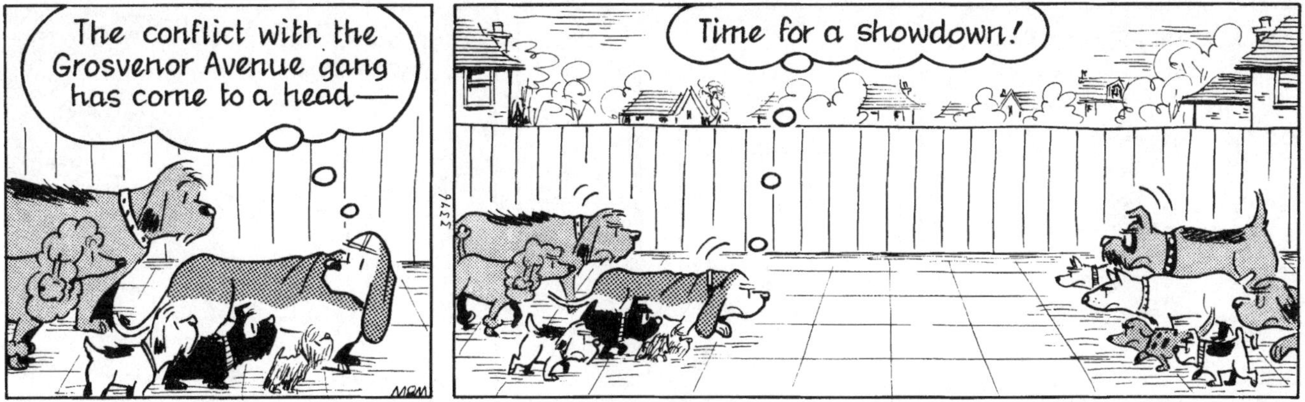
The conflict with the Grosvenor Avenue gang has come to a head—
Time for a showdown!

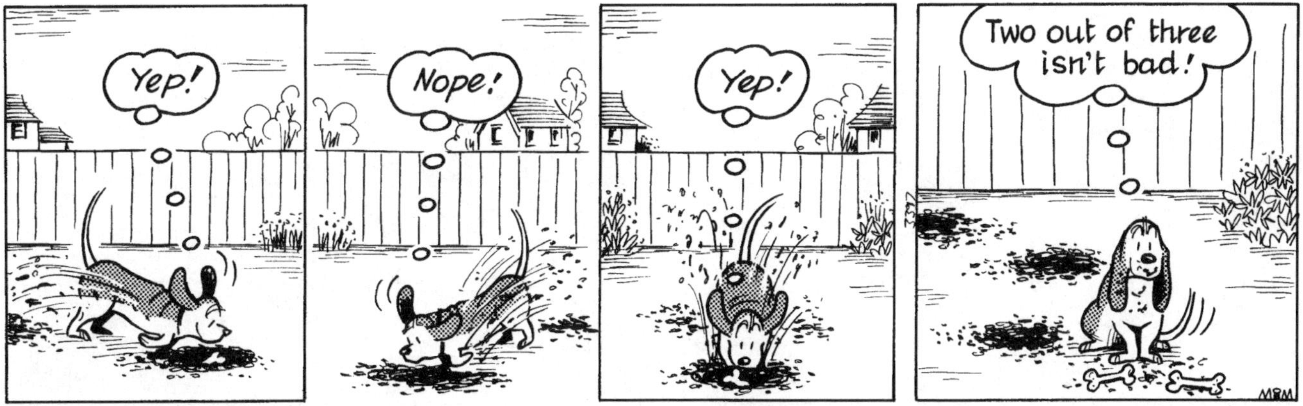
Yep!
Nope!
Yep!
Two out of three isn't bad!

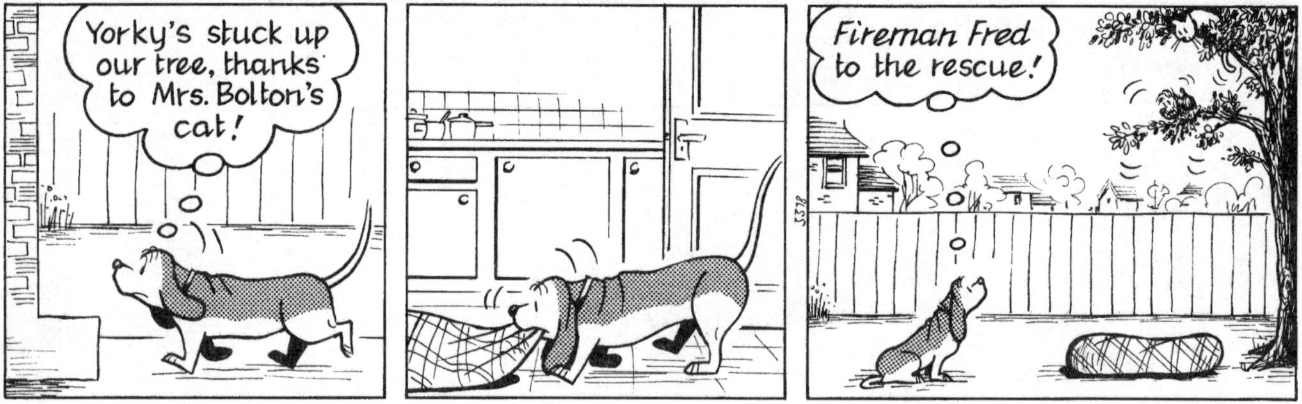
Yorky's stuck up our tree, thanks to Mrs. Bolton's cat!
Fireman Fred to the rescue!

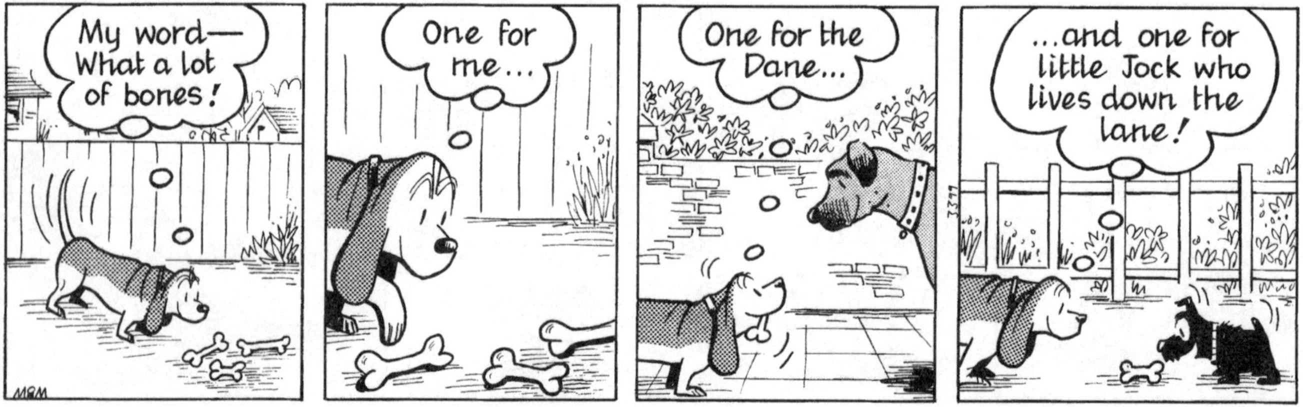
My word— What a lot of bones!
One for me...
One for the Dane...
...and one for little Jock who lives down the lane!

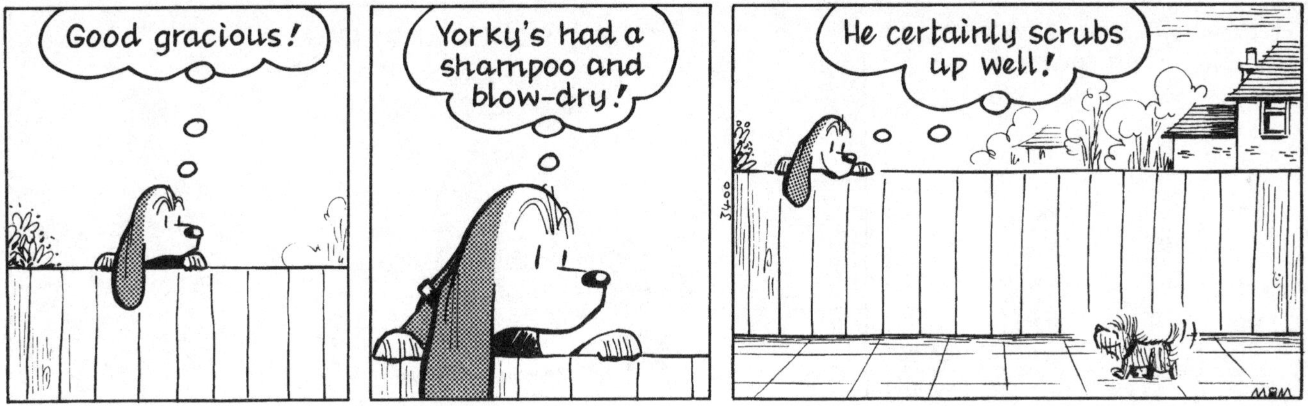

Good gracious!
Yorky's had a shampoo and blow-dry!
He certainly scrubs up well!
MGM

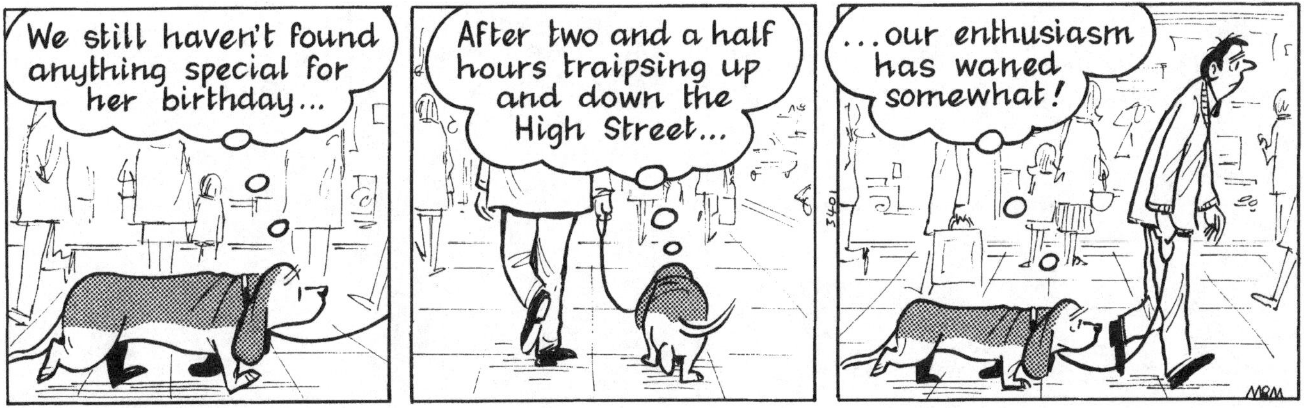

We still haven't found anything special for her birthday...
After two and a half hours traipsing up and down the High Street...
...our enthusiasm has waned somewhat!
MGM

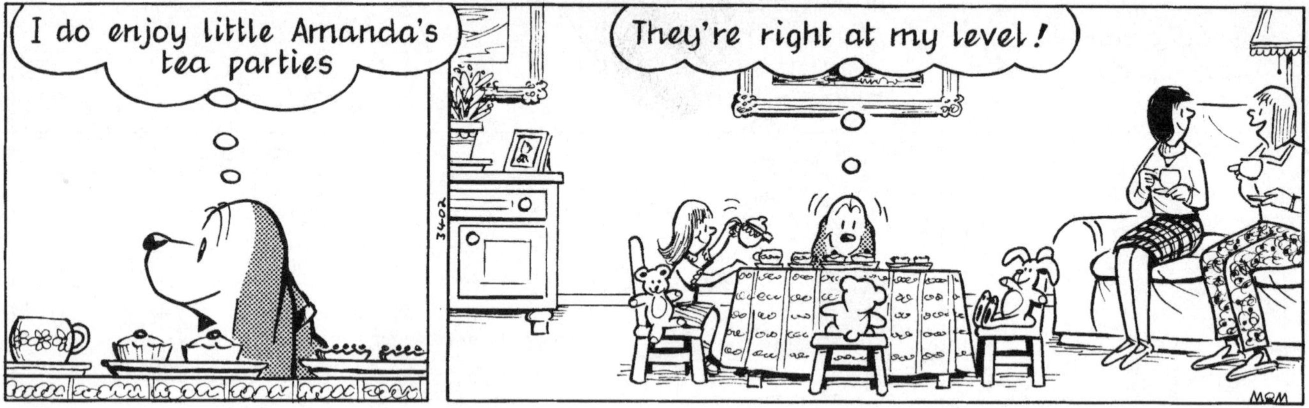
I do enjoy little Amanda's tea parties
They're right at my level!

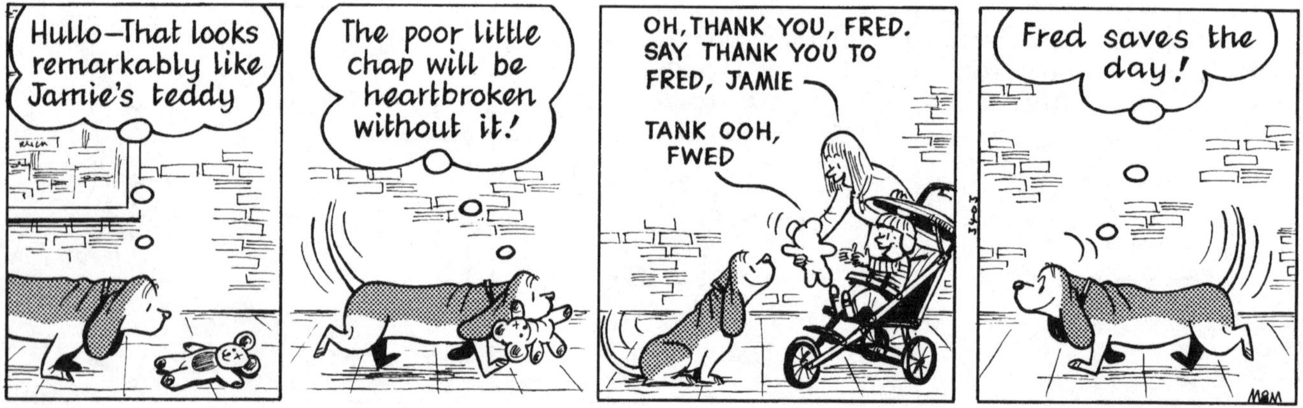
Hullo—That looks remarkably like Jamie's teddy
The poor little chap will be heartbroken without it!
OH, THANK YOU, FRED. SAY THANK YOU TO FRED, JAMIE
TANK OOH, FWED
Fred saves the day!

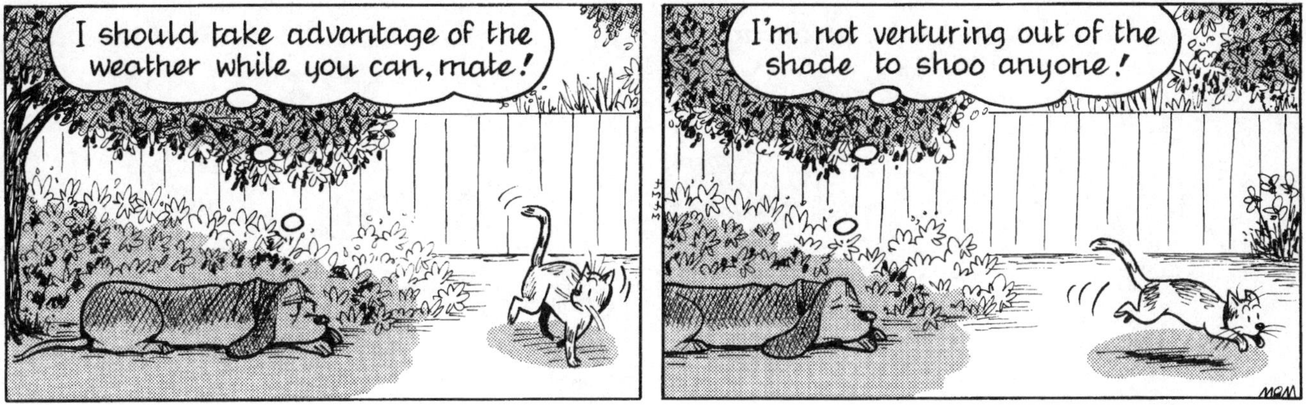
I should take advantage of the weather while you can, mate!
I'm not venturing out of the shade to shoo anyone!

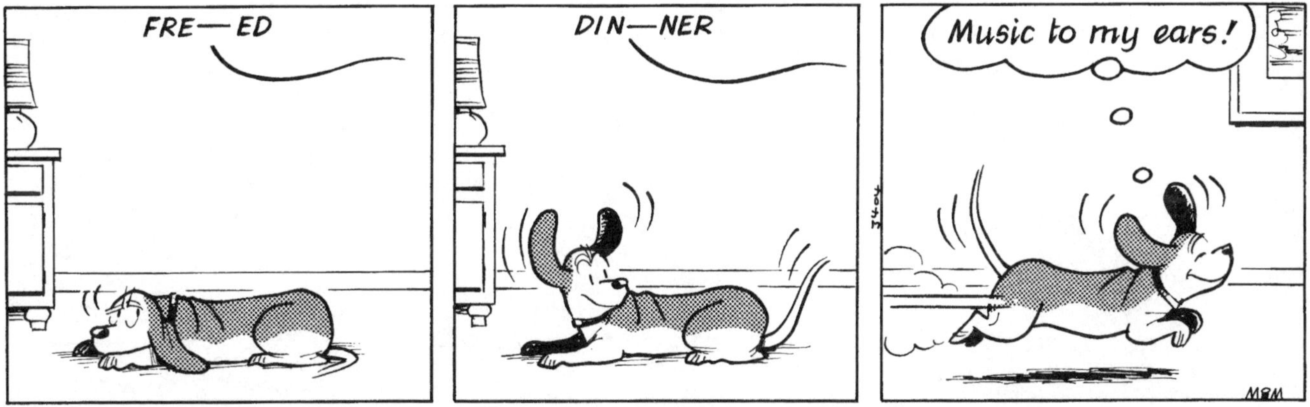
FRE—ED
DIN—NER
Music to my ears!

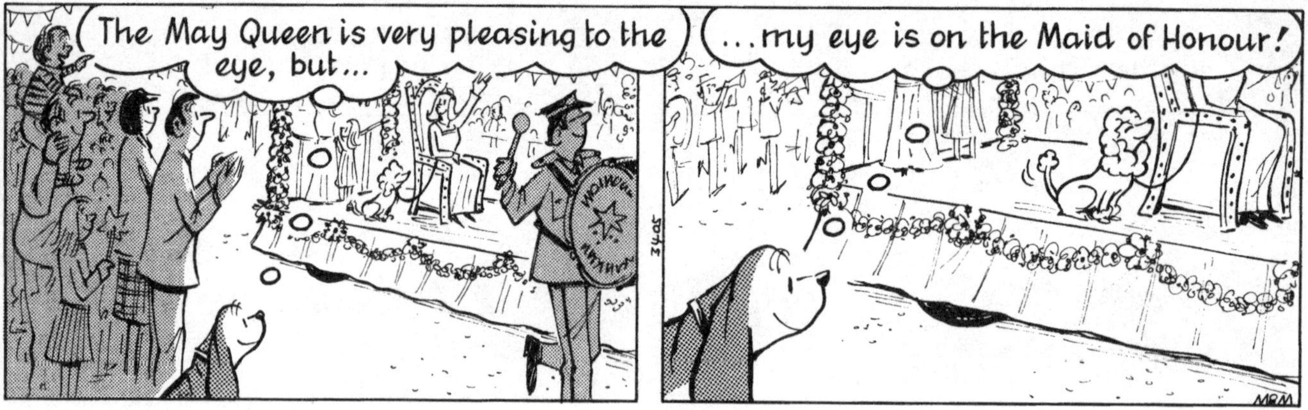
The May Queen is very pleasing to the eye, but...
...my eye is on the Maid of Honour!

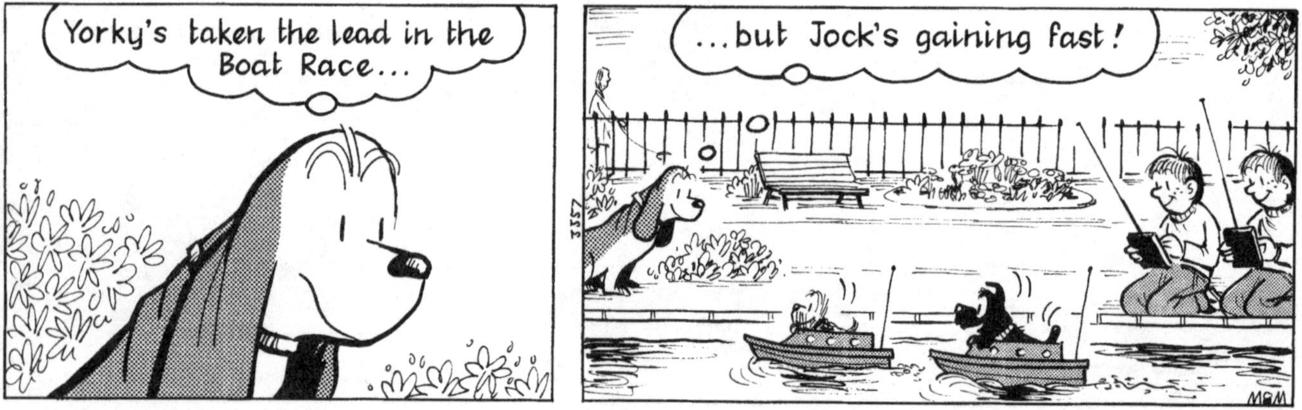
Yorky's taken the lead in the Boat Race...
...but Jock's gaining fast!

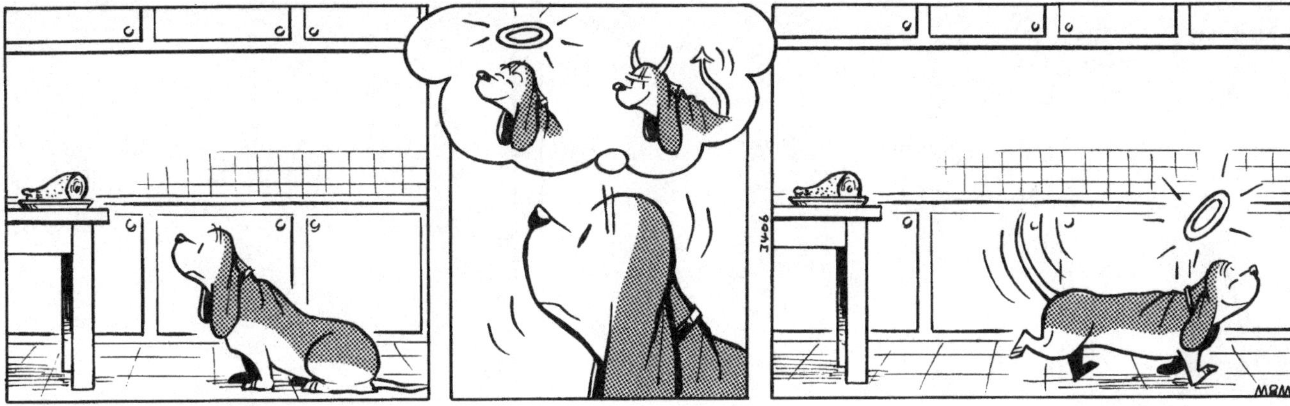

3406
M&M

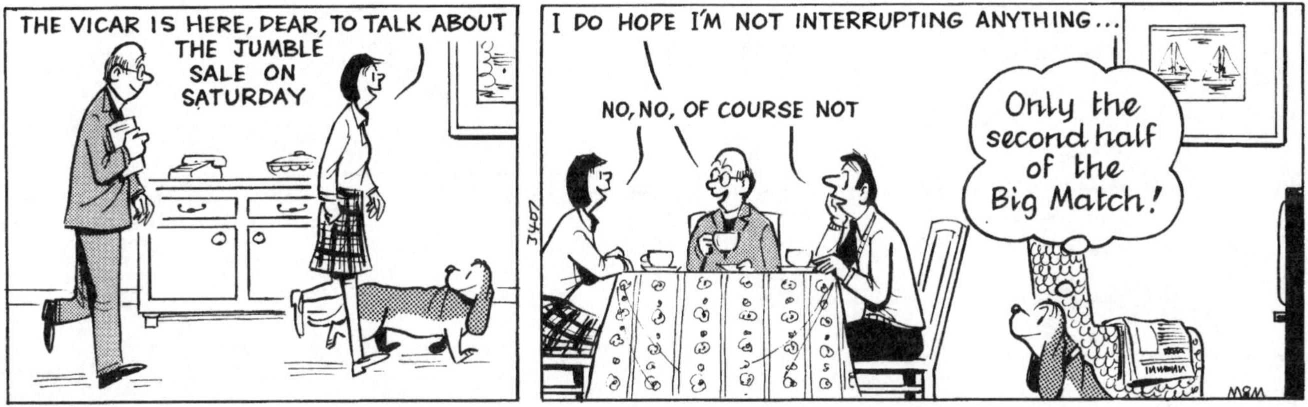

THE VICAR IS HERE, DEAR, TO TALK ABOUT THE JUMBLE SALE ON SATURDAY
3407
I DO HOPE I'M NOT INTERRUPTING ANYTHING...
NO, NO, OF COURSE NOT
Only the second half of the Big Match!
M&M

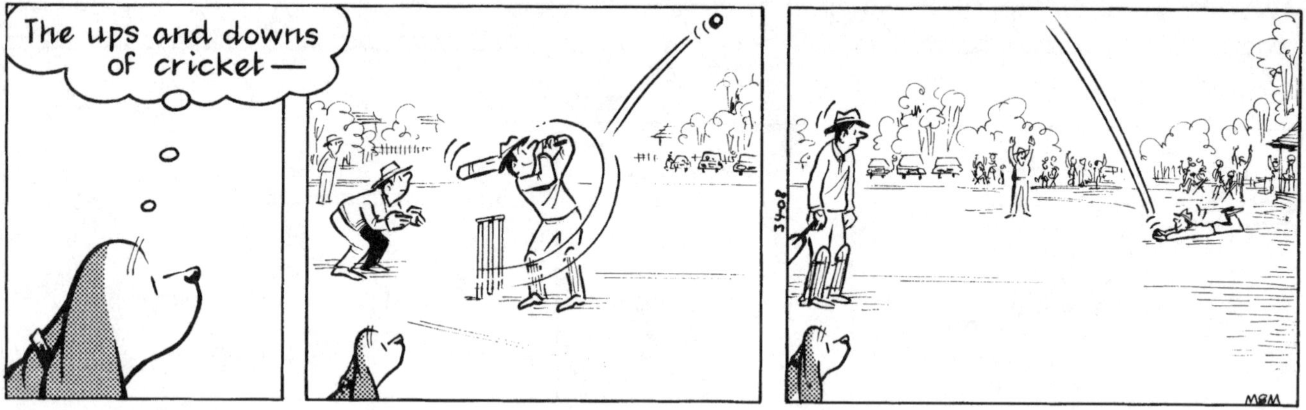
The ups and downs of cricket —

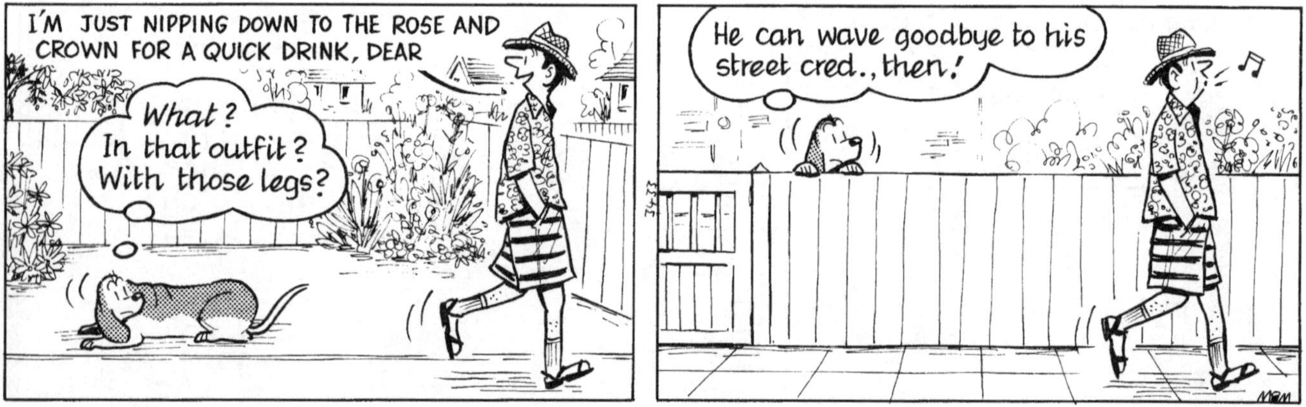
I'M JUST NIPPING DOWN TO THE ROSE AND CROWN FOR A QUICK DRINK, DEAR
What? In that outfit? With those legs?
He can wave goodbye to his street cred., then!

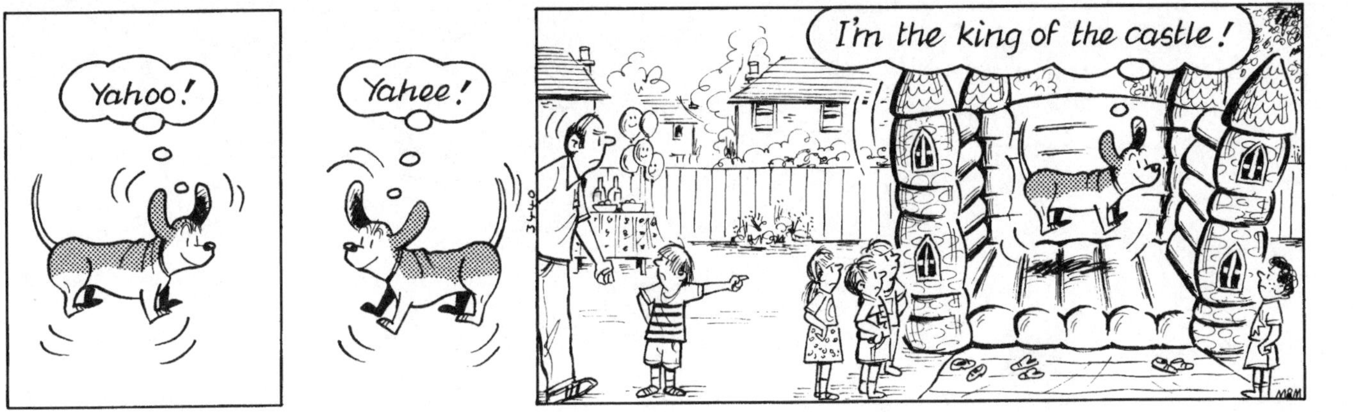
Yahoo!
Yahee!
I'm the king of the castle!

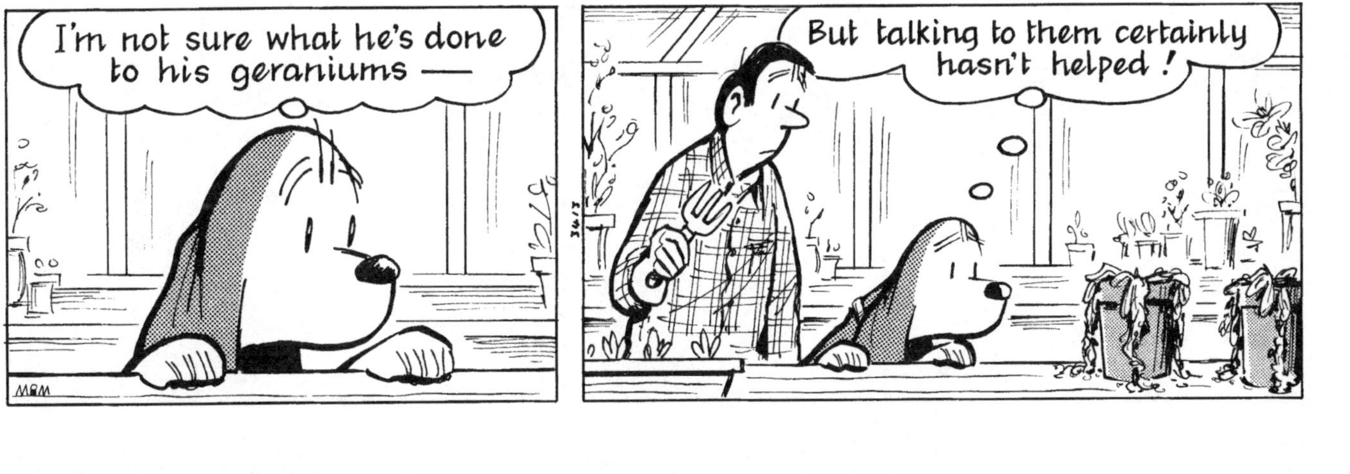
I'm not sure what he's done to his geraniums —
But talking to them certainly hasn't helped!

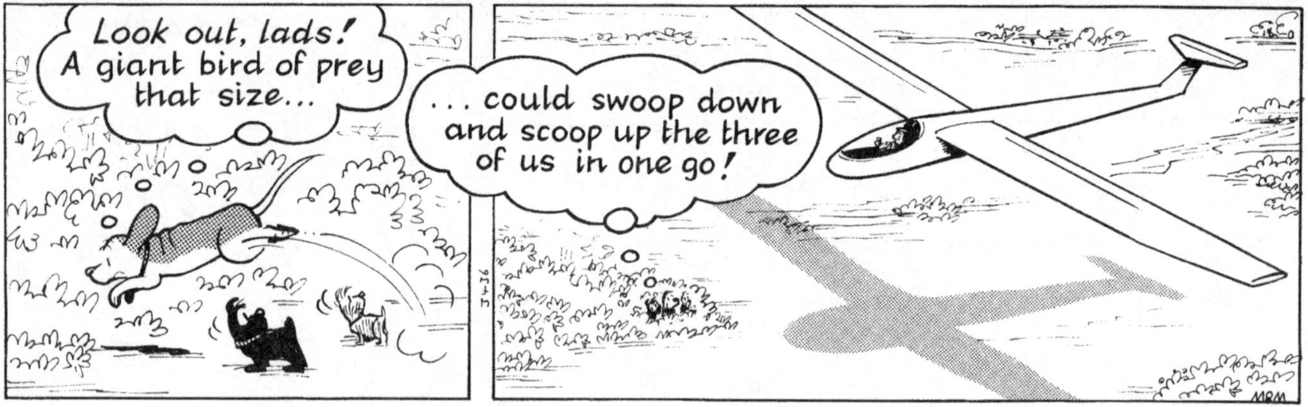
Look out, lads! A giant bird of prey that size...
... could swoop down and scoop up the three of us in one go!

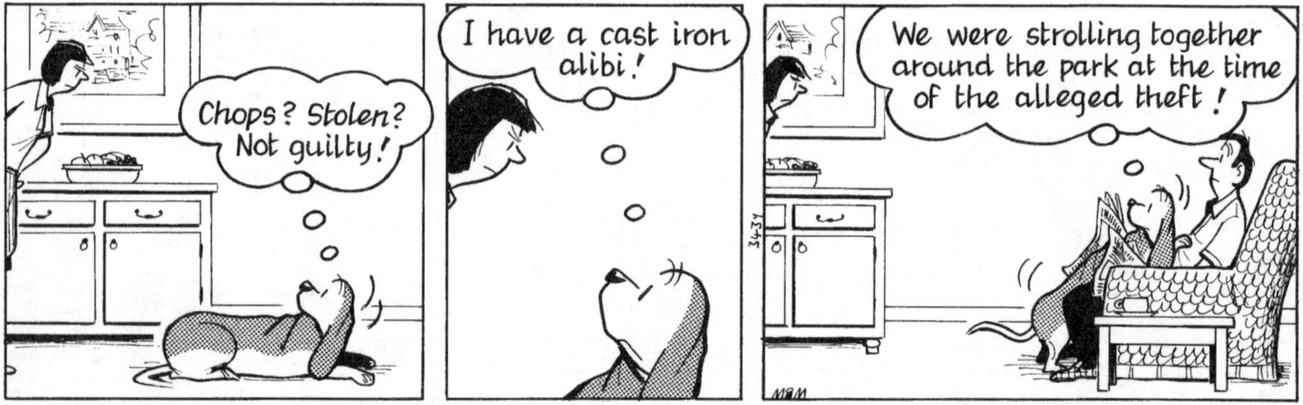
Chops? Stolen? Not guilty!
I have a cast iron alibi!
We were strolling together around the park at the time of the alleged theft!

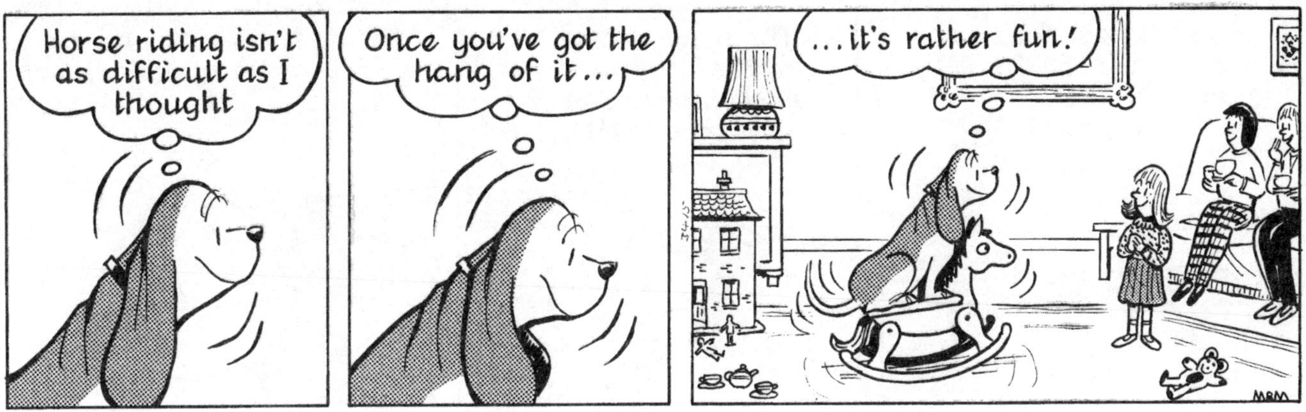
Horse riding isn't as difficult as I thought
Once you've got the hang of it ...
... it's rather fun!

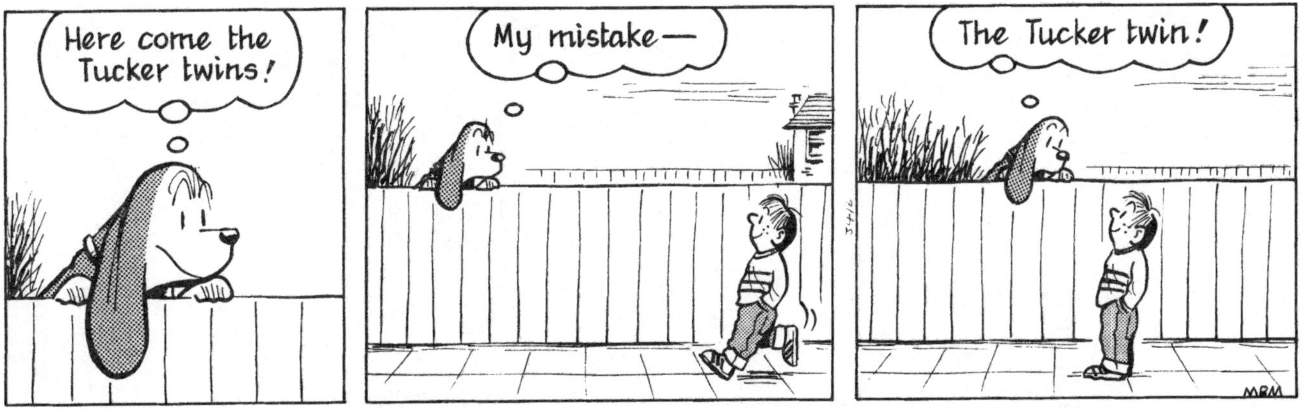
Here come the Tucker twins!
My mistake—
The Tucker twin!

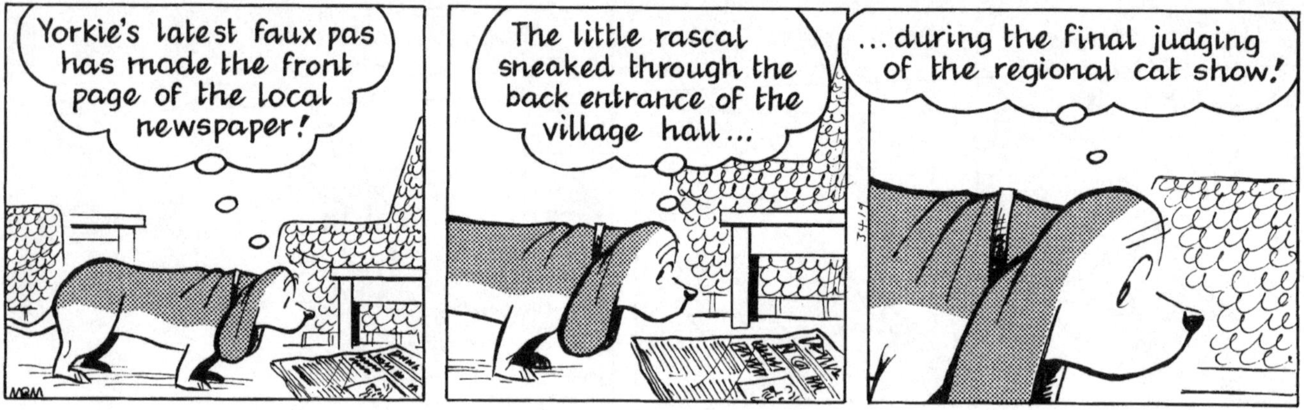
Yorkie's latest faux pas has made the front page of the local newspaper!
The little rascal sneaked through the back entrance of the village hall...
...during the final judging of the regional cat show!

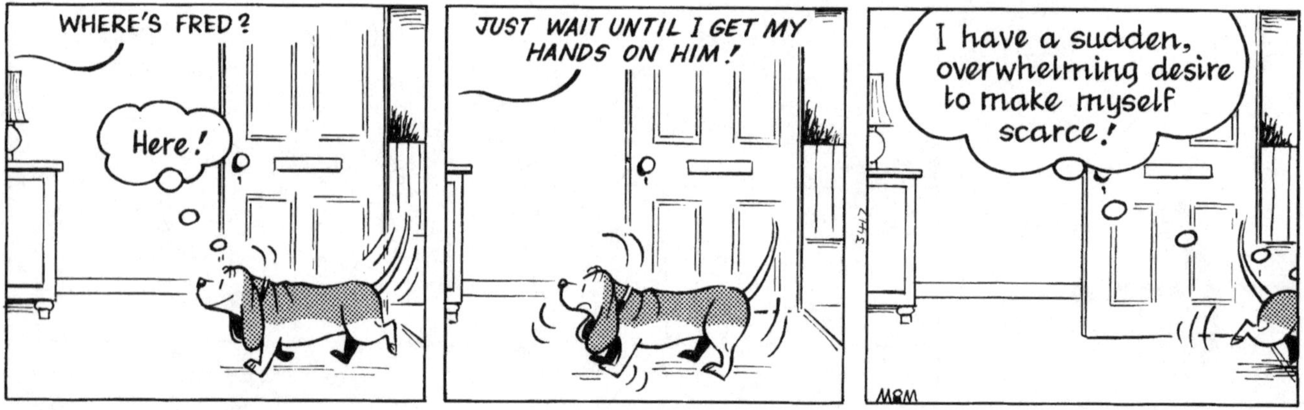
WHERE'S FRED?
Here!
JUST WAIT UNTIL I GET MY HANDS ON HIM!
I have a sudden, overwhelming desire to make myself scarce!

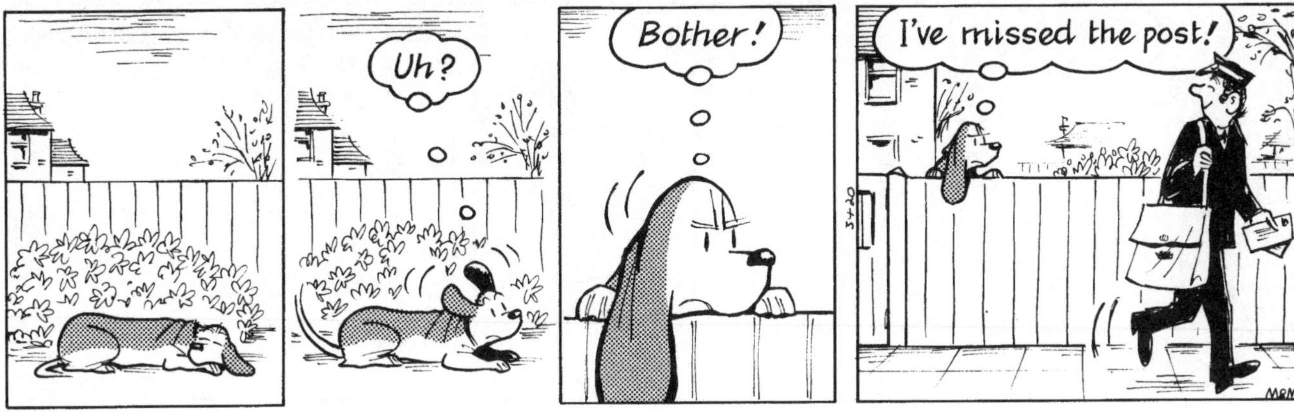
Uh?
Bother!
I've missed the post!

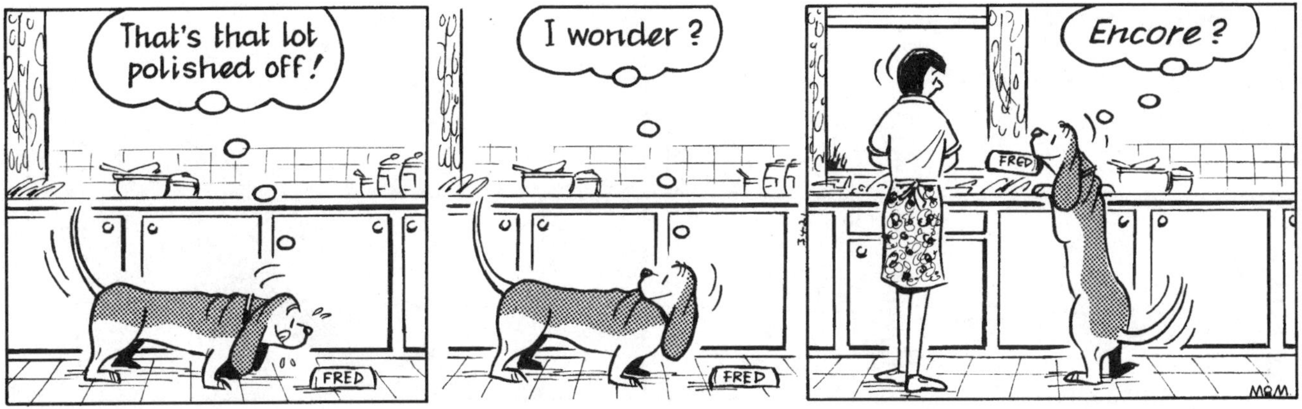
That's that lot polished off!
FRED
I wonder?
FRED
Encore?
FRED

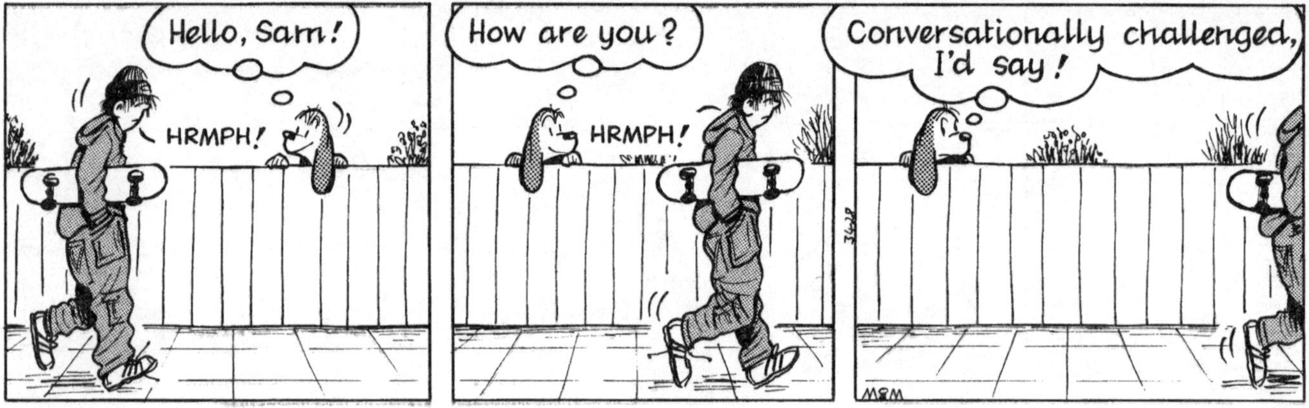
Hello, Sam!
HRMPH!
How are you?
HRMPH!
Conversationally challenged, I'd say!

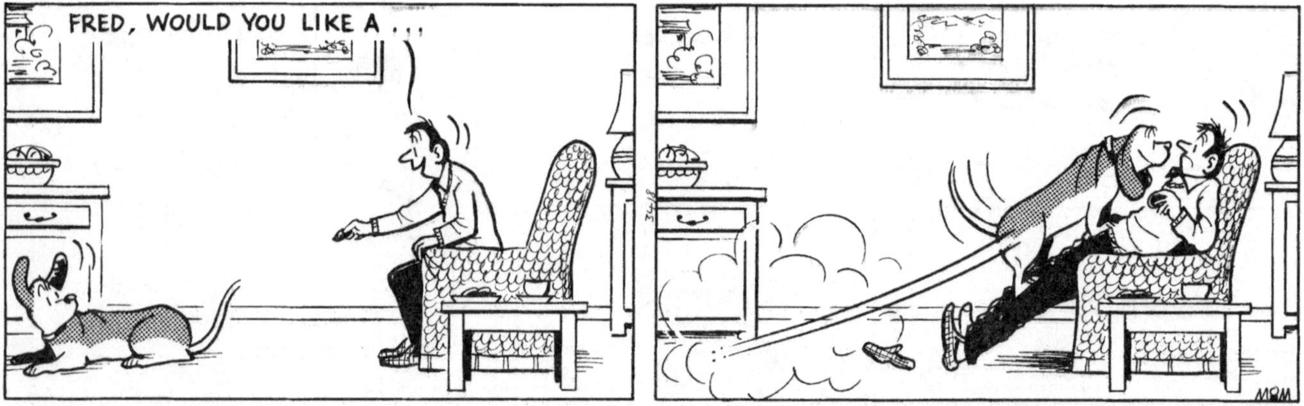
FRED, WOULD YOU LIKE A . . .

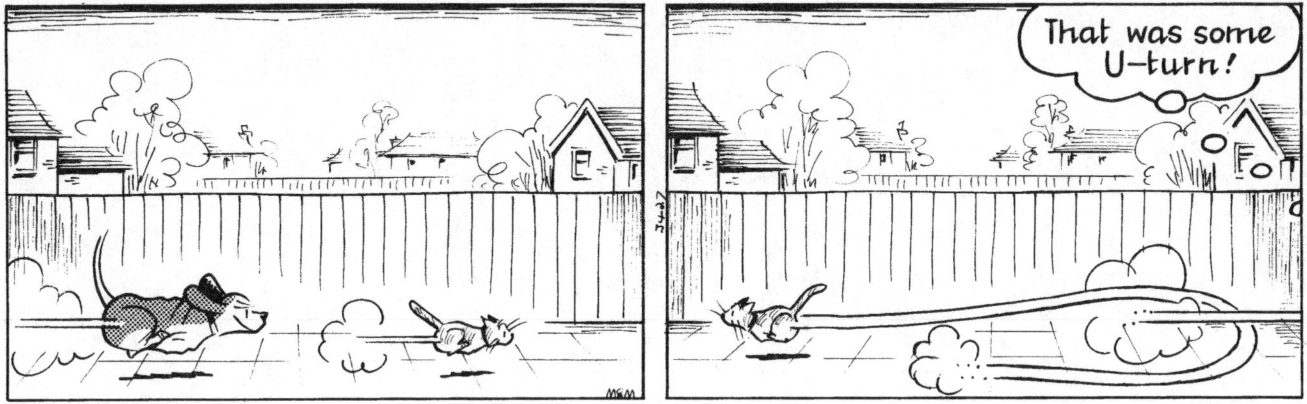
That was some U-turn!

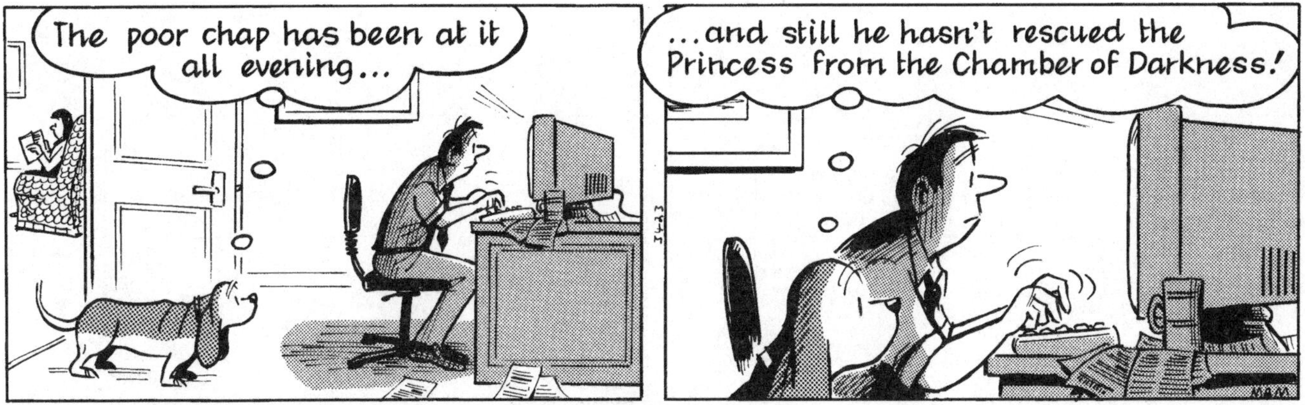
The poor chap has been at it all evening...
...and still he hasn't rescued the Princess from the Chamber of Darkness!

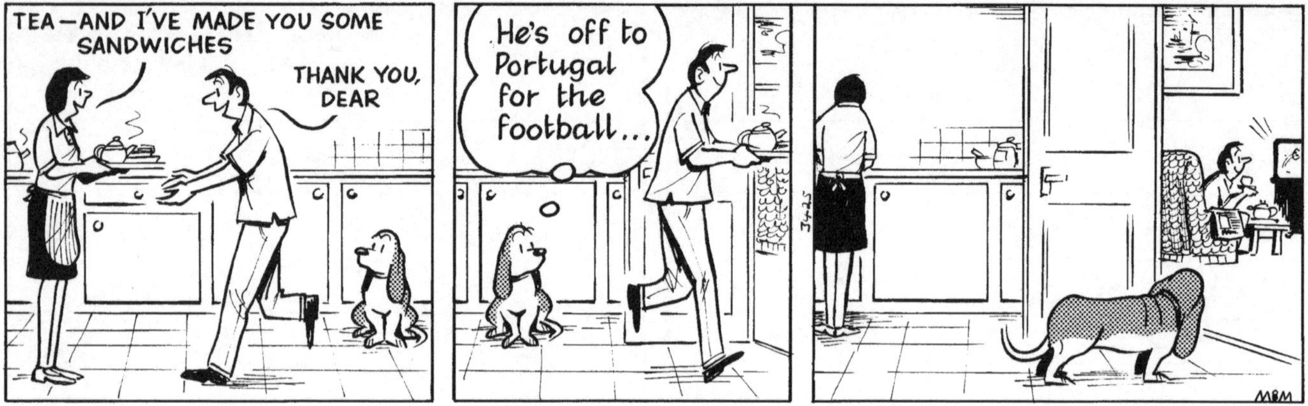
TEA—AND I'VE MADE YOU SOME SANDWICHES
THANK YOU, DEAR
He's off to Portugal for the football...
3425
MBM

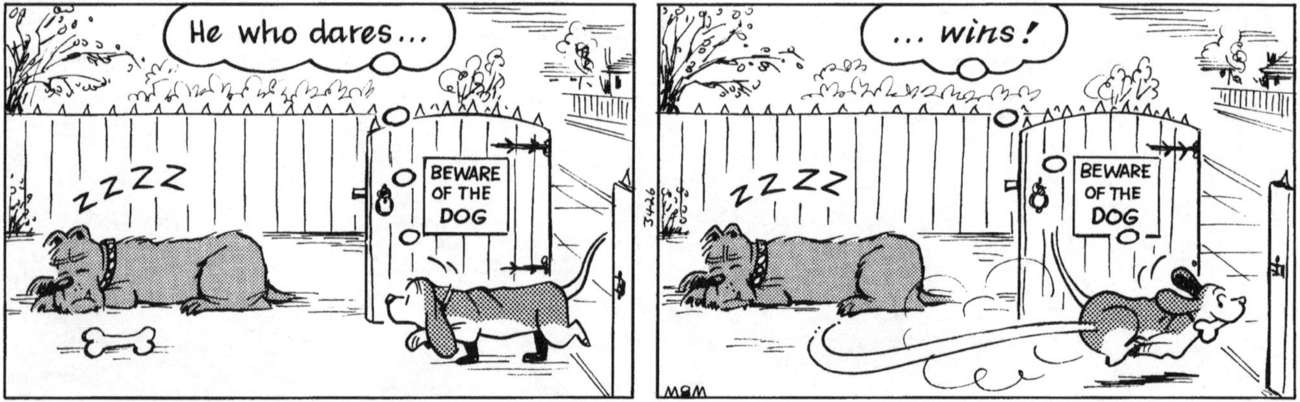
He who dares...
ZZZZ
BEWARE OF THE DOG
3426
MBM
... wins!
ZZZZ
BEWARE OF THE DOG

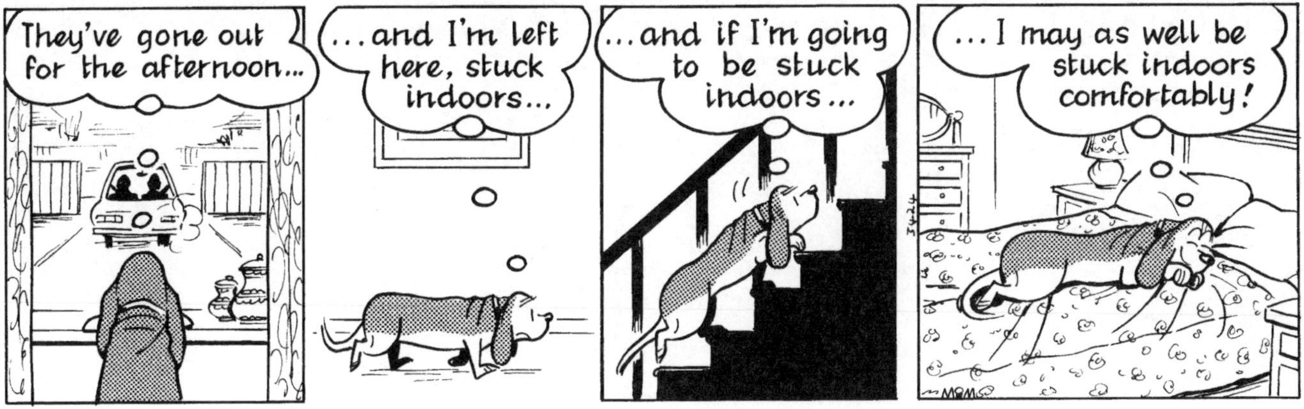
They've gone out for the afternoon...
...and I'm left here, stuck indoors...
...and if I'm going to be stuck indoors...
...I may as well be stuck indoors comfortably!

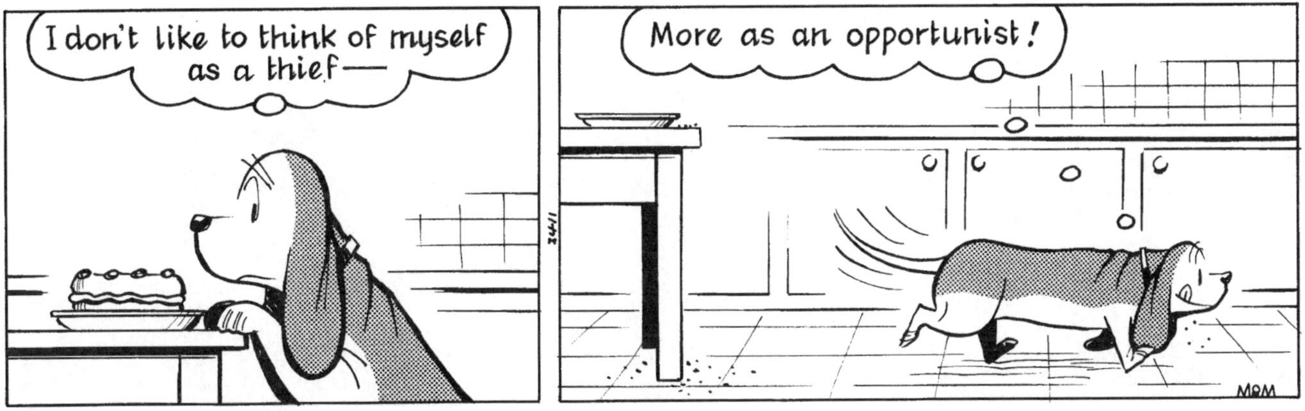
I don't like to think of myself as a thief—
More as an opportunist!

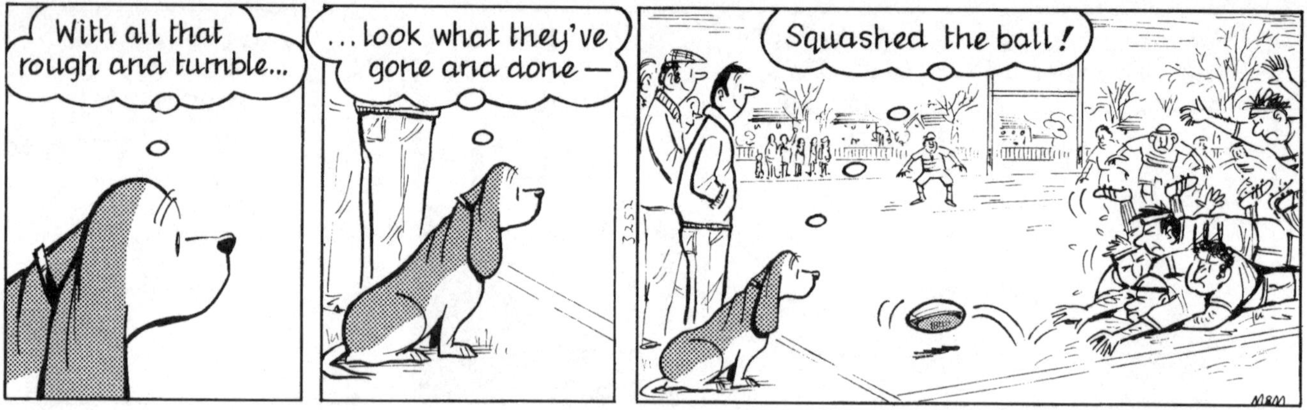
With all that rough and tumble...
... look what they've gone and done —
Squashed the ball!

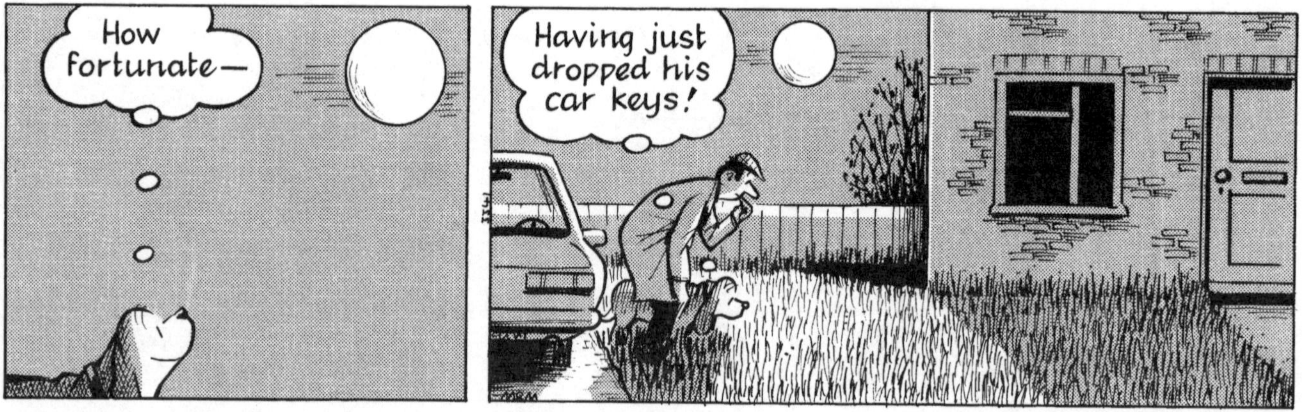
How fortunate —
Having just dropped his car keys!

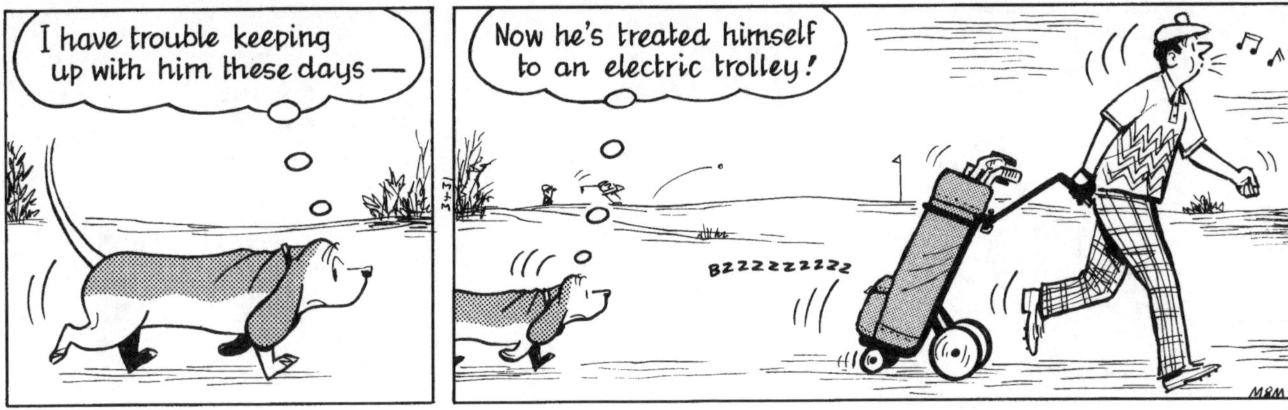
I have trouble keeping up with him these days —
Now he's treated himself to an electric trolley!
BZZZZZZZZZ

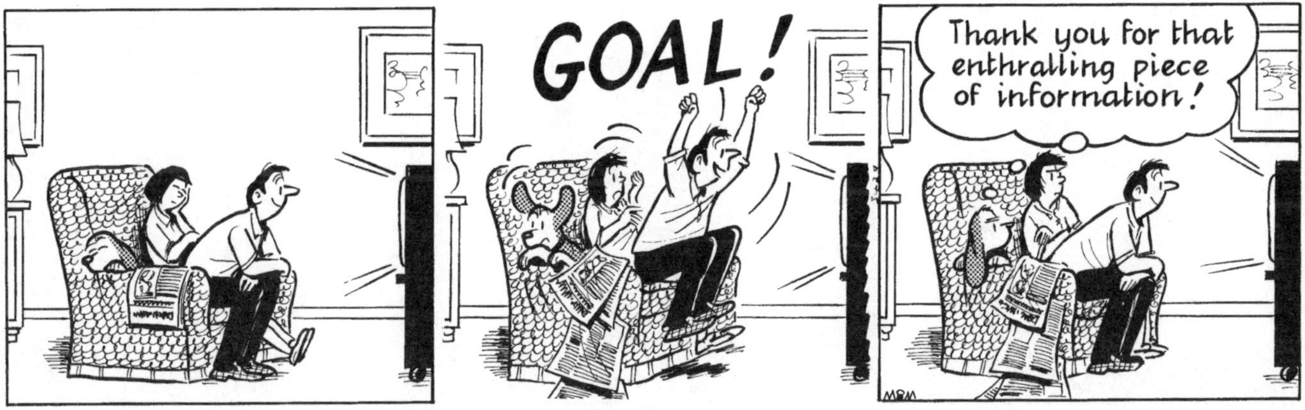
GOAL!
Thank you for that enthralling piece of information!

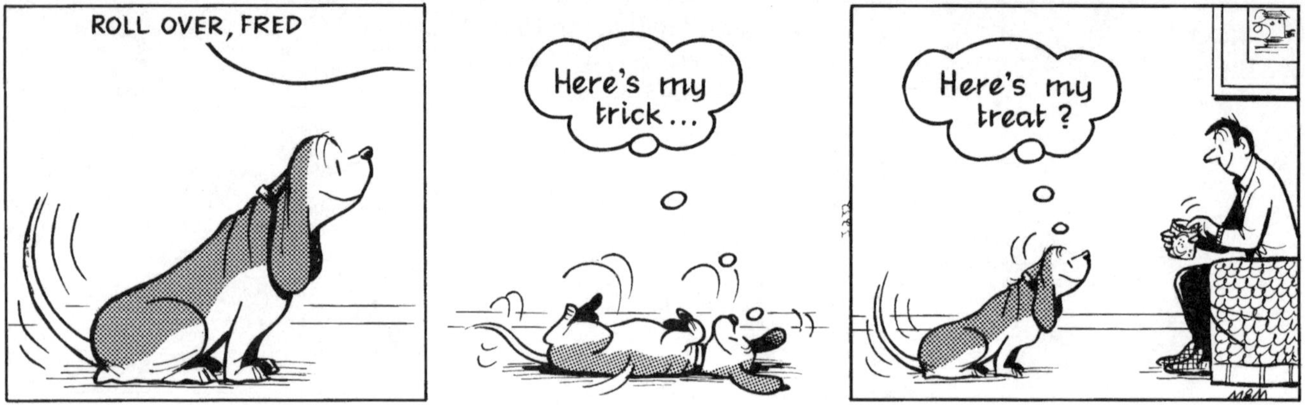
ROLL OVER, FRED
Here's my trick...
Here's my treat ?
MBM

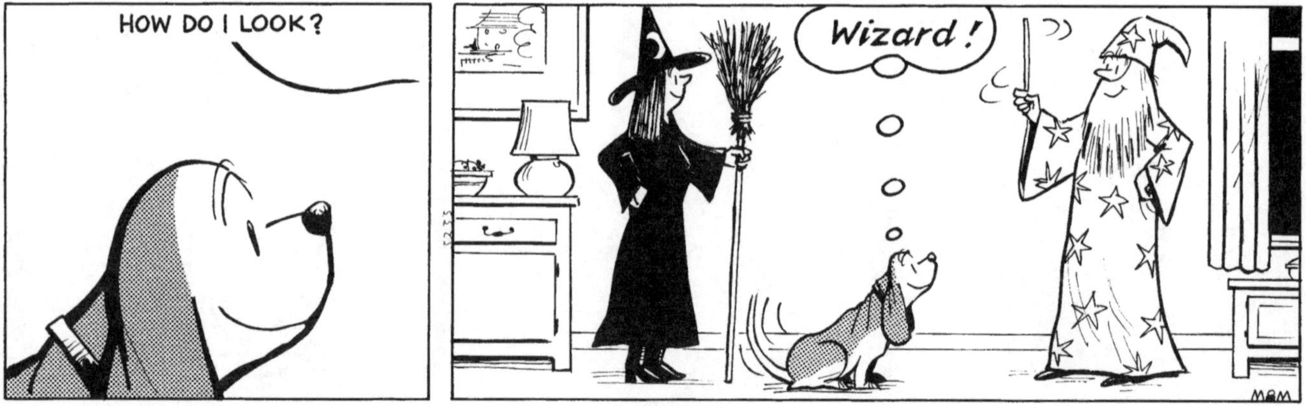
HOW DO I LOOK?
Wizard !
MBM

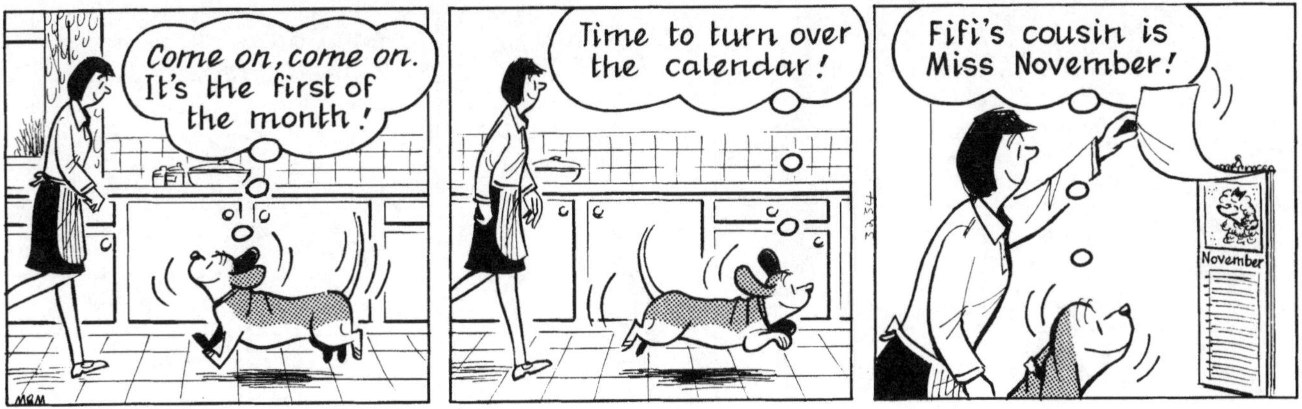

Come on, come on. It's the first of the month!
Time to turn over the calendar!
Fifi's cousin is Miss November!
November

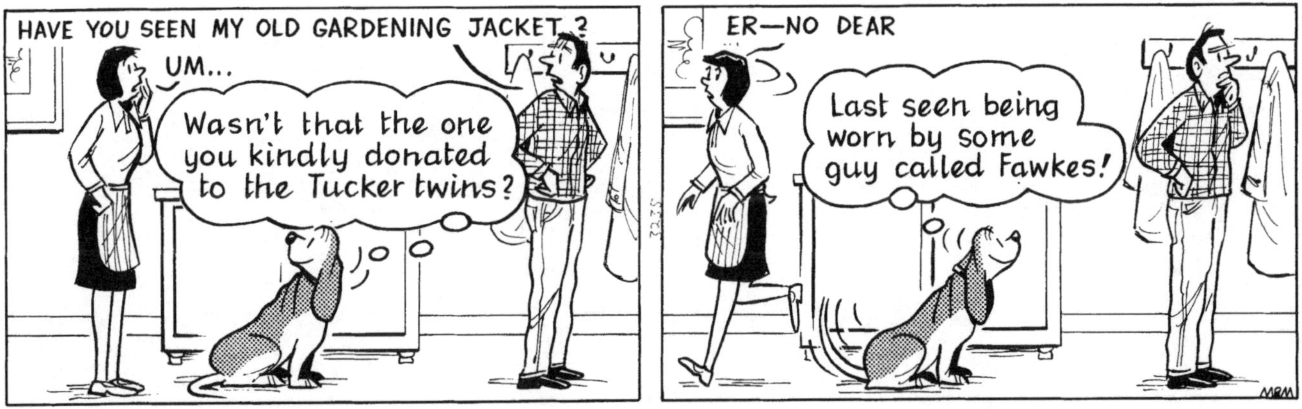

HAVE YOU SEEN MY OLD GARDENING JACKET ?
UM...
Wasn't that the one you kindly donated to the Tucker twins?
ER—NO DEAR
Last seen being worn by some guy called Fawkes!

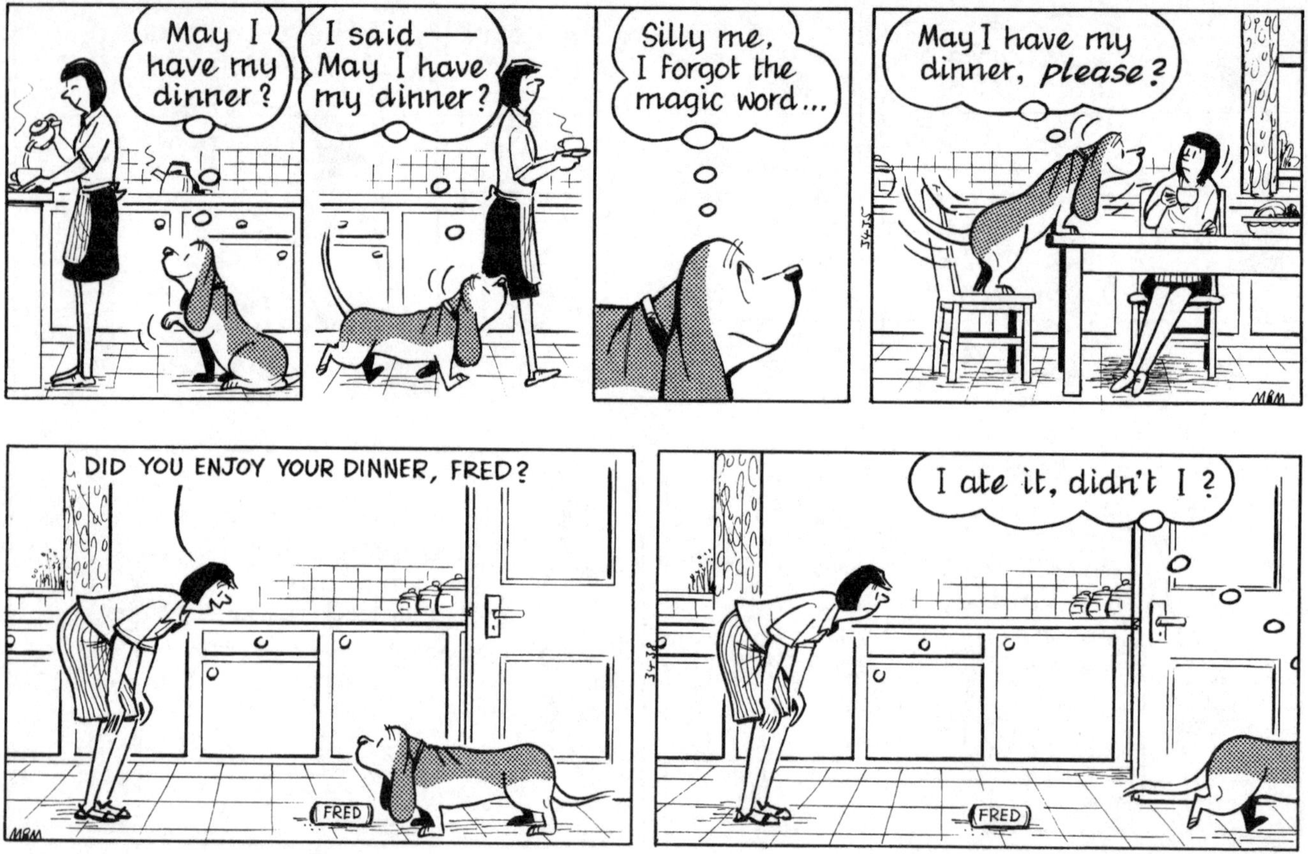
May I have my dinner?
I said — May I have my dinner?
Silly me, I forgot the magic word...
May I have my dinner, *please*?
MBM
DID YOU ENJOY YOUR DINNER, FRED?
FRED
MBM
I ate it, didn't I?
FRED

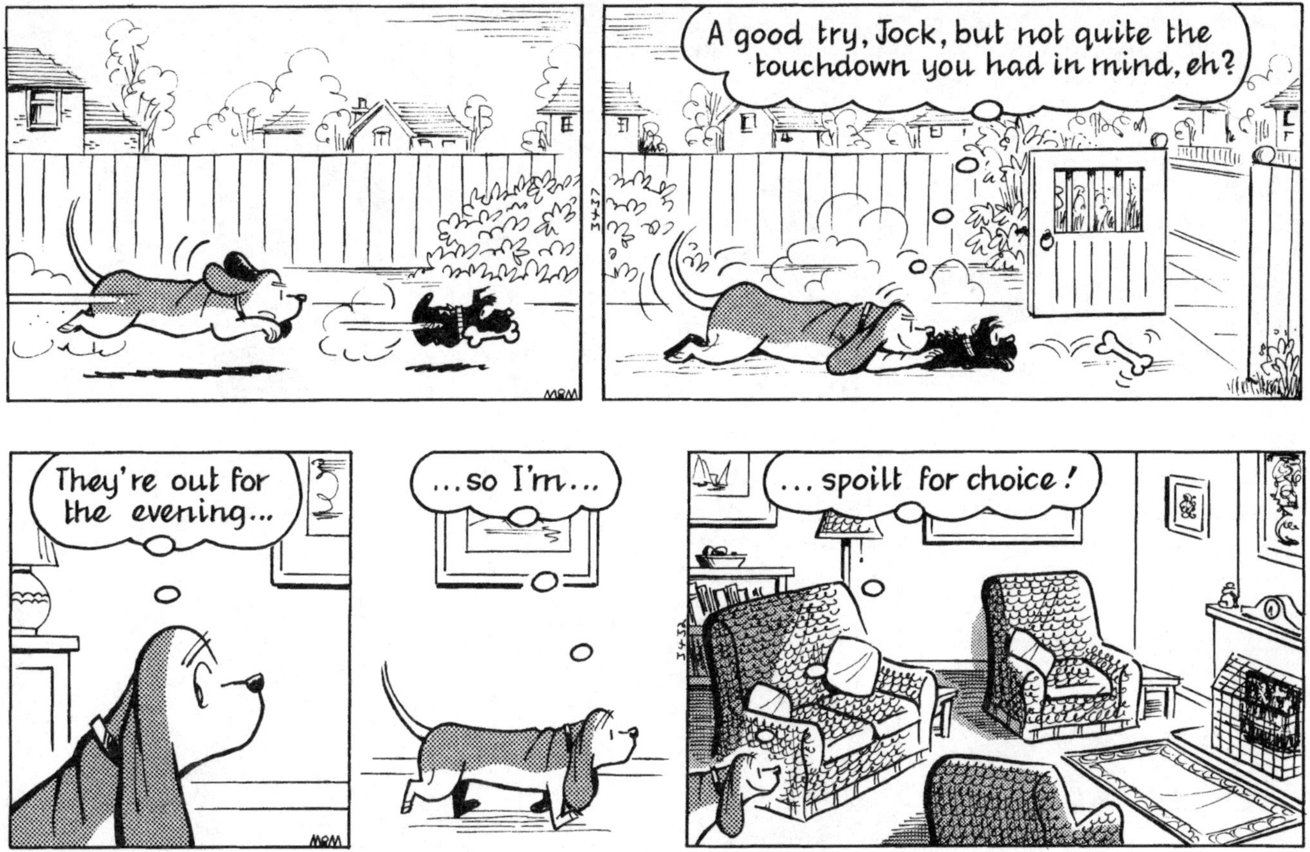
A good try, Jock, but not quite the touchdown you had in mind, eh?
They're out for the evening...
...so I'm...
...spoilt for choice!

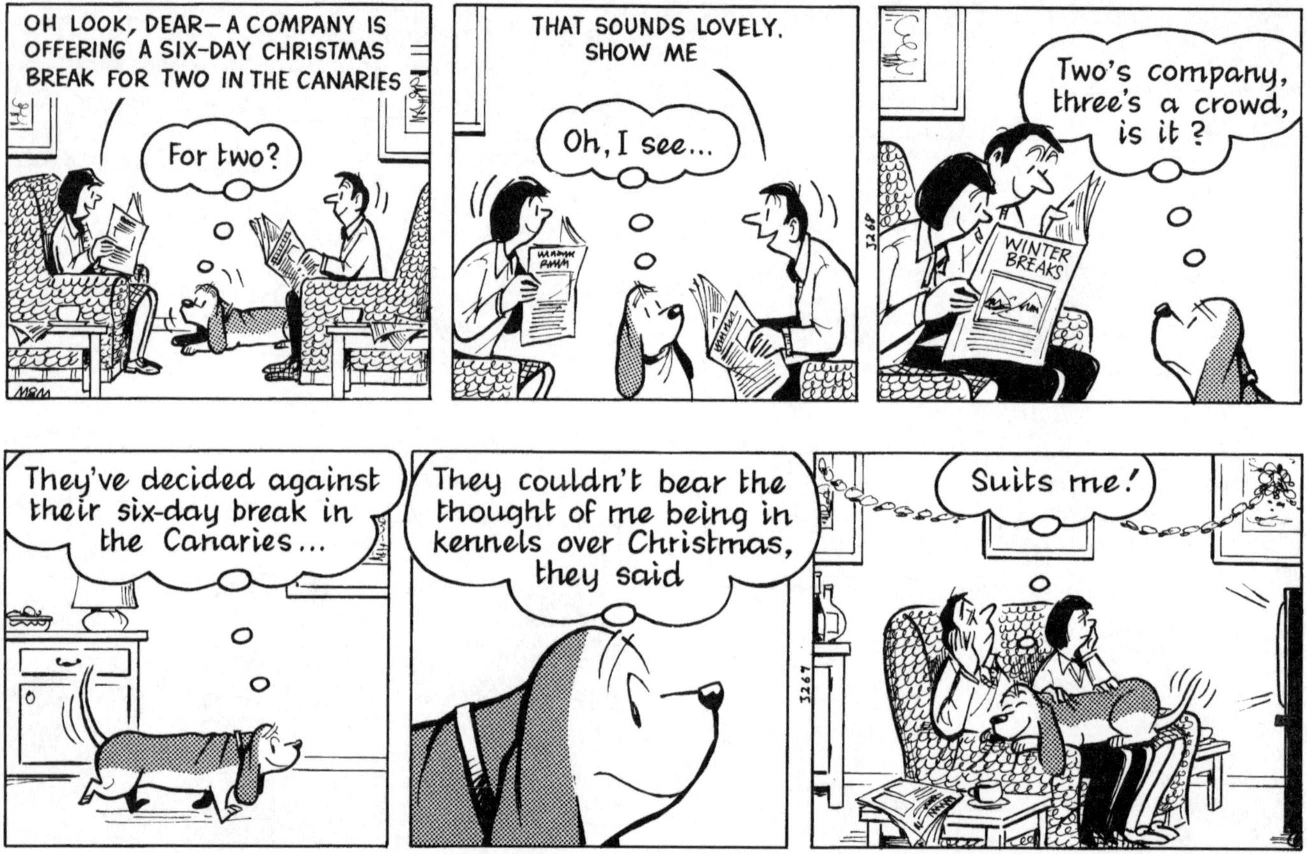
OH LOOK, DEAR— A COMPANY IS OFFERING A SIX-DAY CHRISTMAS BREAK FOR TWO IN THE CANARIES
For two?
THAT SOUNDS LOVELY. SHOW ME
Oh, I see...
Two's company, three's a crowd, is it ?
WINTER BREAKS
They've decided against their six-day break in the Canaries...
They couldn't bear the thought of me being in kennels over Christmas, they said
Suits me!

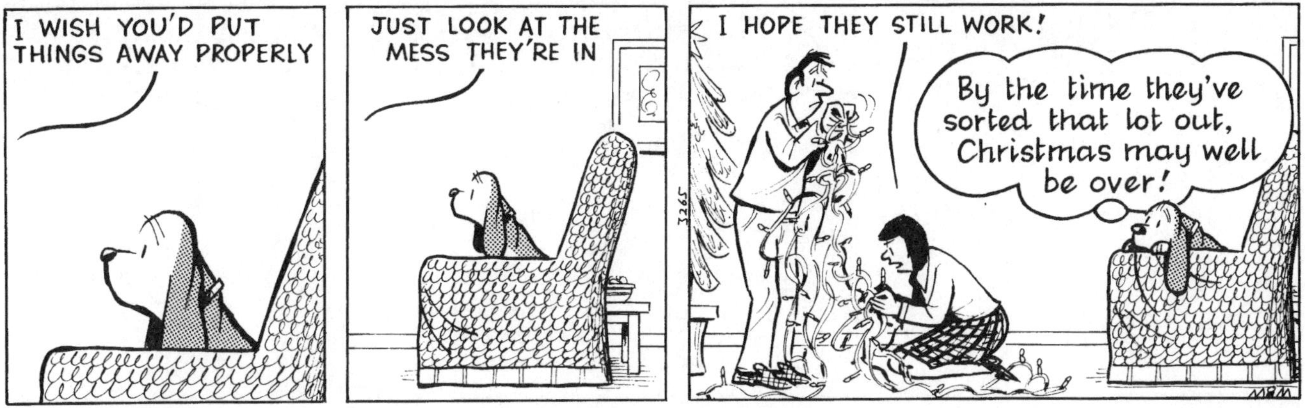
I WISH YOU'D PUT THINGS AWAY PROPERLY
JUST LOOK AT THE MESS THEY'RE IN
3265
I HOPE THEY STILL WORK!
By the time they've sorted that lot out, Christmas may well be over!
MRM

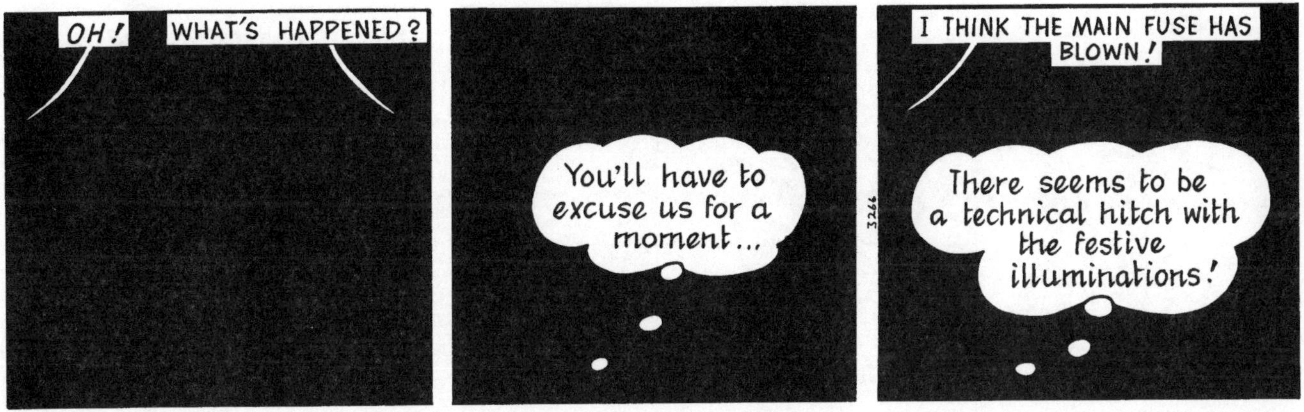
OH!
WHAT'S HAPPENED?
You'll have to excuse us for a moment...
3266
I THINK THE MAIN FUSE HAS BLOWN!
There seems to be a technical hitch with the festive illuminations!

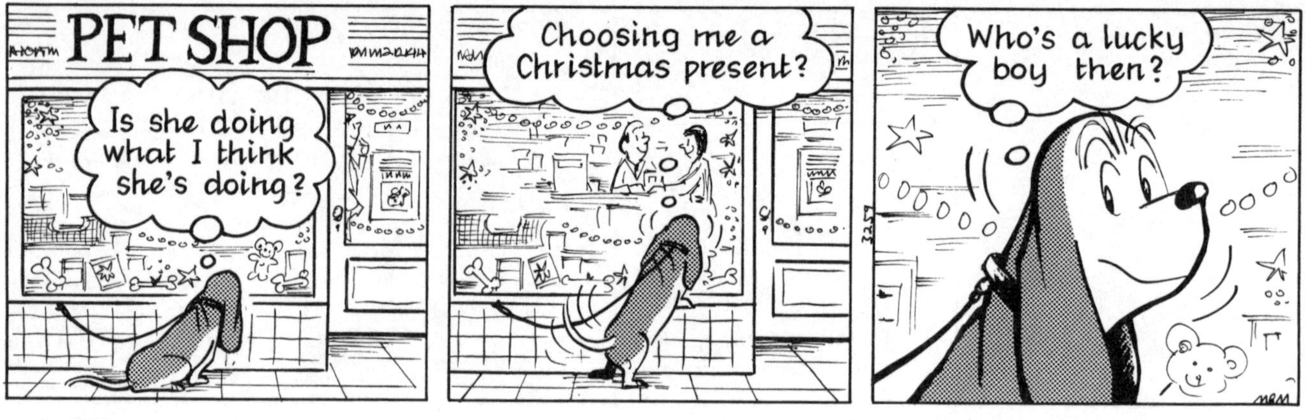
PET SHOP
Is she doing what I think she's doing?
Choosing me a Christmas present?
Who's a lucky boy then?
MBM

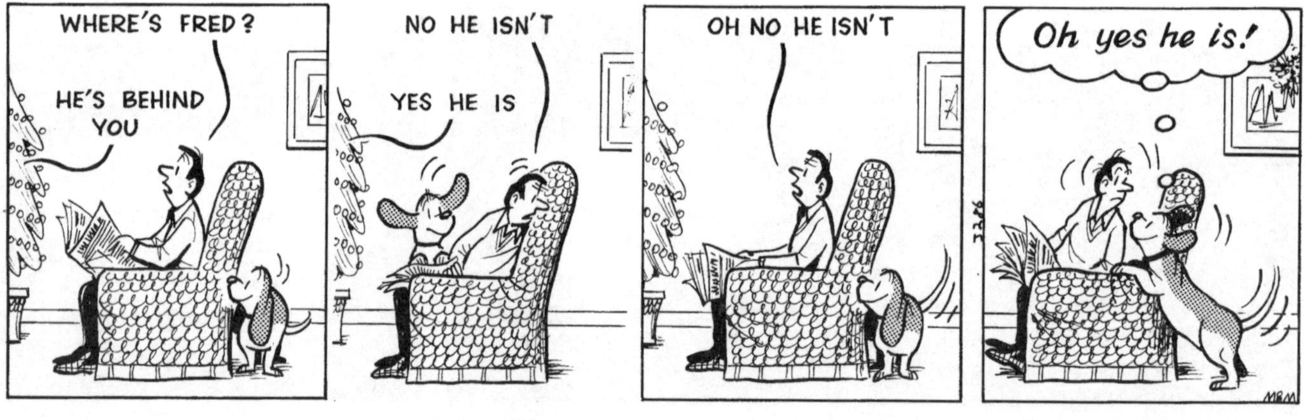
WHERE'S FRED?
HE'S BEHIND YOU
NO HE ISN'T
YES HE IS
OH NO HE ISN'T
Oh yes he is!
MBM

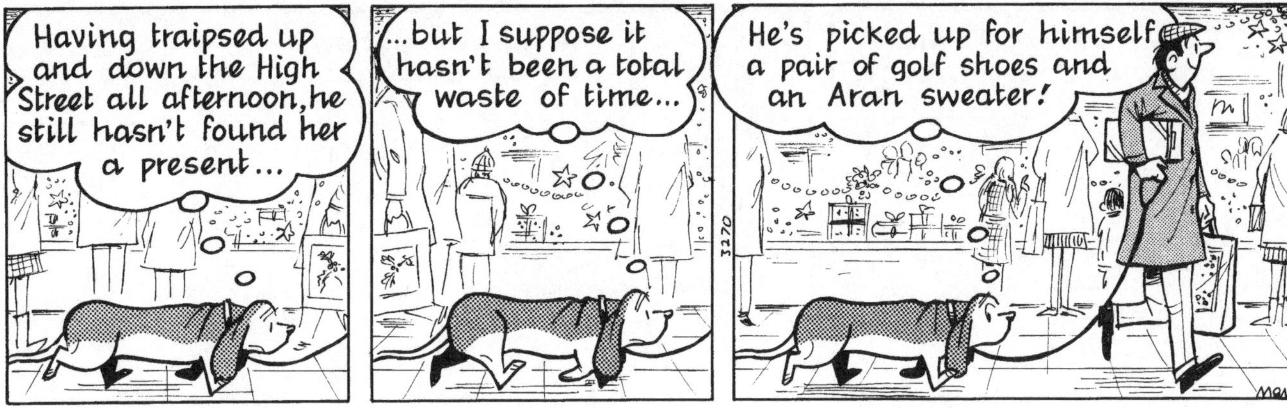
Having traipsed up and down the High Street all afternoon, he still hasn't found her a present...
...but I suppose it hasn't been a total waste of time...
He's picked up for himself a pair of golf shoes and an Aran sweater!

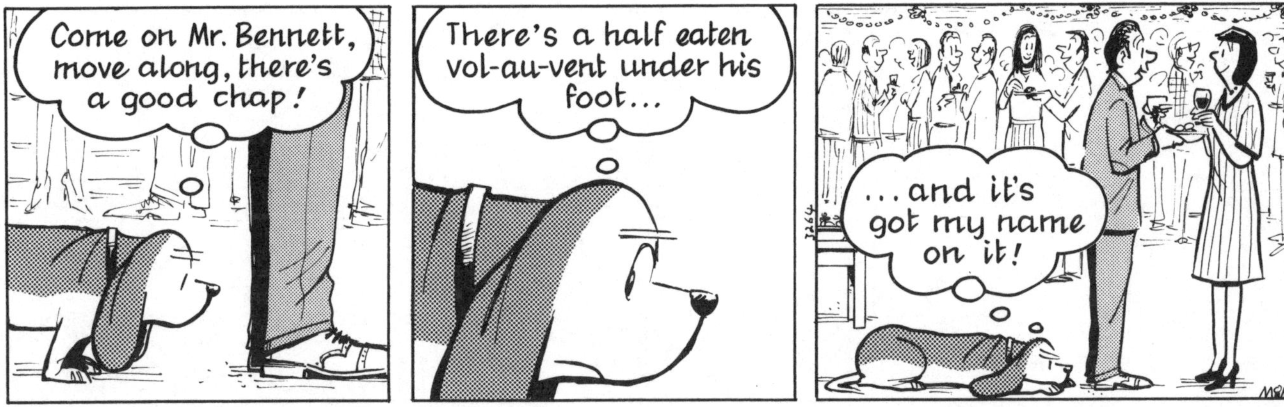
Come on Mr. Bennett, move along, there's a good chap!
There's a half eaten vol-au-vent under his foot...
...and it's got my name on it!

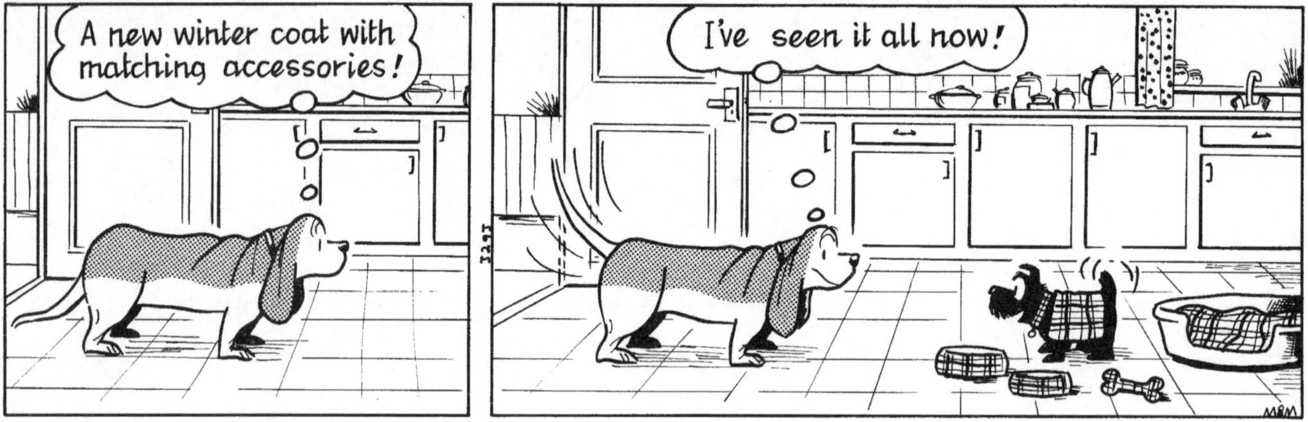
A new winter coat with matching accessories!
I've seen it all now!

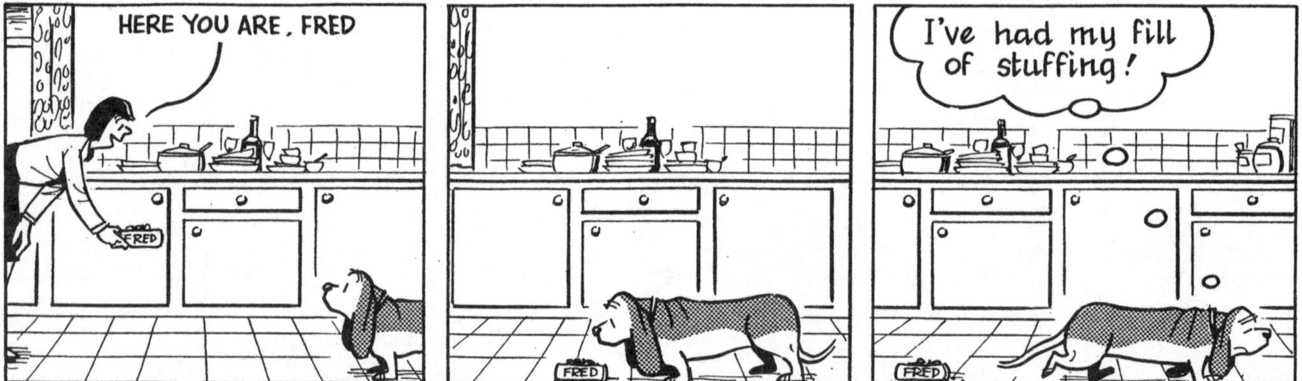
HERE YOU ARE, FRED
FRED
FRED
FRED
I've had my fill of stuffing!

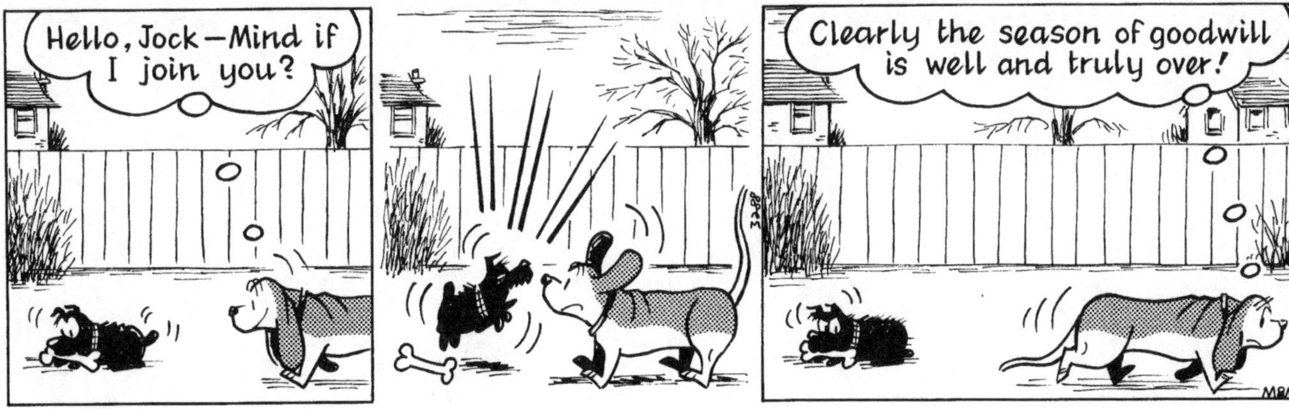
Hello, Jock—Mind if I join you?
Clearly the season of goodwill is well and truly over!

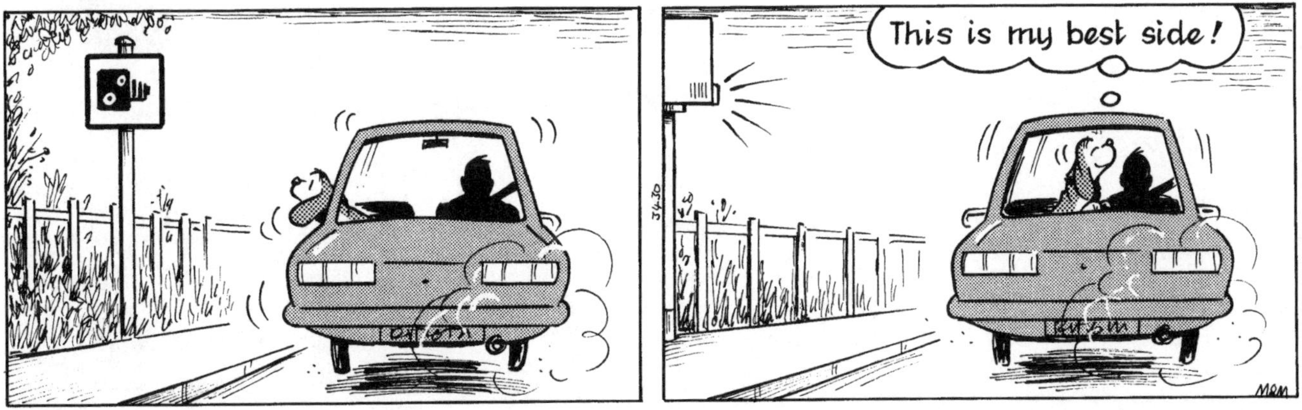
This is my best side!

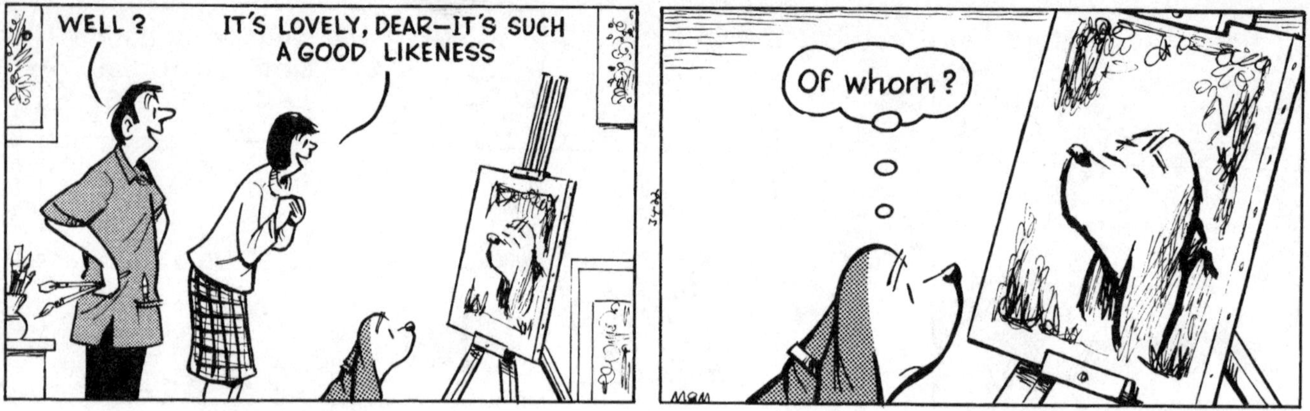
WELL ?
IT'S LOVELY, DEAR—IT'S SUCH A GOOD LIKENESS
Of whom ?

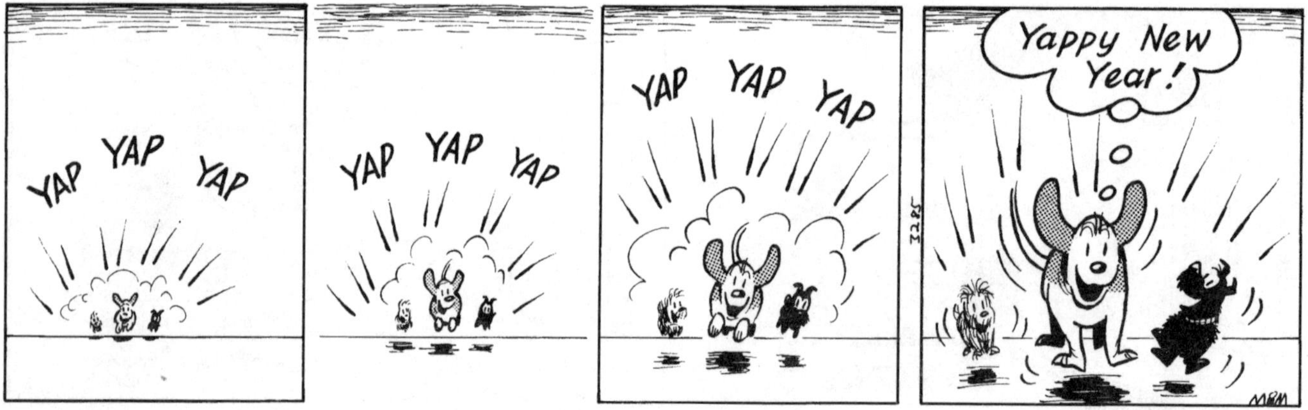
YAP YAP YAP
YAP YAP YAP
YAP YAP YAP
Yappy New Year!